LAN Performance Optimization

LAN Performance Optimization

Martin A. Nemzow

Windcrest®/McGraw-Hill

FIRST EDITION
FIRST PRINTING

© 1993 by **Windcrest Books**, an imprint of TAB Books.
TAB Books is a division of McGraw-Hill, Inc.
The name "Windcrest" is a registered trademark of TAB Books.

Library of Congress Cataloging-in-Publication Data

Nemzow, Martin A. W.
    LAN performance optimization / by Martin A. Nemzow.
      p   cm.
    Includes index.
    ISBN 0-8306-4277-3 (pbk.)
    1. Local area networks (Computer networks) I. Title.
    TK5105.7.N46 1992
    004.6'8—dc 20   92-24077
                               CIP

Acquisitions editor: Neil Levine
Editorial team: Art Cronk, Jr., Editor
                Joanne M. Slike, Executive Editor
Design team: Jaclyn J. Boone, Designer
               Brian Allison, Associate Designer
Cover design and illustration: Sandra Blair Design, Harrisburg, Pa.   WT1

LAN Performance Optimization is dedicated to my love, Carol,
and our family for enduring the hours and efforts devoted to
researching and writing this book.

Contents

Acknowledgments

Babcock, Kathleen, Hewlett-Packard Corp., Boulder, CO 80302.

Barry, Diane, Cabletron Systems, Rochester, NH.

Bernardi, Fred, McGraw-Hill, NY, NY, 10011

Bradner, Scoot, Harvard University, Cambridge, MA.

Burke, Kathleen, Hewlett-Packard Corp., Andover, MA.

Castellian, Lee, Hewlett-Packard, Fort Collins, CO.

Conner, Deni, Thomas-Conrad, TX.

Cutler, Scott, SE Area Manager, MicroCom, Atlanta, GA.

Dauber, Steve, Product Marketing Manager-Network Analysis Products, San Jose, CA.

Eggers, Barry, Major Accounts, Business development manager, Cisco Systems, Orlando, FL.

Fetterolf, James, AMP Inc. Valley Forge, PA, 01776.

Endy, Daniel, SEI Corporation, Malvern, PA, 01778.

Galvin, Peter, LAN Products Marketing Manager, Andrew Corporation, Chicago, IL.

Garafallo, Brian, Headquarters Sales Representative, Novell LANalyzer Group, Provo, UT.

Grieser, Elizabeth, Triplett Corp., Bluffton, OH 45817.

Healy, Bob, Associate Publisher, Windcrest Books, Blue Ridge Summit, PA, 17294-0850.

Hollingsworth, Robert, Datapoint Corporation, TX.

Kilker, Jeanne, PR Manager, Microtest.

Kirby, Scott, Area Support Manager, Cisco Systems, Orlando, FL.

Larsen, Andy, executive director, ARCnet Trade Association, Arlington Heights, OH.

Lee, Ronald, Novell Systems Engineer, Provo, UT.

Levine, Neil, Acquisitions Editor, McGraw-Hill Computer Science, Communications, New York, NY.

MacLean, Kevin, Cabletron Systems, Incorporated, East Rochester, NH 03867.

Network Performance Institute, Inc., PO 41-4371, Miami Beach, FL 33141-1350. (Product successor to SST Company, PO Box 771, Brookline, MA, 02146-0771.)

O'Brien, John, Nova University, Ft. Lauderdale, FL.

Ostrander, Bob, Executive Editor, Windcrest Books, Blue Ridge Summit, PA, 17294-0850.

Rauch, Peter, Director of Developer Relations, Thomas-Conrad, TX.

Rohan, Perry, Cabletron Systems, Rochester, NH.

SST Company, PO Box 771, Brookline, MA, 02146-0771.

Schachter, Charles, Network General Corporation, San Jose, CA.

Schlafly, Laura, Network General Corporation, David Browns Group, Miami, FL.

Sparks, Chuck, Area Sales Manager, Cisco Systems, Orlando, FL.

Templeton, Don, Spider Systems, Burlington, MA.

Thirion, Walter, CEO, Thomas-Conrad, TX.

Turner, Dave, Senior Technical Consultant, Cabletron Systems, Rochester, NH.

Wallach, Jeff, Network General Corporation, Miami, FL.

The text and artwork for this book was prepared by the author unless otherwise indicated. Text was prepared with Micropro WordStar 4.0, Aldus PageMaker 4.0, Fox Pro 1.2, and Xerox Ventura Publishing Professional 4.0 Windows Edition software. The typeface is Times Roman and Helvetica. Final camera-ready copy was prepared by a Linotronic Imagesetter 530. Artwork was prepared with Hewlett-Packard Scanning Gallery 4.2 and Corel Draw 3.0. Spreadsheet data and graphical charts were prepared using Lotus 1-2-3 2.0. Software was provided by Network Performance Institute, Inc. and programmed in MS C 5.0, MS SDK, and MS Visual Basic under MS Windows 3.0 and 3.1.

Introduction

Expected readership

LAN Performance Optimization describes pragmatic methods to optimize network performance. It shows how to establish appropriate goals and related performance benchmarks, assess network performance, and test assumptions to produce effective network improvements. The book is an advanced book about local area networks (LANs), specifically ARCnet, Ethernet, FDDI, and TokenRing. The book assumes the reader understands principles of networking; it presupposes basic knowledge of network configurations and how data communications and attached workstations interact.

Content of book

LAN Performance Optimization demonstrates how to analyze the performance of data communication networks, assess performance data, and optimize performance for local area networks. (A companion book, *Enterprise Network Performances Optimization*, demonstrates how to optimize performance for networks with complex configurations, which encompasses diverse computing platforms, multiprotocol connections, encapsulation or translating bridges, routers, and gateways, as well as enterprise-wide linkages.) This book addresses the problems of network bottlenecks, shows how to gather appropriate data to locate bottlenecks, and explains how to tune a network for optimal results. *Bottlenecks* range from slow network response to saturation, including insufficient channel capacity, network overloading, network configuration oversights, inappropriate partitions, network node obstacles, excessive hardware or software overhead, as well as other typical and unusual limitations obstructing network operation.

LAN Performance Optimization includes the *LANModel* software for performance estimation and evaluation. While the tool utilizes complex statistical techniques, its application would be apparent to most readers. Chapter 4 details tool usage, how to interpret its findings, and how to optimize LAN performance based on those results.

1
Chapter

Overview

Network performance optimization represents a crucial goal for computer maintenance groups, management information systems (MIS) departments, and data processing (DP) organizations. As such, it parallels an earlier and similar development in performance optimization for mainframe computers and timesharing service providers. It is an essential consideration since performance enhancements improve efficiency as much as 80 percent, shave maintenance costs, and postpone adding incremental capacity. Optimization is crucial for those traditional centralized computing environments; this urgency is accentuated only when that computing power is distributed and inextricably networked into daily operations throughout an organization.

Performance optimization becomes imperative given the complexity and limitations of local area networks (LANs). An underutilized resource provides viable opportunities for competitors to challenge your organization; it is critical with today's competition to maximize resource utilization from already-installed or planned LANs, and downsizing strategies. This provides the most obvious financial and strategic reasons to optimize LAN performance.

Throughout this book, the terms *LAN* and *network* will be used interchangeably. Both terms refer to a *local area network*. Although optical fiber-based or hybrid networks extend beyond 20 square kilometers, network architecture and management techniques, nonetheless, qualify them as LANs. Networks that span cities, states, and countries with heterogeneous protocols and transmission methods are *metropolitan area networks* (MANs) or *wide area networks* (WANs). Since MANs and WANs also comprise simple remote terminal support for mainframes, the term *enterprise-wide network* refers to premise networks, MANs, WANs, and networks for dispersed organizations that service heterogeneous requirements.

LANs have invaded small businesses, not-for-profit organizations, schools, universities, government agencies, and corporations. While this infiltration is not news to any reader or an isolated and unusual occurrence, the expectation for LANs has changed. LAN Data communications networks often dispense essential services and mission-critical client-server and host linkages throughout an enterprise. LANs connecting personal computers, host servers, or engineering workstations provide computing resources comparable to mainframes. Furthermore, the LAN configuration lends itself to smaller incremental units of computing power than a mainframe computer configuration can. Sadly, the data transmission capacity of the LAN is not as easily increased incrementally. This limitation is the most obvious technical reason to optimize LAN performance.

Two metaphors are reiterated and expanded throughout this book and are pertinent to help the reader visualize the full complexity of LANs. They are also relevant to help the reader visualize the LAN as a system of inherently subordinated and intertwined elements. The first metaphor equates networks to traditional (mail) delivery systems, as Fig. 1-1 illustrates. Data communications network delivery represents another substitute for (or enhancement to) mail delivery systems; it

1-1   A mail system as a metaphor for a LAN.

supports various securities, reliabilities, cost factors, and delivery speeds. Just as first-class mail delivery is not inherently better than courier or even bulk mail, different network protocols and configurations are not inherently better than any other. Efficiencies, suitabilities, intramural politics, and finances ultimately establish the "best" delivery system. Similarly, other—though parallel—external constraints and factors establish the "best" network system. LAN performance optimization must recognize the LAN protocol differences, organizational network requirements, goals, application demands, and financial limitations for effective results.

The second metaphor equates a data communications network to an interstate highway system. This system includes junctions to other highways and major roadways, local access roads, commuting traffic patterns, accidents, and only indirectly related slowdowns. Figure 1-2 shows a LAN as a system of access roads, junctions, and highways. This analogy is pertinent because networks interconnect like road systems: loads on a network are called *traffic*, and overloads on a data communications transmission channel are called *bottlenecks* and *traffic jams*. Furthermore, standard techniques for optimizing highway traffic and toll services are pertinent techniques for tuning LAN segment traffic and network services.

Nonetheless, there is a significant dissimilarity between highway traffic and LAN traffic. Highway traffic can crawl to a halt without functional repercussions or

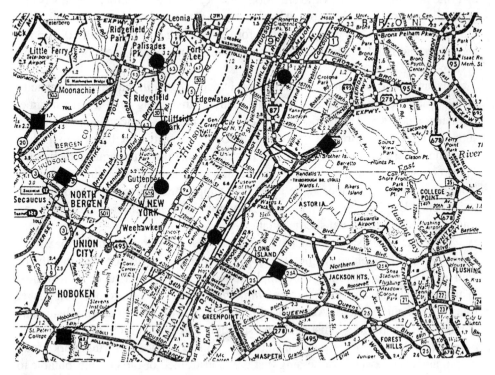

1-2 Highways as a metaphor for a LAN.

3

maintain varying and mixed speeds. Vehicles can violate speed limits or keep up a slow and steady pace. In contrast, LAN traffic propagates at enforced signal transmission speeds. Highway traffic is delayed and inconvenienced by errors and traffic jams; some vehicles make spontaneous U-turns or seek local side roads. In contrast, LAN traffic tie-ups reverberate throughout the system to create a massive infrastructure failure. LAN client-server jams inhibit any client activity (unless clients detach from LAN); there are no side roads.

Purpose for optimization

Optimization increases the financial value of a local area network. The LAN investment is an involved installation of cabling and wiring, network attachment hardware, computer equipment, expensive software, application development, and support staff. A dysfunctional network decreases productivity, slows production, and delays results. A slow network diminishes results—whether the results are as a new product release, a company newsletter, sales literature, customer support, shipping manifests and bills of lading, searches through online libraries or extensive data-bases, or an exploration through the daily electronic mail (E-mail) messages. A slow network translates into lowered productivity, additional labor expenses, and reduced profits. While computing capacity and disk storage facilities can be added in incremental units, the LAN transmission channel itself is a facility not always so gradually expandable. Therefore, it is wise to assess network performance. Discover if a network facility can be optimized before embarking on a potentially disruptive and uncertain path to subnet, recable, or upgrade protocols and network operating systems (NOSes).

Just as additional mainframe capacity is expensive, additional network capacity is too. Incremental mainframe capacity can mean adding another mainframe. Similarly, incremental network capacity can mean adding another channel, building subnets, creating a "firewall" which is a logical or physical barrier to isolate segments in case of network failures, or upgrading to a faster transmission channel. These changes incur major expenses. While incremental mainframe time is available from a time-sharing vendor, there is no such supplemental capacity for networks. Incremental LAN capacity entails a permanent investment; alternate channels and routing trees require actual site installation.

Therefore, the customary goal of LAN performance optimization is to maximize capacity and throughput within the *available* data transmission bandwidth; of course, this is subject to software application and application server constraints. Within a strict and simple assessment, *throughput* refers merely to network packet transmission and capacity. Assessing throughput as work group accomplishments demonstrates a more sophisticated perspective and recognition of the primary purpose for the network. However, since few tools exist for measuring work group output and even fewer for assessing that part constrained or directly attributable to a network, most practical methodologies view packet transmission and capacity as a practical substitute. This book, in fact, concentrates on this utilitarian approach.

As white-collar productivity is increased substantially for office workers—via a local area network—LAN performance optimization gains importance. The network becomes an inseparable cog in operations. Networked computers displace traditional data processing activities, such as data entry and retrieval. Therefore, the relative efficiency of networks translates into bottom-line profits. As networks gain influence and importance, effective optimization translates into sizable organizational benefits.

Definition for optimization

Optimization is the process that maximizes outcomes. When applied to computer systems, optimization usually refers to using as much available central processing unit (CPU) capacity as possible per unit time for constructive work. This process comprises tuning the computer configuration, replacing existing code with more efficient software algorithms, routing and balancing tasks to the most suitable timeslot and processing platform, and establishing concurrent processing (multiprocessing). Optimization is important since a CPU cycle provides no value unless used; otherwise, it is wasted. This is just like the way an empty mail cargo bay on an airline retains no future value. Similarly, just as mail is assigned delivery priorities, CPU usage has a priority value. Some work is more important and accordingly is charged more for that high priority and processed faster or completed sooner. Other work waits in a stack, or is "queued," on a first-come first-served basis. This lower-priority work is processed as the system has free time; "time shifting" minimizes otherwise wasted capacity.

When applied to networking, optimization is a similar, although a more complicated issue. Optimization for a local area network means that performance, costs, and benefits are maximized. While ideally this would refer to human work group output, in reality, optimization refers to maximizing network throughput and capacity for practical reasons. Nonetheless, maximizing throughput and network capacity remains a complex statistical and operational task.

Network capacity corresponds to more than the network channel speed or "bandwidth." Capacity refers to the data communication channel bandwidth, protocol efficiencies, overhead effects, utilization levels, and distribution or composition of traffic loads. A topic that will be reiterated and expanded throughput this book is the crucial assumption that a data communications network is not a singular entity. It is often no faster than its slowest critical component. From a LAN performance optimization viewpoint, the local area network comprises more than just the network data communications facility—cable or wiring medium, the network attachment devices, or the protocols and procedures. A LAN is the total aggregation of *all* physically and logically connected components. This not only includes the network facility itself but also all node hardware devices, firmware, software, applications, and management practices. Any single component could cause significant bottlenecks.

Network optimization might require optimization of one or more of the following: workstation memory, transmission buffers, direct memory access (DMA) wait states and transfer speeds, disk drive seek times, disk controller transfer rates, numbers of active bus or SCSI (small computer system interface) devices, disk or disk array file fragmentation, BIOS (basic input output services) and VLSI (very large scale integration) chip sets and their efficiencies, workstation (or server) load factors, software performance, client requests and server paging, database gateway efficiency, and graphic screen repainting times. LANs seldom support multiprocessing and transmission priorities to balance network usage; revision two of the Fiber Data Distributed Interchange (FDDI-II) is an exception. While network traffic can be delayed for short periods of time (seconds), that work cannot be queued for later processing as it would be in a mainframe batch environment. Instead, delays in the network correspond to delays in interactive computer processes. This in turn prevents users from completing their tasks.

Preferably, organizations seek to maximize the utility of all assets. Just as optimizing the use of the mainframe and tuning constituent components are both viable options, LANs can be optimized and tuned as well. The LAN performance optimization process is more complicated since priorities, utilities, and political issues cloud the definitions of what it means to optimize the LAN. Also, the LAN is not a single resource; it is a dispersed and very complex system made even more complex when the LAN supports true distributed processing and client-server activities.

Performance confusion

Nontechnical executives often confuse the reasons for network failures, misunderstand network performance bottlenecks, as well as misinterpret the complex issues of security, uptime, and reliability. Often, such managers might not realize the differences between tools, information, and causes for unreliable network performance. Such managers might insist that a $16,000 protocol analyzer is supposed to fix the network or that such tools are adequate and sufficient to resolve all network problems. Alternatively, such managers might insist that, clearly, subordinates just do not understand how to use the tools. LANs are more complex than that simplistic view. Operational continuity and performance optimization are separate issues. LAN continuity encompasses three key charters:

- Compatibility
- Consistency
- Credibility

Performance issues transcend these charters. Networks are complex. The intricacy is shifting from physical issues to software, management, and the interrelationships between the operating system, the network operating system, and application software. Additionally, the scope and necessity for many networks have shifted from merely support activities to *mission-critical* operations. Before even considering optimizing performance, be certain that the basic network operational charter is fulfilled. While network management is not the topic for this book, realize that LAN performance optimization is not fundamental for most networks; reliable, secure, and useful LAN operation is.

Optimization tradeoffs

The crucial realization is that LAN performance optimization is not always a tradeoff between cost and performance. LAN performance optimization is relatively inexpensive and highly beneficial. The relationship is not linear. As Fig. 1-3 indicates, successful optimization might alter the cost to benefit relationship so that marginal amounts of hardware (or capital) might provide significant benefits. For example, twenty hours spent examining the hardware with a tester and checking the data delivery with a protocol analysis tool might reveal that poor installation and specific oversights are causing network problems. Poor client-server performance might result not from network overloads but rather from disk file fragmentation, excessive random access memory (RAM) swapping, and slow network server controllers. Improving performance might entail only time to swap existing components between computers and fix cable errors instead of building new subnetworks, replacing bridges and repeaters with routers that discriminate packet destinations, or upgrading the network from a 4 Mbits/s Token-Ring to a "faster" 16 Mbits/s ring.

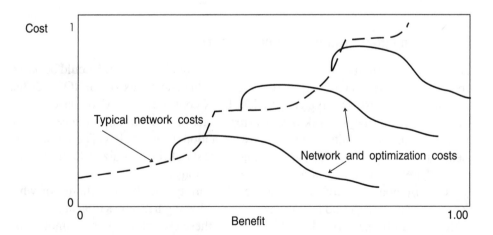

1-3 Optimization is a nonlinear tradeoff between cost and performance and is practical when a negligible cost yields a prominent gain.

Optimization procedures

The procedure for network optimization is four-fold. First, it establishes relevant network goals and explicit benchmarks to measure network performance. Second, measurements are collected and compared against the benchmarks. Third, variances from the expected benchmark values form a basis for reviewing where a network is suboptimal and what can be done to better network performance. Fourth, changes to the network are performed based upon that analysis. The second, third, and fourth steps tend to be iterative since any change to the network should be tested to ensure that it actually is beneficial. Figure 1-4 charts the optimizing sequence.

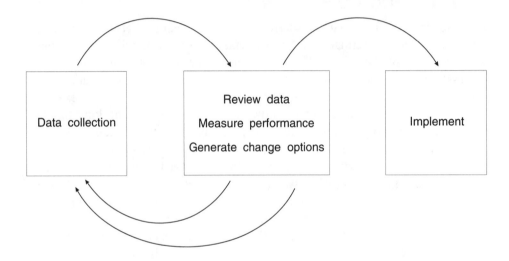

| Data collection | Review data

Measure performance

Generate change options | Implement |

1-4   LAN performance optimization sequence.

Establishing goals and related benchmarks

There are few definitive network goals. Every network is different. It could be based upon ARCnet, Ethernet, FDDI, or Token-Ring. Other choices exist too. NOSes differ. Few standards exist for a typical physical LAN configuration. Also, performance and capacities of the network devices (repeaters, bridges, multiport access units, attachment interface units, and network workstations) vary widely. There is also no clear-cut meaning about what part of the network should be optimized. Optimization generally refers to some desirable though ambiguous improvement.

Concise goals are crucial because of the variety and the uncertainty of what aspect of a network should be optimized. The following list shows typical questions with which to frame network goals. Note that these questions comprise more than performance-related issues; they include organizational objectives, strategic values, and political concerns. Some benchmarks are substantive, while other criteria are

- What is the purpose for the LAN?
- What are strategies for LAN applications?
- What are critical LAN tasks?
- What are priorities for the LAN?
- What is expected will be achieved with a LAN?
- What is LAN capacity?
- What is LAN speed?
- What is the LAN configuration?
- What are appropriate measurement standards?
- How will measurements be collected?
- What are the objectives for benchmarks?
- Who benefits from the LAN?
- Who is in control of the LAN?
- Who funds LAN activities and maintenance?

subject to the whims of the organization. These less-objective goals, while important, play a minor role in this book.

While goals define what aspects of the LAN are to be optimized, benchmarks define the precise terminology for gathering data and the applicable measurement system. Both goals and the related benchmarks are important. There is a difference between goals and benchmarks. Goals establish an objective while the benchmarks provide a means to assess how to reach that objective and show progress toward that end. For example, the goal to improve LAN response time might require a benchmark for average token acquisition time, average packet delivery time (including Ethernet deferrals and collisions), or include the time required for a spanning tree bridge to reroute traffic around a failed segment.

These benchmarks, or *metrics*, are the measurement standards used to evaluate network performance. Functional network metrics must reflect initial expectations. These benchmarks define the purpose, the function, and the expected performance for a network in unambiguous terms. The benchmark must include the formal terms for measurement. For example, network speed might be defined as packets per second, average network response time, SQL transaction time, or average packet delivery time. A failure to formalize such seemingly clear descriptions will undermine the optimization process. Also, it is unreasonable to begin the optimization process without a concise objective because the process might be jeopardized when informal benchmarks acquire importance beyond the initial consideration.

While it is possible to capture and retain years worth of network performance data with a protocol analyzer, those statistics serve no purpose until an objective is established. Note, however, this does not suggest that those statistics are worthless without an objective. In fact, collecting network data periodically often provides irreplaceable insight into network performance over a long period; it often establishes base levels for network operation. Such base values provide necessary and comparative documentation. Also, when the networking is not working as intended, as a result it is almost impossible to gather useful network statistics.

Measurements can be relative, such as "the network is running well," or "network users are happy and are getting work done." Ideally, metrics consist of formal and measurable information, such as channel capacity, percentage utilization, error rates, hours of network availability, estimated mean time to failure, or average waiting time for token acquisition. These unambiguous terms and values establish a credible, independent, and consistent system for evaluating network performance. Metrics should be repeatable.

Data collection

Once the organization has established goals and benchmarks, the second step of the network optimization process is to collect data against the formalized benchmarks. A protocol analyzer is a method of capturing network performance data. The hardware analyzer is a stand-alone hardware network station, such as the Novell LANalyzer, Spider Systems' Spider Monitor, and the Network General Sniffer. A software protocol analyzer, such as FTP Software's TCP/IP Protocol Analyzer, is a software application that collects network data while running on a network workstation. Other examples include NETSTAT, PERFORM, Simple Network Management Protocol (SNMP), and Common Management Information Protocol (CMIP). These tools either analyze data on the network to build a performance picture or expect network devices periodically to transfer *device agency* data into a network performance database. This database is called the *management information base* (MIB).

Measuring performance

The third step in the optimization process—and it might be iterative, as Fig. 1-3 previously illustrated—is to generate the variance from the expected benchmark norms. This determines what is suboptimal and might represent minor or critical performance bottlenecks. For example, if network utilization is 23 percent, does that mean performance is poor? Is that acceptable to the users? Will an additional database server perform well? Answers to such questions are conditional upon the established benchmarks. If normal utilization is 5 percent, 23 percent might suggest a significant new process on the network or a transmission problem. On the other hand, a Token-Ring showing only 23-percent utilization might be highly satisfactory and easily support a 300-percent increase in usage. Whether such a load is acceptable to users can even depend upon how they perceive the increased utilization and the initial objectives.

Consider, for another example, an Ethernet collision rate of 12 percent and waiting time (collisions and deferrals) of nearly one second. Whether that is a bottleneck depends upon network benchmarks. It might not matter for a network servicing E-mail, but this traffic level seriously hinders a user from loading several

4 Mb 24-bit color images from a networked file server to a client workstation running page composition. Each image of the multiple images might require 1000 to 2000 packets with each packet experiencing that one-second delay. Delays of that magnitude hinder productive results.

Frequently, there is no precise determination for the cause of an observed bottleneck. Bottlenecks result from complex and intertwined circumstances. It is hard to differentiate cause and effect. For example, a router ostensibly creating a bottleneck might merely reflect traffic saturation on outbound channels or even itself be adversely affected by the lack of timely transmission acknowledgments. The router is not the cause of the bottleneck, just the site of the bottleneck. This traffic backlog is typically seen on expressways at rush hours. While the highway itself is jammed, the bottleneck is often caused by the inability of backlogged traffic downstream to exit into the city or merge quickly into other highways at junctions. Clearly, it is imperative to recognize where bottlenecks are visible, thereby separating the true causes from peripheral reactions.

Variances from benchmarks merely reflect that there is indeed a problem without determining why there is a problem. Repeated instances for the ARCnet burst reconfiguration, high Ethernet collision rates, low throughput for FDDI, and frequent Token-Ring beaconing are symptomatic, but they might not be the cause. Chapter 6 contains essential information in the structure of cross reference symptoms and causes. Because there are many causes for observed or inferred symptoms—and many plausible solutions for each cause—it is vital to explore as many causes and relevant solutions as possible.

Performance optimization

Actual performance enhancement begins after network data is evaluated subject to the established benchmarks. Enhancement might require physical LAN configuration. As often as not, optimization might include only a thorough testing of all network hardware—the wire or cable and every individual connector—and some simple tightening of connectors or replacement of suspect parts. Hardware might be upgraded or a new release of the NOS might be installed to overcome routing and gateway problems. Even so, the process would be incomplete.

Test causes. Implement simple solutions. Capture more network data and perhaps even revise the benchmarks or the type and form of the network statistics. Perhaps reassess even the benchmarks. LAN performance optimization is an iterative process if only because the symptoms, causes, and pragmatic solutions are so incongruous so as to seem unrealistic. It is important to realize that some perfect solutions are simply suboptimal due to management, organizational, or financial constraints. Balance the network goals with what is possible—and optimize within that framework.

In fact, LAN optimization often is an ongoing process. Every change must itself be evaluated for its potential to enhance network performance, its risk for making the network worse, its cost for implementation, and its effects upon users and the organizational strategies. Frankly, some changes do not work. They might not solve the problem, and might even add to the immediate problem. For example, excessive data collection (such as through passive SNMP activities) from remote devices degrades performance because that activity requires bandwidth. It is even possible that a protocol analyzer will not list such activity because it is a connectionless protocol. Some enhancements optimize one or more objectives but degrade more crucial ones. It is also likely that changes destabilize the network and reliability suddenly becomes a far more important objective than previously considered. Later chapters in the book discuss specific solutions and improvements.

Optimization goals

Optimization represents a multifaceted goal. Optimization can mean maximizing data throughout from point to point without concern for data damage, timeliness, or delivery reliability. Bulk-rate mail is one such example where throughput is maximized to the detriment of other considerations. Optimization can mean maximizing delivery speed without concern for data clarity, accuracy, or full utility. Consider, as an example, fascimile delivery. Although fax delivery of a simple signed document is nearly instantaneous, the transmitted imaged is blurred and jagged. Further, it is not legally binding.

Optimization instead can mean providing the lowest-cost delivery of large data streams without a second thought about the arrival time. Train or barge transport, for comparison, provides the lowest-cost delivery of bulk commodities when delivery time is not important. Optimization can also mean improving speed of delivery *and* receiving verification that the intended recipient actually received the delivery. For example, courier, express, or registered mail guarantees qualified and rapid arrival to the detriment of the expense account.

Likewise, LAN optimization can mean any of these and other characteristics. Typical network performance optimization goals are listed here:

- Capacity
- Average speed of delivery
- Incidence speed of delivery
- Work throughput
- Guarantee of delivery
- Reliability of delivery
- LAN availability
- Length or reach of the network
- Access to bulk data
- Security
- Service levels (priorities)
- Cost of delivery
- Overhead requirements
- Manageability

Benchmarks are an essential for these goals to be useful. These individual goals are illustrated in the following pages. They are useful to establish a common framework for establishing and assessing benchmarks in the remainder of the book.

Capacity

Capacity usually refers to the ability of a network to transport data bits independent of protocols, overhead costs, and introduced errors. For uniformity, network capacity is usually represented by speed in a useful and comparable format, usually bits per second. The *channel capacity* of ARCnet is 2,500,000 bits per second (2.5 Mbits/s), ARCnet *plus* is 20,000,000 bits per second (20 Mbits/s), TCNS ARCnet derivative (Thomas-Conrad Network System) is 100,000,000 bits per second (100 Mbits/s), Ethernet is 10,000,000 bits per second (10 Mbits/s), Fiber Distributed Data Interchange (FDDI) is actually 125,000,000 bits per second (125 Mbits/s) although this protocol employs a 4 bit translation into 5 bits for effective throughput of 100 Mbits/s, and IBM Token-Ring is either 4,000,000 bits per second (4 Mbits/s) or 16,000,000 bits per second (16 Mbits/s). Other token-ring networks do exist with different transmission speeds. These relative measurements (fixed by transmission oscillators or a signal-quality heartbeat) represent data delivery channel upper limits. At face value, a network can be optimized by merely substituting FDDI, the LAN protocol with the greatest capacity. Network utilization is a typical formal benchmark. *Utilization* often refers to throughput as a function of channel capacity.

Average speed of delivery

The average speed of delivery recognizes that all data communication networks impose protocols, errors, and overheads that detract from full channel utilization. This is important when comparing the performance of networks with different delivery rates. For example, while a 16-Mbits/s Token-Ring sounds faster than a 10-Mbits/s Ethernet, a populous and active ring might impose unsatisfactory token acquisition delays, or the size limitation of Novell 4 KB IPX packets might create a token rotational time (TRT). Likewise, the enormous capacity of FDDI might be reduced to a virtual standstill by time-consuming and wasteful encapsulation of smaller Ethernet packets into the larger FDDI frame format. Alternately, an overloaded Ethernet can become saturated with collisions and provide no data delivery. Therefore, an optimizing goal is represented by the average speed of delivery for a typical message or completion of a typical operation. A formal benchmark is usually a time to move a standardized file from point to point over the network, the time required to perform a typical (and rigorously defined) operation, or packet delivery time.

Incidence speed of delivery

The *incidence speed of delivery* is the fastest or slowest time required to deliver a message or complete an operation. Sometimes, it is called *latency* or comprises a component of latency. This can be expressed as the *minimum* and the *maximum*, or as *confidence intervals*. While average speed of delivery provides a general assessment of network performance, a network user who experiences several minutes delay in loading a word processing document will not appreciate that the twenty-four-hour average is several seconds; that user does not want to work at off-peak hours. The minimum provides a benchmark for what might be achieved with optimization, while the maximum represents the worstcase that must be optimized for the network manager's continued employment. The benchmark consists of minimum, expected, and maximum times with statistical confidence intervals for transmission of a single packet.

Work throughput

Work throughput is an ill-defined term that can refer to record transactions per time period, files updated per hour, or actual data moved across the network channel per second without protocol messages, errors, and overheads. Note that this goal is ambiguous until formalized by circumstance—usually an organizational imperative or strategic plan. Throughput is a function of how you define it and apply it, and is thus context sensitive. Generally, work throughput is optimized in situations where the transport mechanism and processing platforms are the limiting factor. Examples include data entry and retrieval operations, packetized transmissions of single keystrokes in network terminal service to a host (as in IRMA, TTY, and typical personal computer mainframe terminal emulations), transaction reporting, forms processing, and other distributed or client-server events. The benchmark for work throughput include timings or counts for a standardized operation during a period with a regulated traffic level.

Guarantee of delivery

The *guarantee of delivery* is analogous to a return receipt indicating accurate and appropriate delivery. It is a function of the network protocol and the supporting application software. It is optimized, for example, by using IP as a transport-layer protocol, a NOS request with transmission acknowledgment (ACK) and negative acknowledgment (NAK), or by selecting an E-mail software application that verifies message delivery and informs the sender that the intended recipient has actually read the message. This goal has no quantitative benchmark; it is a function of the chosen NOS or network protocol and is how applications support delivery verification.

Reliability of delivery

Reliability of delivery is a factor of the network cabling and wiring plant, the design or configuration of the actual network, the quality of the network interface hardware, the protocols employed, the dependability of system software, and the error-recovery capability of application software. Reliability can be optimized through knowledgeable network design, adherence to network specifications, careful installation, attention to network alarms and user-indicated problems, wiring hubs, quality components, fault-tolerant designs, and IEEE 802.1 spanning bridges. The benchmark for reliability is represented by error rates and numbers of transmission retries or repetitions.

Availability

Availability of the network is a function of reliability of delivery, but there is also a time element. For example, consider the difference between reliability and availability. It is possible that 100 percent of all data is reliably delivered when the network is available, but the network is so unstable that it is rarely available. Essential services and mission-critical operations are optimized for reliability *and* availability since failure of the network represents a serious disaster to the organization in terms of lost revenue, loss of goodwill, and the actual endangerment of human life. The benchmark for the goal of network reliability is usually indicated by the number of hours per day that the network is available.

Length or reach of the network

The length or reach of the network are important factors for widely scattered or campus-wide organizations. For example, several thousand users might access a LAN network over a several kilometer expanse. While each Ethernet network is limited to a maximum of 1024 devices when repeaters are used, normally a network is not as populous. In fact, a network node typically supports multiple workstations (via multiport repeaters) and each workstation could support multiple users. Although Ethernet and even Token-Ring device placement and utilization could be optimized to facilitate such numerous users, repeater delays and the increased network slot time—sometimes called "latency" (caused by collision delays or lengthy delays for token acquisition)—degrade network reliability and availability. In such a situation, partitioning networks into a subnet hierarchy, limiting access, and substituting FDDI (which supports 1000 devices at a maximum of 2 km intervals) represent optimization scenarios. There is no benchmark for this goal; it is a function of the network specifications, store-and-forward gateways, and the extensibility available with repeaters, bridges, routers, and gateways.

Bulk data access

Distributed or networked processing might also require access to bulk data in the form of enormous databases, image files, and graphical information systems (GIS) vector data. When such information is distributed on many different computing platforms, the virtual cross-mounting of disk partitions might destabilize the network by creating a domino effect. Inability to access one source for data required by another might halt transactions and possibly even disable network operations altogether. This event is called a "fatal embrace." In such a situation, optimization might indicate a restructuring of data storage and segmentation of processing, but no *network* changes per se. There is no clear metric to benchmark this goal. It is a function of the accessibility to large storage devices and the support offered by the NOS.

Security

Security might represent a goal for networks supporting financial transactions. Optimization of security surely suggests avoidance of wireless network transmitters in favor of more secure optical fiber links or FDDI, the implementation of scrambled or encoded transmissions, and installation of rigorous validations and maintenance procedures to limit and track user access. A true ring structure—rather than the open architecture of a star (Token-Ring and 10Base-T) or bus (Ethernet)—optimizes security because any tampering or additions of new devices would create an observable domain failure. New devices or splices in optical fiber alter clarity and noise; a time domain reflectometer (TDR) trace photograph or printout documents any such changes. Other benchmarks for security are difficult to assess, although there are ways to improve security and monitor it. Realistically, we know that security is insufficient only after it has been breached.

Cost of delivery

The costs for most networks are optimized within some organization parameters. Certainly budget restrictions, the need to justify additional expenses, applications of costly technologies, and the need to resolve network bottlenecks temper how money is spent. Ethernet is less costly than Token-Ring. Twisted-pair wiring might lessen the overall site cost, although network length, reach, and expansion requirements might require that coaxial cable is a better means to optimize cost. Both are less costly than FDDI, yet FDDI might optimize costs for internetworking connectivity by minimizing the need for repeaters and additional channels to handle throughput. The only realistic benchmark for the cost of delivery is performance within established budgets. It is possible, of course, to assess the costs for networks and data delivery for *different* protocols and network standards.

Overhead requirements

Transmission overhead is rarely a concern in local area networks because NOSes usually designate protocol overheads and packet efficiencies rather than the hardware. Hardware, end-user software applications, sunk costs, and political decisions usually define the obligatory protocol. Protocol, or rather the choice of the protocol, therefore, is rarely optimized for a LAN installation. Additionally, by the time it is obvious that a LAN has a bottleneck due in part to the protocol, it is disruptive and expensive to shift to a better protocol. It is rarely attempted except in critical LAN applications; and then only when absolutely essential. Examples include installation of FDDI backbones for connecting Ethernet or Token-Ring subnetworks or FDDI to the desktop for medical or scientific imaging.

However, certain Novell networks *might* benefit from using Token-Ring rather than Ethernet, or visa versa, because the minimum and maximum frames differ in size. Protocol optimization does become an issue when packets must be encapsulated or translated into another protocol. For example, terminal emulation between a host and a network device requires bidirectional transmission of a single keystroke per packet and any resulting screen refreshes.

Protocol waste and overhead costs degrade actual channel utilization while encapsulating and translating data degrades speed of delivery and data throughput. Optimization might indicate a normalization of network protocols—dispensing with multiple protocols—in order to minimize overhead and maximize data throughput. Benchmarks for assessing network transmission overhead are irrelevant except within the context of contrasting different protocols and network standards.

Manageability

Optimizing manageability is accomplished by designing simple networks, qualifying components, installing a network correctly, and acquiring good tools. Manageability is also improved by establishing usage standards, minimum connectivity requirements, and understanding what goes wrong with the network. It is also possible to optimize network management time by using Token-Ring rather than Ethernet, assessing the time requirements for adding and switching star-wired connections versus the time required for extending a bus, or by minimizing the functionality of the network. There are no real benchmarks for assessing manageability. Proxy benchmarks for manageability might be reliability, availability, and work throughput. Similarly, it might be prudent to rate the skill level of the staff, or the relative complexity and need for the network.

Elusive and iterative optimization

LAN performance optimization is possible and, realistically, beneficial. Networks that perform badly, once optimized, are likely to realize 80-percent gains in data throughput. Enhancements might not be simple, straightforward, obvious, or financially possible. As such, network optimization is an elusive and iterative task. Often, some aspect of performance can be improved discernibly but with a secondary performance degradation or unsatisfactory organizational consequences. Often, too, some improvements just don't work. This is relevant for extensive, complicated, and true distributed networks.

Optimization techniques are as much an art as a science. Knowledge of network specifications, management experience, and troubleshooting practice are pertinent and valuable. But optimization is also a science. Statistical methods are available that are pertinent and valuable too. In fact, this is a major reason that this book includes the *LANModel* estimation and evaluation software. The art does not succeed without the science. Nonetheless, the application of the optimization science remains an art—one that is often elusive and iterative.

Often the network choke point is correctly identified while causes are not. When this happens, the bottleneck is only moved upstream or downstream. As previously stated, it is often difficult to distinguish the cause from the effect. Some network users might experience better performance to the detriment of others. The net result on average is negligible (unless better service for some users is the real priority). But, despite that evaluation, optimization can achieve cost-effective LAN improvements.

LAN performance optimization is also elusive because goals and benchmarks tend to evolve with practice and improvements. Improvements in performance beg for more enhancements. New optimization goals supersede the old. People forget and lose perspective, too. As networks are perceived as a reliable and consistent resource, formerly ad hoc tasks and nonessential chores coalesce into expected applications. Such activities become essential; some are stamped as "mission-critical" operations, without which the organization is jeopardized.

LAN throughput optimization

This book is about optimizing LAN capacity and data throughput because other goals are amorphous, difficult to measure, or politically biased. While these other ambiguous goals are valid, LAN performance optimization works best when it is based upon unambiguous goals and credible, independent metrics. One of the most common and recurring goals for optimization is to maximize data throughput within the existing network channel bandwidth.

LAN performance optimization becomes an important consideration for local area networks as they grow from initial ad hoc designs and become fundamental to organizational operations and even critical to success. Effective optimization can yield performance improvements of an average of 80 percent or as much as 4000 percent. It is crucial for those traditional centralized computing environments; this urgency is only accentuated when that computing power is distributed by a LAN and inextricably networked into daily operations throughout an organization.

Structurally, the network bandwidth is a significant limitation since it cannot be increased incrementally. Bandwidth is subject to peak traffic levels and stress from networked applications. Although the bandwidth itself is rarely the limiting factor, it is incorrectly perceived as the single most important factor for initially exploring suboptimal LAN performance. Furthermore, the metrics for assessing throughput performance are formal and unambiguous. For these reasons, *LAN Performance Optimization* and the included *LANModel* software stress maximizing LAN throughput as a prevalent goal. This book does explore other goals, although throughput optimization remains the primary focus.

2

Chapter

Network
bottlenecks

This chapter describes a variety of critical bottlenecks that diminish LAN performance. LAN performance optimization is the process of diagnosing which critical bottlenecks impede network performance—then eliminating or circumventing them. Frequently, DP managers, consultants, and other networking experts speculate that no clear methodology exists for assessing LAN performance. In fact, there are several effective methods to evaluate performance and locate bottlenecks—statistical modeling techniques and experimental trials, as Chapters 3 and 4 demonstrate, and as the *LANModel* network simulation and evaluation software establish.

The most common assumption for poor network performance is that the network channel is too slow or overloaded; that guess is usually wrong. It is common to hear someone say, "ARCnet is only 2.5 Mbits/s, Token-Ring is only 4 Mbits/s, and Ethernet is only 10 Mbits/s. 100 Mbits/s FDDI is what we need!" Transmission speed is actually relevant in less than 10 percent of bottlenecks. Given the premise that channel capacity is rarely the cause for bottlenecks, LAN performance will improve only slightly (25 to 50 percent) by increasing network bandwidth. It is more important to review physical LAN infrastructure, station performance, and software application demands. Figure 2-1 charts the most common network bottlenecks that actually degrade performance.

In general, defects in signal transmission qualities will adversely affect performance; there is usually an uncertain threshold before the cumulative defects affect

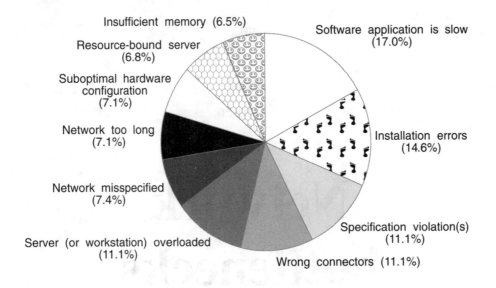

Insufficient memory (6.5%)

Resource-bound server (6.8%)

Suboptimal hardware configuration (7.1%)

Network too long (7.1%)

Network misspecified (7.4%)

Server (or workstation) overloaded (11.1%)

Software application is slow (17.0%)

Installation errors (14.6%)

Specification violation(s) (11.1%)

Wrong connectors (11.1%)

2-1 The top ten network bottlenecks.

performance. While specification violations do not guarantee poor network perform-ance, aggregated violations do.

Significantly, installation errors, specification violations, suboptimal configura-tions, poor network node performance, poor placement of *firebreaks*, and overloaded file servers represent the bulk of all bottlenecks. Furthermore, the premium is significant for upgrading a 4-Mbits/s Token-Ring to 16-Mbits/s operation, supple-menting ARCnet with ARCnet *plus*, or installing compliant FDDI optical fiber or copper wiring for copper-based FDDI (CDDI) to the desktop. All three are budget busters, and thus often impractical and unjustifiable optimization techniques.

Since channel saturation is an infrequent culprit, this book discusses channel limitations as part of the performance model in Chapter 4. However, due to the high cost of upgrading to a faster network protocol, this option is presented only as a last resort. More often than not, suboptimal network performance results from other causes, as listed in decreasing likelihood on page 21. Some network consultants, experienced installers, and vendors might want to rearrange this extensive list. However, this order does provide progressively more complex questions for quali-fying the performance of a local area network.

Usually, LANs perform badly because the installation is faulty. Examples include grounding it improperly, mismatching cable and wire grades or types, or attaching connectors poorly. Other faults include placing transceivers too close together or making the cable too long. As easy as it is to extend a coax-based network and exceed the 500-meter (m) limitation, it is even easier when the coax limit is 200m. Although LANs built upon twisted pairs are more reliable when installed correctly, and manageable due to the centralized star-configured wiring, this medium imposes more rigorous length

- Installation errors
- Specification violation
  Too many nodes
  Network too long
  Wrong physical medium
  Wrong connectors
- Network misspecified
- Suboptimal physical LAN configuration
- Suboptimal logical LAN configuration
- Network devices overloaded
  Repeater
  Router
  Bridge
  Frame relay
  Gateway
  Modem
- Server (or workstation) overloaded
  Slow disk access time
  Too many disks
  Disk full or fragmented
  Corrupted files
  Slow bus
  Slow memory
  Slow memory paging/swapping
  Suboptimal memory configuration
  Overloaded with requests
  Resource-bound
  Software not installed properly
  Software application is slow
  Suboptimal hardware configuration
  Improper interrupt settings
- Heterogeneous environment (mixed equipment)
- Heterogeneous protocols
- Incompatible network devices and nodes
- Slow internetwork protocol translation
- Slow internetwork protocol encapsulation
- Transmission errors
- Protocol errors
- Slow protocol
- Transmission timing errors
- Overloaded channel capacity
- Overloaded internetwork linkage
- Significant burst-level transmissions
  Network devices
  Stations
- Electrical magnetic interference (EMI)
- Radio-frequency interference (RFI)

limitations and noise difficulties. The riser heights—vertical distances between cable conduits and the actual outlets—and the actual stair-stepped route are often miscalculated. Installers frequently use the wrong cable grade, mismatch connectors, or mix phone and data lines.

Frequently, network managers will blueprint and substantiate network performance at a hardware level by examining signal transmission qualities and characteristics. Poor signal clarity, signal dispersion, improper electrical resistance, capacitance, signal propagation speed, or crosstalk from parallel channels or external radio sources often lead to suboptimal network performance. Optical networks, while immune to electrical signal distortions, are adversely affected by optical signal dispersal, excessive splices, lack of transmission medium clarity, transmitter strength and coherence, and receiver sensitivity.

For example, these possible LAN problems are analogous to anyone's experience with international telephone calls. Consider trying to comprehend a conversation over a poor international telephone connection. Although a particular instance of a bad connection might not lead to confusion, it might. The likelihood of communication problems increases if you add a non-native speaker to that example. Signal delays, phase shifts, crackles, hisses, and pops, or background ghost conversations cumulatively add to the possibility of a bottleneck. Language dialects, much like XNS, LAT, DECnet, IPX, Ethernet, 802.3, can increase the confusion until the communications obstacles reach the bottleneck threshold.

While specification violations do not guarantee poor network performance, aggregated violations do. It is worthwhile to obtain network protocol, configuration, and connectivity specifications. Read them. Learn them. Understand the implications of the formally and scientifically stated specifications. Plan networks to conform within these limitations, or realize that carefully planned violations require special attention. For example, it is possible to successfully construct a 3.8km FDDI link (by minimizing cable splices, installing superb-quality optical fiber, picking the most luminous transmitters, and selecting the most sensitive receivers) in spite of the 2km maximum specification. Bottlenecks often result from cumulative errors, most of which are minor and therefore, all too often, disregarded as insignificant. Cumulatively, insignificant violations and errors will break a LAN.

Vendors have frequently created network methodologies, marketed them, and hoped for economic successes. To a large degree the successful network protocols preceded formalization of official standards. Ethernet, Token-Ring, and ARCnet are the best examples. Standards became important only when customers recognized that multiple sources for network protocol provided better technology and allowed less reliance upon single and thus risky sources. Some network specifications have failed because the lengthy time and effects of design by committee doomed them to economic oblivion. Group FAX IV and FDDI (OSI protocols) are perhaps two such protocols. Pertinent network specifications are provided in the following list, with sources.

- ANSI X3.139 FDDI MAC-layer protocols (ANSI)
- ANSI X3.148 FDDI Token Ring (ANSI)
- ANSI X3.166 FDDI PMD (ANSI)
- ANSI X3.184 FDDI SMF-PMD (ANSI)
- ANSI X3.186 FDDI-II (ANSI)
- ANSI X3T9.5 Transitional FDDI Specifications (Global)
- ARCNET Cabling Guide (ARCNET Trade Association)
- ARCNET LAN Standard (ARCNET Trade Association)
- ARCNET Protocols (ARCNET Trade Association)
- ARCNET *plus* LAN Standard (ARCNET Trade Association)
- TCNS (Thomas-Conrad)
- IEEE 802.1 Spanning Tree Bridge (IEEE, NY)
- IEEE 802.2 LAN LLC protocols (IEEE, NY)
- IEEE 802.3 Ethernet (IEEE, NY)
- IEEE 802.5 Token ring protocols (IEEE, NY)
- IEEE 802.6 MAN protocols (IEEE, NY)
- TCNS, a 100 Mbits/s ARCnet derivative, (Thomas Conrad)

These flaws often masquerade for insufficient channel capacity. While specification violations and installation faults are the major causes for network bottlenecks, there are many others. The list below identifies the significant network bottlenecks addressed within individual sections in the remainder of this chapter.

- Channel constraints
- Physical configuration constraints
- Protocol limitations
- Compatibility
- Hardware limitations
- Software limitations
- NOS limitations
- Connectivity
- Applications limitations
- Overloading
- Saturation
- Discrepancies

Channel constraints

Although the data channel capacity is responsible for critical bottlenecks in less than 10 percent of networks, data communications channels will become saturated under sufficient load. Three basic loading conditions exist to saturate the network data communications channel. Sufficient load consists of demand consistently exceeding bandwidth, periodic channel capacity overloading for short durations or at peak work periods, or errors that jam the bandwidth regardless of its capacity.

First, ample demand for bandwidth can overload any network. Demand can be chronically high, high during peak work hours, or high for special software applications. Chronic overloads occur when the infrastructure (that is, network management, network design, and user requirements) are mismatched. For example, small rural towns might employ just a single mail employee to handle window sales, mail sorting, and actual delivery. Second, peak overloads might occur when processes or users request large block transfers. For example, large priority packages quickly fill mail trucks during holiday season and squeeze out other mail. Sporadic and sudden demand for peak bandwidth might oversaturate the channel. For example, last-minute tax return submittals might clog the mail sorting facility; this is a typical routing error. Third, the most likely explanation, errors and management problems can clog any channel no matter the bandwidth. For example, misaddressed letters, missing addresses or zip codes, and letters that open and jam the sorter might delay all mail delivery or even disable mail routing for an extended period. For an additional example, management that decides moving bulk mail is a higher priority than critical tax returns will create a postal bottleneck.

Figure 2-2 illustrates chronic, peak, sporadic, and application-related channel overloading. Network management software will typically show average and peak utilizations, or chronic overloading. Also, data gathered with a protocol analyzer can be plugged into *LANModel* to show why the network is overloaded. Under most conditions, though, channel constraints result from error conditions and installation flaws. High error rates create additional packet traffic as bad packets are transmitted again. Poor installation and creeping divergence from the formal network specifi-

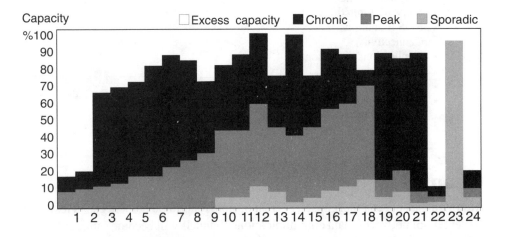

2-2   Chronic, peak (application-related), sporadic, and overloading.

cations increases signal slot times, incidences of marginal quality signal, and data bit loss. Before assuming that the channel is clogged, test other assumptions as well, such as suboptimal physical network configurations.

In the improbable situations when channel capacity is overwhelmed for peak periods or consistently overloaded, avoid the "obvious" conclusion that greater channel bandwidth will optimize performance. Other causes are numerous. Often, there might be a "stampede" of users signing onto the network at the beginning of the workday, after lunch, or after a server crash. Runaway processes could pump substantial load to create a nonproductive traffic bottleneck. Good examples include network management software that, when traffic loads become high, creates alerts that begin a cascade of automated debugging operations. These, in turn, could themselves create a broadcast storm. The *Heisenberg Uncertainty Principle* suggests that as a situation is observed, that observation itself accentuates or accelerates that situation, as described previously with the connectionless SNMP messaging. Typically, suboptimal physical network configurations create channel overloading.

Physical configuration constraints

Network configuration dramatically affects performance. The network refers to the data communications channel and network attachments as well as all the aggregated network station components. Two fundamental reasons for this include unbalanced placement of stations and an unbalanced mix of stations on a network. Figure 2-3 illustrates these constraints.

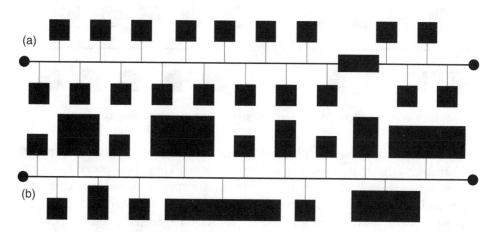

2-3 Physical network configuration constraints; (a) shows an unbalanced placement of stations, and (b) illustrates an unbalanced mix of stations in terms of performance and network loading.

Primarily, inadequate station performance results when the workstation is CPU-bound, memory-bound, or disk-bound. A database or file server with either full hard drives or slow hard drives, or providing maximum CPU operations is a bottleneck.

A server with too many onerous clients or overloaded with requests to construct SQL views is a serious network bottleneck. Similarly, diskless workstations will tend to overtax that server—by requesting the initial bootstrap segments, loading a large operating system (such as a Unix kernel) into memory, swapping and paging memory overlays, and requesting all applications and data from that single source. The network data communications channel might randomly experience full utilization while the server is topping out at capacity most of the time. Another equally likely possibility is that the server is limited by its ability to pump out traffic through its network port, or manage multiple networks ports.

Secondarily, too many stations or a unbalanced mix of stations on a single network segment or subnetwork creates channel overloading. An excessive number of servers and clients on a single network in aggregate might well saturate the channel. In addition, although a host mainframe serving as the corporate data repository could adequately service all its clients, that composite load could create a traffic bottleneck if concentrated on a single network channel.

Configuration oversights like these are easily solved. Solution might entail little additional hardware; often, the solution is nothing more than load balancing. Star-wired networks (Token-Ring, 10Base-T, FDDI with SAS stations) simplify such efforts because the subnets can be administered centrally from the wire closet, as can remote configuration hubs. Ethernet bus and FDDI rings might complicate load balancing to some degree, but adding additional parallel channels for subnetting is inexpensive for localized networks. Figure 2-4 illustrates how network load can be balanced.

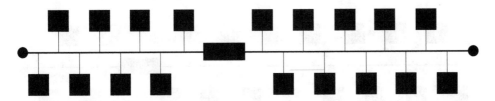

2-4   Balance network configurations by rearranging placement of stations and repeaters.

Usually, the lack of network blueprints undermines any effort to review network performance. Blueprints are essential documentation. They show actual placement and accurate lengths of the network wiring. Blueprints should reflect current alterations and enhancements. Use this information to calculate wiring lengths; append riser heights for accuracy. Match each length against the formal specifications. Length violations do not necessarily cause a bottleneck, although it is a reasonable error to review. Figure 2-5 shows a network blueprint for a twisted-pair network. Cable type is not specified; it could be UTP, STP, or European data ribbon.

For example, ARCnet and Token-Ring signals are audible for distances that exceed formal specification. Ethernet tolerates longer buses, drop cables, and

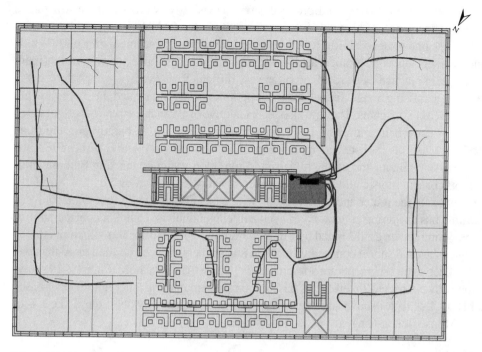

2-5   LAN wiring blueprint.

multiport repeater segments. FDDI can support segments twice the specification distance with high-quality fiber (or wire), superior transmitters, and sensitive receivers. Although a single violation is merely questionable, many violations should be perceived as a stability problem. Minor violations tend to creep into a network as it is expanded, lengthened, or modified. Station nodes are added, relocated, recabled, or rerouted. Connectors corrode, are jumpered, and are tortured.

Marginal violations in aggregate will increase the network error rates and transmission times to impede overall LAN performance. If the installation contractor failed to provide accurate wiring (twisted-pair, cable, or fiber) blueprints, a time domain reflectometer or sophisticated cable tester is the appropriate tool to generate wiring run-length measurements. Combine generated wiring measurements with site inspection before drafting physical blueprints.

However, the blueprint indicates only structural connections and not the logical LAN configuration. It rarely indicates repeaters, bridges, routers, gateways, or even any existing subnets. This is particularly relevant when networks utilize twisted-pair wiring or centrally managed physical networks. While a bus structure is almost obvious from the coaxial cable runs, twisted-pair wiring is completely plug-switch-able from the central wiring closet. A proficient manager can reconfigure the logical structure of a complex network in an hour.

In fact, it is so easy to swap cables that a "temporary" bypass or emergency repair often becomes permanent. As a result, it is important to document the logical structure of the network too. Bottlenecks will be visibly obvious when the structure is clearly documented. Also, this information is basic for *LANModel*. How many nodes does a segment support? How much traffic (packets) does the segment transport? Which logical segment is the protocol analyzer tracing? While these three questions might seem simple, in practice they are all too often very difficult to answer.

A surprising range of network configurations are illustrated in the following sequence of six figures. They are also representative of alternate network configurations to consider when optimizing LAN performance. They are all based upon the same wiring blueprints, as listed in Fig. 2-5. Figure 2-6 illustrates a typical Ethernet 10BASE-T segment utilizing the wiring blueprint. A multiport router connecting Ethernet multiport concentrators could replace the token network, as shown by Fig. 2-7. Similarly, exchanging the router and concentrators with a bus master switch (not to be confused with a bus mastering *controller*) or even a intelligent hub is a quick reconfiguration at the wiring center, as illustrated by Fig. 2-8. Figure 2-9 transforms this structure into the logical bus and subnet configuration. Note that subnets are not cascaded more than one unit deep so that segments are not separated by more than three hops. Figure 2-10 shows logically connected Token-Rings based upon the same wiring blueprint. Copper-based FDDI (CDDI) for single attachment stations (SAS) is logically configured like a 4- or 16-Mbits/s Token-Ring, as Fig. 2-11 illustrates.

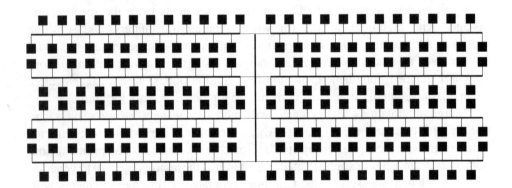

2-6   10Base-T logical configuration for LAN wiring blueprint.

Protocol limitations

The LAN protocol not only establishes physical configuration limitations, it also sets transmission times, overheads, and throughputs. Protocols incorporate multiple levels of data encapsulation, encoding, and calculated checksums. Typically, the multiple levels include the physical packet signal (PHY), a media access control

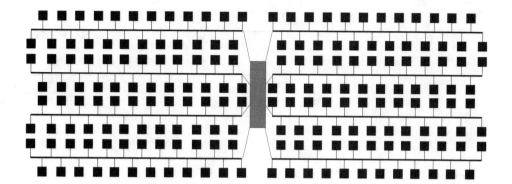

2-7 Router and concentrator logical LAN wiring configuration.

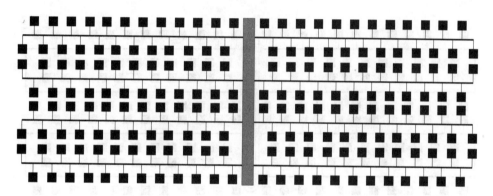

2-8 Bus master or intelligent hub configuration.

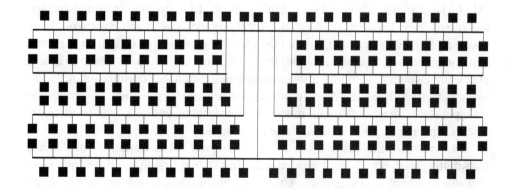

2-9 LAN wiring blueprint for bus and subnet configuration.

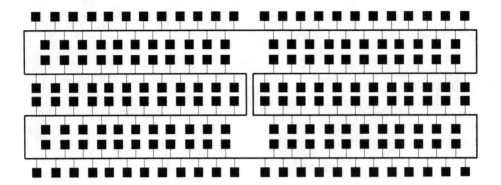

2-10 LAN wiring blueprint for token ring logical configuration.

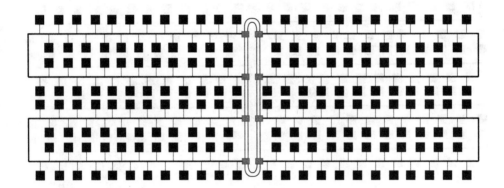

2-11 LAN wiring blueprint for copper-based FDDI (CDDI) configuration.

(MAC) layer, transmission and logical link controls (LLC) to coordinate and manage the interchange between sending and receiving devices, and application layer encoding and data sequencing so that the receiver gets the message in an expected and comprehensible format. Protocol limitations include encapsulation overheads, checksum calculations, initial transmission request signals, transmission acknowledgments, fixed latencies, random intervals for channel acquisition, overheads for multiple stacks, packet size minimums and maximums, and slot time restrictions. The list on page 31 gives some of these limitations.

For example, the basic ARCnet hardware protocol is designed such that a transmitting station polls the intended receiving station first to see if it is available and able to accept incoming data. After data transmission, it then expects a confirmation transmission. Ethernet protocol states that two simultaneous or overlapping transmissions generate a collision and followed by a random period without any

- Data encapsulation overheads
- Checksum calculations
- Minimum packet sizes
- Maximum packet sizes
- Channel acquisition methods
- Transmissions priorities
- Stack overheads
- Data field padding
- Slot time restrictions
- LAN protocol complexities

network traffic (collision backoff). Additionally, every TCP/IP data transmission usually initiates a response from the receiving stations. Server application software might require that the clients are periodically polled for status. Although TCP/IP and application-based transmission are seen as data packets, the TCP UDP and SNMP transmissions are *connectionless* and thus not always observed as traffic loads.

Compatibility

Bottlenecks arise from incompatibilities between all network components. Nothing is immune. Although substandard twisted-pair cabling is a frequent cause of signaling problems that create traffic bottlenecks, delays, and significant retransmissions, incompatibilities can be more subtle. While many are transient and might occur during certain operations or combinations of events, some are intermittent and recurring. The list below provides some typical sources for incompatibility-based bottlenecks.

- Cabling
- Connectors
- NICs
- NIC power draw
- Network devices
- Contention backoff algorithms
- Network timing stability
- Network signal frequencies
- Deviation from protocol specifications
- Network operating systems
- Protocol stack interpretations
- Memory buffer sizes
- Number of buffers
- Operating systems

LANs supporting multiple protocols are frequently affected by incompatibilities in the protocols. For example, although Novell, LAN Manager, LAN Server, and

IBM Advanced System 400 (AS/400) share Token-Ring hardware and even the actual wiring plant, broadcast packets are apt to confuse the different operating systems. Similarly, DECnet, LAT, XNS, Ethernet 1.1, Ethernet 2.0, and IEEE 802.3 represent the Ethernet protocol family. While stations might coexist within the same physical cabling plant, collision handling hardware and mechanisms are fundamentally different. Signal frequencies, heartbeats, and jams, as well as multicasts and broadcasts, are handled differently. When TCNS, ARCnet, and ARCnet *plus* coexist, the speed incompatibilities between these fundamentally similar protocols often create a routing bottleneck.

The primary purpose for most local area networks is to promulgate peer-to-peer resource sharing or to connect servers with their client workstations. Host computers (mainframes), terminal servers, and other stand-alone systems can piggyback onto an existing LAN. Although these systems might not interoperate, let alone interconnect to the LAN servers, they increase LAN traffic and the tendency for a performance bottleneck. At a minimum, this supplemental traffic creates meaningless overhead for the primary client-server activities. More likely, supplemental traffic will not conform seamlessly to the client-server network operating system protocols. This spawns processes that try to decipher traffic and reroute it. This also increases network traffic and frequently overburdens network servers.

Hardware limitations

While each network protocol imposes speed and performance limitations, node devices influence the aggregate LAN performance. Node devices are active computers that include workstations and connectivity devices (bridges, routers, and gateways). This section concentrates on the typical computing nodes: workstations, servers, and hosts. Connectivity devices are amplified in a subsequent section. LANs, in general, experience most performance limitations due to wiring errors and installation flaws; marginal signal timing; frequency, quality, or strength differences; and mechanical degradation—throughout the life cycle of the network.

Although this book is indeed about performance optimization, and effective LAN performance requires that these hardware-based errors be resolved, other books explain in detail how to use voltmeters and multimeters, time domain reflectometers, and the newest combination of all these tools, the cable scanners. Other McGraw-Hill books, such as *The Ethernet Management Guide, The Token-Ring Management Guide*, and *How to Install and Manage FDDI*, provide excellent resources for basic network design, installation, and network management. Computer-aided design tools, such as *LANBuild* from Network Performance Institute, also provide a means to design a sufficient network and bypass some of the typical hardware-based and infrastructure errors. However, it is often the case that underlying infrastructure flaws accentuate problems with the node workstations and connectivity devices.

Computing node hardware

As previously stated, actual data transmission channel performance is ordinarily adequate. Instead, overall network operation is severely restricted by inferior workstation, server, or gateway host performance. Just as the LAN is a complex entity, these network stations (or nodes) are complex aggregations in their own right. A station is the total aggregation of all physically and logically connected components. This includes not only the LAN hardware access facility itself but also all other hardware devices and software processes. Any one of these components could cause significant bottlenecks—and often do. Figure 2-12 illustrates the complexity of typical node hardware.

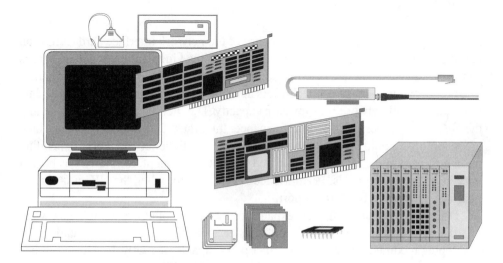

2-12 Complexity of typical node hardware.

LAN adapter performance

All computing devices access the network by means of a hardware *and* software attachment. The attachment hardware, of course, transmits and receives the signals. It also buffers outgoing and incoming packets, and assembles and disassembles the data within those packets. The hardware additionally resolves or indicates errors at the media level, such as collisions, packet misallignments, jittering, jabbering, channel breakage beacons, as well as late, lost, and duplicate tokens. The IEEE and ISO standards also define other hardware and software processes strictly related to the transmission flow. Figure 2-13 graphically simplifies the actual transmission process.

Although most transceivers or transmitter and receiver units (network interface cards) are perceived as a predefined network component, the choice of the actual units, the configuration process, and the design teams' interpretation of the specifications do affect network performance. For example, consider the following: The

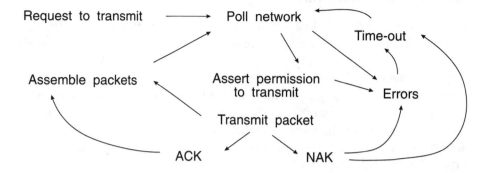

2-13 Simplified transmission process flow diagram.

number of chips on the LAN adapter board of the network interface card (NIC) can determine process speed and power draw. Local bus video and network interfaces can decrease wait state time and bus conflict for improved local node performance. The number and/or size of packet buffers determine whether a card can provide data burst rates at full network transmission capacity. The method for actually attaching the NIC to the processor affects performance. Integrated data ports are NICs, which are incorporated onto the motherboard, and can be both better and worse depending upon how communication was optimized for that component. Similarly, bus boards vary in performance levels. Performance is also a factor when the NIC is a plug-in board or attached to the parallel port.

LAN adapters that fit in a bus expansion slot might not utilize the full data width of the bus. To overcome bus and port transfer speed limitations, some vendors are developing modified bidirectional parallel ports capable of nearly 16 Mbits/s. When these high-speed ports appear on laptops, the attached NIC is unlikely to create a process bottleneck at current network speeds. Nonetheless, such bus-mastering access ports might create a bottleneck at 100-Mbits/s Token-Ring or FDDI speeds.

Bus architectures

Bus architectures restrict station performance and as a result, network performance. PC bus architecture—such as ISA (industry standard interface), EISA (enhanced industry standard interface), or MCA (micro-channel adapter)—affects node performance as well. ISA is limited to 512,000-bits/s bus transfer speeds, EISA to 38 Mbits/s, and MCA to 42 Mbits/s. Effectively, EISA and MCA provides only 4 to 6 Mbits/s. Clearly, a heavily utilized file server with an ISA bus can spawn a bottleneck if the LAN or application software can sustain greater data burst rates. These bus DMA transfer speeds will be discussed again because they are a factor in internal CPU, display, and disk transfer limitations.

Software limitations

The *LANModel* software (on the companion disk) explores the actual channel transmission capacities. Frequently, the traffic levels are measured by protocol analyzers that capture and tally data packets while overlooking the NAK, ACK, higher-level protocols, and software overheads. Most protocol analyzers simply cannot translate and collect traffic data at full network transmission speed; the best track 87 to 95 percent of channel traffic. As a result, view the accuracy of these devices with some skepticism, and realize that even the most accurate might ignore the hardware protocols or misinterpret them. Software limitations include poor NIC drivers, complex software, poorly tuned application software, code swapping, and memory constraints.

NOS limitations

The network operating system frequently influences network performance. The protocols, complexity, processing required for any activity, and memory requirements clearly represent overheads that might well inhibit a station from attaining full channel capacity. The network operating system software, the vectors that interrupt and redirect underlying operation system functions and calls, the packet assembly and disassembly, and the hardware device drivers all impose a cost in terms of time, disk space, and memory. The list below gives some NOS limitations that affect network performance.

- Operating system device drivers
- NOS overhead requirements
- NOS disk space and memory requirements
- NOS stack space
- NOS buffer space
- NOS environment space
- Multistack packet buffers
- Multistack protocol overheads
- Vector interrupt processing time
- Redirect processing time
- Station address construction
- Station address resolution
- Protocol overheads
- Protocol communications
- Network requests process time
- Coding standards
- NOS code efficiency
- Code implementations
- Code optimization
- Error recovery
- Transparency (with other NOSes)
- Interoperability
- Speed of overall station operation
- Runaway processes
- Unauthorized or undesirable processes

Even though every network operating system affects data communication performance, some network operating systems necessitate more considerations than others. In fact, some implementations might be better than others. For example, there are many vendors providing TCP/IP for Unix, PC-DOS, and OS/2. Some are faster, require less memory overhead, page less to and from the hard disk, and have better error handling than others. Overheads might include NAK or ACK pretransmissions, response frames, or a "keep-alive" message for connection-oriented LLC (Logical Link Control of MAC-layer protocols) to verify a continued Token-Ring connection between stations. The active monitor issues a request for a response from every active node every seven seconds as part of the Token-Ring protocol. ARCnet is a simple protocol requiring efficient software drivers, while open systems interconnect (OSI) is not. OSI requires more code, more system memory, and because it is hierarchical (i.e. "layered"), it has more steps in the transmission and reception process. As a result, an MS Windows application can be expected to respond more slowly under OSI than for ARCnet.

Similarly, Novell limits data transfers to a maximum of 4Kb under the IPX protocol and 512 bytes under Token-Ring for hops across bridges (without burst mode packet support). Therefore, an Ethernet with low traffic levels will efficiently transfer files within 1500-byte data frames with frequent transmission bursts. A Token-Ring with similar traffic levels will not be as efficient. Although Token-Ring packets can include a maximum of 18Kb, the IPX limit applies. (64Kb packets at 16 Mbits/s was originally inferred by the 802.5 specifications based upon a "reasonable" TRT delay.) Additionally, spacing between sequential packets requires at least the token rotation time of the full ring. More often than not, the network operating system is predetermined. Principle software applications are based upon selection of a specific NOS. It might be LAN Server, LAN Manager, OS/2 LAN, NFS, Novell, Banyan, Ungermann-Bass, Artisoft peer-to-peer connections, TCP, or even a connectivity protocol such as NetBEUI or NetBIOS. Realistically, it is rare that suboptimal network performance can be improved by replacing a NOS. It is simply such a massive undertaking and so disruptive to users that replacing a NOS is an unlikely solution to network performance problems.

Connectivity

LAN performance is greatly affected by connectivity configurations. NICs obviously influence station throughput, server performance, and diskless client operations. However, few LANs are so simple as to consist of a single bus or hub and a handful of stations. Many LANs have expanded in incremental stages with repeaters, bridges, and routers. Performance-oriented linkage products include intelligent hubs, packet switches, and store-and-forward gateways. This books focuses upon optimizing performance for a local area network. As such, more complex internetworking issues are discussed in *Enterprise Network Performance Optimization*. The appendix contains a glossary for these linkage products. However, the next sections describe bottlenecks created by linkages devices, such as those listed below.

- Repeaters, bridges, routers, and gateways
- Store-and-forward gateways
- Packet switches and bus mastering backplanes
- Client-server
- Distributed computing environments (DCE)
- Database gateways

Repeaters, bridges, routers, and gateways

Repeaters, bridges routers, and gateways extend a LAN by allowing a longer physical network or more stations. These linkage devices are lumped together in the same set because they all serve the same function. The complexity differs for each type of device—they operate at progressively higher levels in the seminal OSI networking model. Although there is much doubt that there will be widespread endorsement for this OSI networking standard, it nonetheless provides a meaningful standard for evaluating LAN architecture, interconnectivity standards, and LAN interoperability, as well as performance benchmarks.

Repeaters take a packet from one network and broadcast to one or more attached segments. For most protocols, repeaters become a performance obstacle when they increase slot time and boost collisions or duplicate collisions and other protocol "errors." Repeaters also increase the statistical chance that a marginal signal becomes a inferior signal with bit errors when it is rebroadcast. Repeaters are common for ARCnet and Ethernet. Every station on a Token-Ring or FDDI in effect is a repeater; although for these protocols, errors are minimized through the hardware transmission protocols. Repeaters tend to increase traffic levels on all attached segments to the sum of traffic levels of each individual segment. In other words, if a repeater connects three segments, each originally supporting sustained traffic levels of 8 Mbits/s, interconnected segments will then experience 24 Mbits/s—if the protocol supports that bandwidth. Otherwise, the network will experience saturation or total transmission collapse.

Bridges are repeaters that convert signals from one transmission media to another. The protocol must be the same across the bridge. As such, a bridge induces similar performance problems as a repeater since it multiplies network traffic levels in the same manner as the repeater. A bridge is also a "firewall" when it is designed to overcome the limitations imposed by repeaters. Just as a firewall insulates one area from the immediate effects of a fire, a bridge will prevent collisions and errors on one network segment from infiltrating to another one. As such, bridges *might* filter error, collision, and beacon signals and not propagate these network conditions to other segments. This provides some performance gain. However, signals that convey network conditions also convey information about network configuration and performance that can be important for other segments.

Additionally, a bridge might be unable to maintain full network speed when rebroadcasting signals from one network to others. First, it might be unable to provide the full channel bandwidth. Second, the protocols on destination networks might delay the packet rebroadcast; the bridge might wait for collisions to clear or acquire the token for permission to transmit just like any other network station. In all instances, packets are lost or delayed beyond the network specification. Third, lost packets require extra bandwidth for retransmissions; that is a performance drain.

Routers receive (and process) only those packets directed by network device address to them. The actual destination addresses are conveyed by higher protocols (IPX, IP, etc.) within the data frame. The router interprets and rebuilds that information into a new network packet with the same data, and transmits the modified packet on a new network segment. Routers tend to be slower than bridges because they perform these significant protocol decodes.

Routers filter packets by source, destination, and security factors. Routers do not retransmit error conditions or packets that are irrelevant to the other network segments. Routers discriminate between what should be forwarded and what is unnecessary traffic. As such, routers provide a performance gain for networks with subnets near capacity. This is true with one provision, namely, that all packet addresses must be matched against entries in a routing table. This operation is analogous to mail sorting: this zip code goes here, this one goes here, and this one doesn't have one. Each address match requires a lookup operating in one or more routing tables; routers might maintain a routing table for *each* supported protocol. Each attempted address comparison executes approximately 50 machine instructions in the router's CPU—a router is a computer, of course. Most routers support routing tables with a maximum of 8192 addresses. Good searching algorithms employ modified binary trees for faster response (16 searches or less); poor methods employ sequential lookups (up to 8192 examinations).

While poor searching algorithms take too long, the 50 machine CPU cycles add up to 50 bit times. A busy network can overload the router, which becomes a bottleneck. The router throws away the first (FIFO queue) or last (LIFO queue) packets. Just as in the case for overloaded bridges, lost packets require extra bandwidth for retransmissions, and that implies a performance drain. Some routers incorporate specialized hardware to maintain full network bandwidth transparency. Nonetheless, few computers are fast enough to route at sustained FDDI speeds.

Gateways transform protocols. For example, Token-Ring might talk to Ethernet, FDDI, LU 6.2, or IRMA. Various NOS protocols can interconnect to heterogeneous ones on other networks. Examples include NetWare talking to OS/2, LAN Manager, Appletalk, LAN Server, or NETBEUI. Gateways are usually bottlenecks because the transformation is a complex application-oriented and context-sensitive operation. Examples include keystroke terminal emulation that requires excessive bandwidth, SQL requests that might be optimized for the SQL server but not for the network, and packet format conversion that tend to be optimized for simplicity (such as Novell IPX) rather than transmission efficiency. In addition, gateways incorporate routing functions and therefore suffer all the limitations of routers.

Store-and-forward gateways

Store-and-forward gateways are special forms of a network gateway more relevant within the context of enterprise-wide networking. This device (or process) typically translates or encapsulates data for long-haul transmission or transfer to another network. Store-and-forward gateways improve network performance by delaying transmission of information, pertinent for mail and delivery operations that do not require priority connectivity. However, such a gateway can become an obstacle when a local operation is waiting for data to pass through the gateway. Workstations or servers with multiprocessing capabilities are most likely to be impeded by remote data collection and transmission activities.

Database gateways

Database gateways are software applications that retrieve data from within one environment and translate for use within another. Forest and Trees is one such product that converts and displays from multiple databases. More complex database applications can translate, view, process, and translate data back into the original formats to save or add data into the diverse distributed databases. Not only is this process a software conversion, frequently massive blocks of data must be moved from point to point over the transmission channel. Furthermore, these blocks might be built as complex data views, filtered, and locally processed before they are translated and packetized for network transmission.

Database gateway bottlenecks are likely to occur due to limited data storage device transfer speeds, the burden on station CPUs and memory to create these complex slices of a database, and the channel bandwidth required to transfer these large data blocks in proper synchronization to the actual gateway station. Assembling the slices into a coherent picture on the actual gateway might also pose a significant load to that station. Memory paging speeds, size of available memory, memory and disk caching speeds, and application software efficiencies are the obvious obstacles. The network bandwidth is a limiting factor mostly in instances where that channel is slow or burdened by other network traffic.

Packet switches and bus mastering backplanes

Packet switches and bus-mastering backplanes are specialized network devices that are essentially networks in a single box. They are often high-performance devices essentially installed to resolve existing bottlenecks. They provide interconnectivity for multiple subnetworks and different protocols. While usually designed to concentrate and route multiple networks from a single point, these devices can be overwhelmed by traffic levels. Note that they form a single point of failure.

Since all networks connect into these devices, failure of power supplies, bad routing tables, flawed software, software incompatible with network operating systems, and erratic operation of cards that fit into these specialized computers can readily cause global network bottlenecks. However, packet switches and bus-mastering backplanes are usually designed as high-speed focal points. As such, they perform well until the performance threshold is surpassed.

Client-server networks

LANs have thrived because they provide a distributed computing and interconnectivity environment and a functional platform for client-server computing. They yield cost, data backup, maintenance, and management advantages over peer-to-peer configurations. While client-server networks share all the potential network bottlenecks as previously outlined, the client-server relationship itself is the most likely performance bottleneck. Since most applications and data reside on the server, the server itself is a limiting factor on performance. Insufficient CPU speed, slow memory paging, low disk transfer speeds, few cache hits, nominal disk to network transfer speeds, and overhead for transmission acknowledgments represent the most frequent performance limitations.

Distributed computing environments

Distributed computing environments (DCE) represent a special and advanced case for client-server computing. Functional application execution and coprocessing is performed wherever there is a suitable free resource. Considerable management overhead is required to distribute subsidiary tasks and supervise this complex processing. Management might control process wait states, split computation loads, make judgments on whether a task is best performed locally or globally, and match data communication transmission times with times for acquiring the local or remote data sets.

Additionally, master tasks are not completely parallel nor independent. As such, some tasks might be delayed until collateral tasks are completed and the objects, code, or data are transferred. Bottlenecks are difficult to trace and eliminate since critical paths change from application to application, from iteration to iteration, and are also dependent upon the loads applied to nodes and transmission channels from other ongoing tasks. DCE bottlenecks tend to be randomized and nonprocedural, and thus infuriatingly migrate elsewhere with attempts to resolve them.

Application limitations

Applications represent a complexity and overhead that dwarfs the potential for network bottlenecks caused by hardware, transmission speed, or channel capacity limitations. Software applications represent firmware, operating systems, device drivers, data engines (databases such as SQL, Progress, the Paradox engine, and Btrieve), network operating systems, routers, translating and encapsulating gateways, client-server applications, and end-user applications. Unfortunately, these software bottlenecks are not as controllable nor as amenable to resolution as are hardware and device-based network obstacles. Frequently, software application limitations must be accepted; optimization represents minimal possibilities.

All computer operations are fundamentally limited by CPU cycle speed and the number of steps in operating systems, task multiprocessing, network operating systems, and actual application software. A simple request for data from a storage device might impose several thousand hardware-level commands and acknowledgments. A byte transferred from one memory to a simple network protocol stack can require anywhere from a dozen to several hundred CPU cycles. A complex protocol stack, such as OSI, or a multiple protocol stack, such as ODI and NDIS, might require an additional thousand cycles to route that byte to the correct protocol layer or the anticipated stack when several coexist.

These fundamental computer processing limitations are multiplied millions of times since application software represents complex steps and network interactions. Point-to-point block record or file transfers are fundamentally simple network events. Client-server database activities represent a series of those "simple" record or file transfers. Software must be loaded into memory, large code libraries linked and cached or overlaid into memory as requested, control between sending and receiving stations synchronized and managed, and any intermediate processing and data translating accomplished to parse records or files into meaningful data fields.

Overloading

Network channel overloading is an uncommon bottleneck. Channel overloading represents less than 10% of all critical network bottlenecks. This holds true for ARCnet, Ethernet, FDDI, and Token-Ring. Typically, error conditions or runaway processes overwhelm the channel bandwidth, and the network functions correctly after these flaws are resolved. Examples of error conditions include a beaconing Token-Ring station, a chattering Ethernet transceiver, and a node that does not recognize its own addresses (either hardware, software, or application-specific addresses). Also, overloading does occur when network specifications are violated. Examples include networks with too many stations, those that are too long, and those that intermix incompatible devices and protocols.

Sometimes—through rarely—a channel is overwhelmed by the traffic volume. This frequency coincides with periodic peak periods for network activity, paging-

or request-intensive operations, and ill-tuned distributed processing. Examples include peak E-mail processing during normal employee daily-arrival times, graphic image loading, and SQL or transaction processing. Overloading also occurs when a server supports too many clients on a single channel or when there are too many overlapping servers on a single network. Peer-to-peer networks rarely encounter channel overloading unless there are too many stations on the network.

Saturation

Network channel saturation is a special case of overloading. Saturation develops when the network is chronically overloaded. It also occurs when error conditions so overwhelm the network that data throughput is impossible. The bandwidth is totally used by attempts to clear these errors. Ethernet is a special case where collisions easily overload the channel when traffic exceeds 37% of channel bandwidth.

Although the Ethernet collision is not an error per se—it is a valid component of the protocol—Ethernet saturation occurs when too many simultaneous transmissions continuously saturate the channel bandwidth. No work is accomplished. The full network bandwidth is used by fragmented packets, jam signals, and even some random periods where colliding stations wait for another chance to transmit. Stations repeatedly timeout, and user-initiated actions to restart activities merely recommence the saturation problem.

Discrepancies

Performance drains that include design errors, software bugs, and NOS releases that work erratically with application or OS upgrades fall into the category of discrepancies. This catch-all category is a major offender. Alas, perhaps of all network bottlenecks this grouping represents the most difficult for which to establish benchmarks, capture data, or adequately resolve. It is included here mainly as a reminder that human error and oversight defies scientific or any orderly analysis. (For reference, see the Network General Sniffer example in Chapter 5.) Since it does factor into many LAN performance bottlenecks, consider other approaches; review LAN procedures, plug into BBS and support groups, and cultivate relationships with peers.

Network performance assessment

Recalling Chapter 1, LAN performance optimization requires definition of fundamental goals, establishment of related benchmarks, data collection based upon those benchmarks, and finally, evaluation of variances from expectation. Variations will usually indicate potential bottlenecks. The next chapters start the process for assessing network performance. Chapter 3 shows how to establish benchmarks and collect relevant data. It also shows how to analyze variances and generate solution proposals, as well as assess these trial solutions.

3
Chapter

Optimization data

The network is sluggish. Performance is poor. Users complain. The predominant question is which aspects of the network are gridlocked. Data makes it possible to determine what features of a network are performance bottlenecks. In many cases, resident NOS reporting tools provide interesting although often ineffectual data. Supplemental tools seek to address these shortcomings with the usual result of too much data. Performance evaluation is best based upon a few simple statistics. Specifically, traffic volume, standard deviation or variance of that volume, and network node counts represent the most relevant traffic performance measurements. However, since a network is an aggregation of many components, it is important to assess some component performance measurements and optimize those components that singularly cause network performance bottlenecks.

This chapter describes which data to collect and evaluate. Data is required to optimize a LAN effectively. Many LAN tools—time domain (delay) reflectometers (TDR), protocol analyzers, network management software, management protocols, and packet capture software inclusive—are highly effective LAN information gathering tools. Yet, these are general-purpose tools for collecting and organizing data for making operational decisions. They generate assumptions for making decisions relative to daily network operations. Operational data is inferior for evaluating such long-term and far-reaching issues as logical network structure, best memory or disk configuration, and ideal LAN configuration.

While useful within a daily operational framework, most LAN tools are rarely focused sufficiently to gather the specialized data directly applicable to LAN perform-ance optimization. Most of these and comparable tools can collect so many actual packets, statistics, event rates, and numbers that they often overwhelm most network managers. Consider the following short list of numbers, rates, statistics, deviances from predetermined or preset rates, and alarms. SNMP and CMIP can track more than several thousand distinct statistics for each network device.

- Number of free blocks available on server hard drive
- Number of free directory slots available on server volume
- Cache efficiency
- Number of cache hits or cache misses
- Number of active connections
- CPU utilization
- Number of open files
- Ratio of disk reads to writes
- Protocol cold start trap
- Peer neighbor loss
- Agent authentification reconfiguration
- Last system restart reason
- Ping host from entity method
- Buffer element misses
- Reason for interface change status
- Agent "keep-alives" enabled
- Delay in agent interface (in microseconds)
- Total number of "echoes" and no replies received
- Percent of timeouts acheived
- Number of packets dropped due to a missing route

SNMP and CMIP values represent typical statistics tracked by many protocol analyzers, captured by remote SNMP devices, or concentrated by the Internet-standard MIB-I or MIB-II network management databases. SNMP MIB-I explicitly defines about 500 statistics and MIB-II an additional 300 counts, and neither limit the number of proprietary additions. In fact, the stars of many an Interop show are the MIB-controlled toaster and remote-controlled mechanical toys controlled through proprietary MIB extensions. Not only is the actual data overwhelming, but composite rates and statistics frequently are more confusing than helpful. The operative word is *overwhelming;* most network management tools provide too much data and too many variations on format, presentation, and the actual access to it. In some other cases, access to the underlying primary data is limited by design, lack of tools, lack of documentation, or vendor support policies, or accessed only with great difficulty. The key performance measurements are traffic volume, variance, and node counts.

Furthermore, LAN performance capacity benchmarks and the statistics they generate are fairly meaningless without specific context. All too often, LAN measurements are based upon the particular LAN configuration, not upon any intrinsic performance of the protocol and NOS. Benchmarks must correspond to the production environment for the tests to be an accurate reflection of network performance; they might be accurate and relevant tests for evaluating critical components that singularly cause global network bottlenecks. Rather, most tests are simple LAN component tests—not true LAN system evaluations. Furthermore, most benchmarks create "artificial" or "synthetic" workloads quite atypical of most true LAN environments.[1] When LAN performance is optimized based upon such benchmarks, actual LAN bottlenecks tend to migrate as the workload changes. However, with that caveat, such *relative* LAN performance measurements form a good standard for assessing progress in improving the LAN over some time period. (As an aside, *absolute* LAN performance *estimates* are available only from a mathematically-based calculation as performed by a tool such as LANModel. These are estimates, not measurements, and as such, are critically dependent upon the accuracy and integrity of the input parameters and the quality of the mathematical model.) Nevertheless, do not discount the value of relative measurements. Maintain a database of capacity and performance measurements with dates and other relevant notes. Use earlier values for comparison against current measurements to assess how well the LAN tuning is progressing.[2] The user is wholly dependent upon the developers of network management tools to build pertinent display screens, charts, and graphs, or make intelligent assessments about how the aggregate information will provide the most value. In fact, many protocol analyzer vendors are installing "artificially intelligent" interfaces to boost the value of these complex tools and even more overwhelming databases. Nonetheless—since these interfaces are software products—the user is frequently bounded by the foresight, implementation, and traditional limits of these software products.

It is important to realize that TDRs, protocol analysis tools, and network management software provide specific capabilities based upon what a designer has designed into those tools or envisioned as relevant for the perceived market audience. Superior network management tools provide export facilities. These facilities align captured data within a standard database format (examples include SQL, dBASE, Microsoft Excel, and Lotus 1-2-3 spreadsheet formats) so that users can perform their own particular analysis; this is important for gathering information that is most useful and relevant for LAN performance optimization. With some forethought and experience, the information that these tools gather can be transformed into data applicable for network performance analysis and ultimate optimization.

Another set of standardized and often readily available performance analysis tools includes CPU, system, and network benchmarks. Typical benchmarks for system performance or network performance are based upon iteration of various tasks (sieves, network block reads and writes, video *bitblk* updates, and file copies).

1   Ronald E. Lee, Senior Consultant, Novell Inc.

2   Boggs, Mogul, and Kent; *Measured Capacity of an Ethernet: Myths and Reality*, ACM Journal, Spring 1988

All these benchmarks are interesting. Benchmarks are usually "generalized." Some might even be useful. Assess their utility carefully and the pertinence to viewing LAN performance with a jaundiced eye. Most LANs are more complex with interrelated and convoluted applications than assumed by the benchmark designers. However, as explained above, relative performance benchmarks are useful because they provide values that can be compared to earlier results to show a progression of effective LAN optimization.

Developing effective benchmarks represents one of the most complex software applications. Usually, each benchmark utility is designed to stress a particular feature; thus, *suites* of benchmarks are developed to provide a robust evaluation. Most benchmarks can be acquired from the developer without cost; developers desire that these tools be readily available, openly assessed, and critiqued. Most PC-, Unix-, and LAN-oriented magazines, system journals, trade research organizations, and national consulting organizations have developed published (or available-upon-request) suites of standardized benchmarks.

Specifically, recall that the LAN is the aggregate of all devices and stations on the LAN, as well as all processes, operating systems, and coprocessing interactions. Network performance represents much more than well-designed networks, properly installed cable infrastuctures, and moderate transmission traffic rates. This means that the capacity and throughputs of individual stations, NOS overheads, overlooked background, undesirable processes, plus the LAN and internetworking interactions affect LAN performance, as listed below.

- LAN devices
  Bridge loads and throughput
  Gateway loads and throughput
  Repeater loads and throughput
  Router loads and throughput
  Terminal server efficiencies
- Stations
  NICs
  Caches
  Disk Drives
  Free memory
  Operating systems
  Network operating systems
  Wait states
- Station loads and throughput
- Segment loads and throughput
- Internetworking efficiencies
- Interoperating efficiencies
- LAN loads and throughputs
- Accounting, background, and overhead processes

A LAN optimization method

Because of this complexity, LAN optimization requires specialized data gathered with skilled collection and analysis techniques. It is important to capture global performance data and filter this to a specific station or groups of stations. Additionally, tools such as Norton Utilities *System Information* are relevant for revealing PC station performance. Similar though more sophisticated station performance tools are generally available for MS-DOS, MS Windows, OS/2, Unix, other operating systems in common usage, and network operating systems as well. Use performance benchmark suites.[3] Serious limitations are inherent with any benchmark tools, foremost the relevance of benchmarks to true LAN production workloads.

The methodology for LAN optimization is outlined below. This process begins stepwise, starting with a global view of the network, progressing to individual stations and processes. Global problems, such as deficits in the LAN infrastructure, are traced and explored first. At this stage, no repairs are performed; this is merely a data gathering exercise. Although each step is likely to uncover and substantiate causes for suboptimal performance, endeavor to complete the full analysis *before* implementing network renovation.

- View a LAN as an aggregated object
  Gather aggregated LAN data
  Confirm suboptimal performance
- View a LAN as subsets of station groups
  Gather data for each subset
  Confirm suboptimal performance by group
- Explore station groups as a LAN subsystem
  Gather data for subgroup operation
  Search for interactions
  Trace bottlenecks to stations or processes
- Explore individual station and process performance
  Gather station-specific data
  Confirm suboptimal configurations
  Confirm suboptimal processes

Strive to complete this analysis before developing any strategy or implementing any network changes. It is a mistake to jump ahead and make changes prior to a thorough LAN assessment. Develop a baseline measurement so that changes are assessable. Incomplete information often leads to expensive overhauls that bypass actual performance problems. Furthermore, fragmentary information is apt to mis-

---

3   Some shareware or public domain programs for measuring system CPU and resource performance include TESTNET, PERFORM, CPUUSE, FREEMEM, and RESGAUGE.

lead assessing the network or providing a basis for evaluating the effectiveness of network changes. It is possible that such premature changes might actually *degrade* performance below initial suboptimal conditions.

Avoid implementing station-level changes before completing the full LAN survey for the reasons stated previously. Note that sometimes, nevertheless, improving the local resources might buy time for dealing with the broader-based LAN performance flaws. However, most network problems can ultimately be traced to network-wide deficiencies. It is important to gather data about the network as a whole and analyze its performance as a complete system.

It is certainly reasonable to reverse these progressive steps for political reasons. There is no hard and fast rule that should prohibit gathering data from the station level and progressing outward to the global LAN. In fact, several logical and external reasons might support a reverse order. Not only is it easier to optimize performance for individual stations, but individual users benefit most from optimization at the local level. Also, the political reality is that it is easier to win purchase approval for items designated for individual users than it is for a *global* resource (such as the network) that often transcends functional groups or departments.

Crucial benchmarks

Typical network performance statistics are not always applicable for optimizing total network performance; they lack granularity and have evolved for quick network fixes. Such values are relevant for evaluating single network station operation or analyzing specific cause and affect problems. Examples include a beacon, station errors, and even high rates of collision. These indicators represent a jabbering transmitter, high levels of signal jitter, or a single station that experiences performance problems on an otherwise superb network. They are not necessarily symptomatic of a network-wide problem or chronically suboptimal LAN performance.

Instead, since performance is based upon system-level interaction, it is important to evaluate network performance with system-level statistics. For example, consider capturing throughput data. Review packet counts, packet size distribution, and traffic sources and destinations. Packet size distribution is often overlooked, yet this is an important analysis item since it shows how the network is utilized and the inconsistency of the load. Many client-server networks are awash in minimum-sized requests and acknowledgments. Other networks will exhibit streams of maximum-sized packets with an equal number of minimal-sized interleaved acknowledgment traffic. Some networks support stream delivery, or *packet burst*, of large point-to-point data transfers that do not require interleaved request and acknowledgment traffic. It is rare to see a channel fully saturated by this type of traffic. Figure 3-1 illustrates LAN traffic distribution by packet sizes.

This is consequential information for assessing network bottlenecks. For example, a slow LAN transmitting minimum-sized packets might benefit from an early token release (ETR); the logic for this assessment is that less channel capacity would

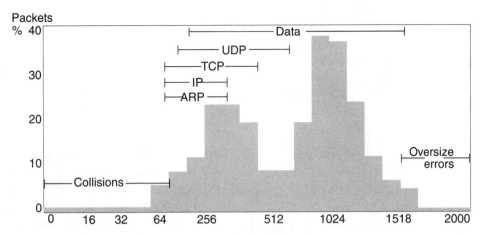

3-1 LAN (Ethernet) traffic distribution by packet size.

be wasted to token latency. Another valid assumption—if these packets represent requests to a file or database server—is that this server has reached capacity. At the other extreme, a slow LAN transmitting an equally interspersed stream of minimum- and maximum-sized packets might be limited by the disk or bus data transfer capacity at either or both the source and receiving stations.

The same assessment is equally valid even if the network supports a more efficient packet burst transfer. Even FDDI or TCNS (100 Mbits/s ARCnet deriva- tive) protocols are sensitive to disk transfer speeds. While a client on network with no other active clients might see data transfer speeds in excess of 20 Mbits/s—faster than the fastest local disk—this transfer rate degrades dramatically as other clients are inserted into this network. Few file servers can sustain such transfer speeds for many stations simultaneously. Buffered data transfers and caches will obviously help. However, packet size distribution along with source and destination informa- tion is key to exploring this type of bottleneck.

Protocol

The network protocol influences performance dramatically. The network architec- tures considered in this book include Ethernet and token-based systems, which comprise ARCnet and derivatives (logical token passing on a physical bus), FDDI (physical token on a logical copper wire or optical fiber ring), and IBM Token-Ring (physical token on a star-configured copper wire logical ring). There are others, including RS-232, X.25, frame relay, and PPP (point-to-point protocol), that are not pertinent within the focus here. Protocols differ in packet sizes, transmission speed, error detection, access and deferral methods, and performance under extreme load. The following list gives some important features for ARCnet, Ethernet, FDDI, and Token-Ring affecting performance.

- Token bits
- Jitter
- Station signal repeater electronic delays
- Signal propagation time
- Data bits
- Overhead bits

Alarms (as a feature of a network protocol, a network management protocol MIB) indicate events or values exceeding preset values that are irrelevant optimization data. Alarms point to occasional incidents or sporadic events, deviations from norms, but not to the chronic problems characteristic of suboptimal LAN performance. It is irrelevant to analyze which is the best protocol since every network has different requirements; it is also immensely time-consuming to create comparable networks. Budget, application software, existing hardware, and other factors almost predetermine which protocol will run on a particular LAN. Political decisions specifying IBM PS/2 workstations virtually predicate that the LAN protocol is Token-Ring. Availability of physical network test tools, cable scanners, protocol analyzers, effective network management tools, operating systems, and application drivers effect the choice of the LAN protocol.

Occasionally, some NOSes—such as FTP, Banyan, and IPX—can drive either ARCnet, Ethernet, or Token-Ring equally well. In those few cases, hardware protocol analysis usually indicate those LANs with special and *repetitious* traffic that benefit from a particular protocol. The simplest view of protocol selection is that persistent protocols (CSMA/CD—Ethernet) are better at low loads. Ethernet is persistent because an Ethernet station transmits when it wants to. Nonpersistent protocols such as those applied in logical or physical token-passing networks (token-based—ARCnet, FDDI, and Token-Ring) are better for network applications with sustained high loads. Some service is always guaranteed, although statistically the latency will always be longer. Nonpersistent protocols are said to be "stable" under high loads. Networks with small packets and frequent acknowledgments benefit from ARCnet. Networks with repetitive file transfers and sporadic though intense traffic benefit from Ethernet. SQL data table requests and intensive IPX traffic is most beneficial with complete 4202-byte Token-Ring frames. However, traffic is rarely the culprit for network bottlenecks.

Ethernet is based upon the premise that a station can transmit only when the network is not busy. When two (or more) stations try to talk simultaneously as often happens, a collision results. The contributing stations stop talking for a random interval and try again when the network is quiet again. Although Ethernet provides 10-Mbits/s throughput when network load is minimal, the throughput drops toward zero as a sustained load exceeds 37 percent (1/e where e = 2.7182....)[4] Hardware overhead is minimal unless the collision rate becomes excessively high. Ethernet supports no hardware error detection. Badly installed nodes, failing transceivers, and other typical Ethernet hardware errors degrade performance with invisibility.

Token-based networks represent a more intuitive environment than Ethernet, which is based upon a random and nondeterministic channel acquisition method, although early token release (ETR) adds a random element to Token-Ring protocols. Permission to transmit is granted by acquiring a token packet that circulates the network ring. Because Token-Rings are closed systems, many types of hardware failures can be diagnosed by the actual network NICs. Stations *beacon* when they perceive certain types of hardware problems, and token-based networks tend to experience fewer overt wiring failures that imperceptibly affect LAN performance. While *soft errors* or *nonisolating errors* might disclose that someone does not know how to locate the faults, these terms actually refer to the automatic feature of Token-Ring where downstream nodes broadcast alerts when packets are corrupted, tokens are lost, or other protocol events are not evident. Find a better tool or learn to use the current ones better so that such errors can be isolated and resolved.

ARCnet, FDDI, and Token-Ring are token-based protocols. ARCnet physically supports a bus-broadcast structure like Ethernet or star-structure like 10BASE-T, but the token circulates around a *logical* ring. FDDI and Token-Ring are physical rings and the token is captured and repeated by each station to the next downstream neighbor. FDDI is both a physical ring with dual-access stations (DAS) and a star-clustered logical ring with single-access stations (SAS). Token-Ring is rarely cabled as an actual ring except in the case of the Apollo domain network; instead, Token-Ring is a star-wired with twisted pairs into multiple access units (MAU), which provides the actual ring configuration. The direction of the ring, upstream or downstream, is predicated by the need to capture and repeat each token signal.

ETR is a protocol enhancement defined in the 16-Mbits/s Token-Ring specifications. ETR allows a token to be released to the next downstream node at the completion of data transmission or when the Token-Ring timer has elapsed. It is a software feature, and is implemented in network operating system software. This enhancement provides decreased latency, higher data throughput, and better LAN performance. It is most effective on large rings and for small packets. TCP/IP, IPX, and Novell query and acknowledgment packets tend to be small packets (32 to 128 bytes) and benefit from this technology. Networks consistently broadcasting maximum-sized packets would see almost no performance improvement since the beginning of the packet will have returned to the source node while the node is still broadcasting that same packet.

Token overhead is comparable to Ethernet. ARCnet is slightly more efficient because it provides for smaller address fields and a shorter minimum packet size, and ACK/NAK support is supported at a fundamental hardware level instead of as part of higher-level protocol like MAC, LLC, connectionless UDP, TCP/IP, or IPX.

---

4   Boggs, Mogul, and Kent, idem.

This is a pertinent fact when optimizing networks with terminal servers and other devices preparing single-character packets.

Token-Ring is also very deterministic. The token rotation time (TRT) is a prime indicator of minimum and maximum LAN performance. Maximum performance occurs when few nodes seek to transmit, although there is a high cost for the extra idle capacity. Token-based LAN performance almost never degrades to saturation. Token saturation occurs where every station exercises its right to transmit when that station acquires the token. The following list charts tuning parameters and the effects on network devices. The actual details are presented later in the chapter.

- **Packet counts:** . . . . All packets on networks
  Packets transmitted
  Packets received
  Packets transmitted with collisions or errors
  Packets deferred
  Packets per node
  By source
  By destination
  By source to destination
  Size distribution (-, 64, 128, 256, 512, 1024, 4096, 18328 +)
  Network period peaks node period peaks
- **Packet errors:** . . . . All packet/frame errors
  Alignment errors
  CRC errors
  Short packets
  Long packets
  Invisible packets
  Incompatible packets
  Misaddressed packets
- **Channel utilization:** . . . . . Throughput
  Peak rate
  Utilization as a percent of capacity
- **Statistics:** . . . . Network usage as a percent of capacity
  Interarrival times (0-100 ms)
  Latency distribution
  Packet size distribution
  Node usage as a percent of capacity
  Node usage as a percent of network utilization packet
  Rate per second
  Bits/s
  Bytes/s
  Retransmission rate
  Delivery error rate

The data required for LAN performance optimization are nearly worthless until cast into the framework of a network traffic performance model. While many benchmarks exist for evaluating network performance, the key ones comprise error levels, collision or protocol response times, throughput, and processor speeds. In effect, these crucial statistics mirror the information that is usual for optimizing highway performance. Below is a list of typical statistics that provide utility specifically for performance optimization. These statistics are the input to a generalized queueing model, and more specifically to *LANmodel*.

- Packet sizes
- Packet interarrival times
- Average traffic loads
- Peak traffic loads
- Throughput loads (traffic volume)
- Error rates
  Collisions
  Frame errors
  Jabber, jitter, and signal frequency errors
  Bad addresses
  Routing errors
  Network size
    Number of stations (nodes)
    Physical network length
    Network configuration
- Network protocol
- Protocol efficiency and ACK/NAK support
- Signal propagation speed

Throughput

Throughput is an indispensable measure for network activity because it conveys traffic volume on a LAN. It is the most useful statistic for analyzing network performance and is the prime input to the LANModel software described in Chapter 4. Throughput is usually presented as a duration of time; without such reference, throughput is meaningless. Furthermore, for example, a throughput-per-second rate is also meaningless unless given context. Consider a throughput of 1235 packets. Without relevant context, it is impossible to know if that is good or bad. How big are those packets? Does it represent adequate performance or not? Typically, a throughput is contrasted with minimum and maximum values. These range limits could be historical service levels or theoretical limits. Some management protocols and analysis tools contrast throughput values with both, or provide statistical confidence intervals (CIs) since traffic varies with user and process loads.

Knowing the peak throughput values is also important. While some networks rarely need to be robust enough to handle all peaks, some mission-critical networks must have some mechanism to transmit even these excessive loads: adjustable bandwidths, alternate channels, complex routing paths, and sophisticated algorithms to balance loads or delay low-priority traffic for later delivery.

Capturing throughput

Throughput tracking is built into most NOSes because it is such an important statistic. Basically, either SNMP, CMIP and other management software, or a protocol analyzer capture throughput information. Traffic (or packet) throughput rates are the ratio of packets per unit interval to maximum theoretical rates. Because packet sizes vary so widely, data throughput rates are better clarified when they are a summation of packet sizes as a ratio of theoretical channel capacity. Be certain to differentiate between numerical counts and ratios. Also differentiate between traffic counts and packet protocol analysis (that is, packet protocol decomposition). Figure 3-2 shows how to calculate these values.

Packet throughput	Number of packets per interval
Packet throughput rate	Packet throughput/theoretical packet
rate Data throughput	Number of transmitted bits per interval
Data throughput rate	Data throughput/theoretical channel capacity

3-2   Calculation for throughput and throughput rates.

Some network operating systems maintain a database of local traffic as bit-level throughputs. Sun NFS, which is Ethernet-based and soon FDDI-based for data-intensive processing, supports a simple NETSTAT application that counts packets transmitted and actual bytes transmitted, packets received and actual bytes received, and errors during a known time interval. Since this includes sufficient detail to construct throughput rates per station, amassing all local station information into a central database is sufficient for generating accurate throughput information.

Throughput measurement shortfalls

Most protocol analysis tools maintain network throughput levels consisting of data throughput during a known interval. It is frequently scaled by the channel bandwidth limits in order to display a "throughput meter." In the simplest analogy, highway traffic engineers measure traffic volume by counting vehicles that compress a pneumatic tube. Simultaneous or co-resident traffic in adjacent lanes are not always counted accurately. Likewise, network traffic volume defies accurate counts.

While most network protocols prohibit simultaneous traffic, many network management tools are unable to count all packets and all errors with serialized traffic. It is crucial to factor any shortfall inaccuracies into LAN performance analysis. Realize that all network management tools have blind spots, performance limitations, and perhaps even poorly defined features. Specifically, some management tools rely upon device agency databases (for example MIB-I, MIB-II, and vendor-proprietary extensions) to retain the necessary information on a per-station basis. When some stations lack a valid agency (that is, the stations are old and incompatible with SNMP, CMIP, or other proprietary management software such as the previous NFS NETSTAT example), obviously data capture will be incomplete. Also, high throughput levels easily overtax the capture and filtering capacity of software-based protocol analysis tools and most hardware-based protocol analyzers.

Such a shortfall is obvious with FDDI and other high-speed multimodal, multiplexed, and multichannel networks; a substantial computer is necessary to capture and trace 100 Mbits/s. Protocol limitations undermine accurate data collection. For example, the protocol limitations of Ethernet mean that packet fragments resulting from collisions might provide sufficient information for a collision count, but insufficient information to trace sources and destinations. Collisions occurring during preamble are not even valid packets, but nonetheless add to network loading.

There exists a serious limitation for evaluating LAN throughput with traffic throughput values. When highway planners count traffic volumes, they also assess throughput speeds and arrival delays (due to backups at toll plazas, exit ramps, and volume overloads). Highway planners often make assessments of traffic deferred by backups that seeks alternate routes. Because LAN protocols enforce transmission at preset speeds, LAN traffic throughput represents total traffic volumes; deferrals and delivery slowdowns are irrelevant and alternate routes rarely exist. Although different networks and media support different transmission speeds, the broadcast signals propagate only at fixed speeds. Delays are handled by deferral or collision mechanisms. Token protocols (ARCnet, FDDI, and Token-Ring) manage delays by permitting transmission only by acquisition of a singular token. Ethernet handles delays by collisions, deferrals, and random waits. Stations on LANs with imposed loads in excess of a manageable level experience excessively long transmission delays and *time-outs* when applications decide that the network is unavailable. The information about work denied network access is not captured.

Since a slow LAN provides suboptimal transmission and this delays user-initiated or coprocessing operations, less work is accomplished during any time period. Instead, assess individual station workload with the supposition that the LAN is perfect and will provide *unlimited* bandwidth. Determine the load that station could place upon the LAN. Extend this analysis to all network stations. This data throughput forecast is important information for LANModel because it bypasses the inherent limitations of inaccurate throughput rates. Chapter 4 shows how to apply this data for effective LAN optimization, and generate realistic estimates for the queueing model analysis.

Error statistics

Error statistics provide an important overview of network performance. Error statistics detail physical network health since errors typically result from hardware-related breakdowns. Error rates provide a highly effective means to evaluate the physical structure of the LAN. Error rates provide little information about the logical structure of the LAN. Figure 3-3 shows a matrix for evaluating error rates.

	High error rates	Low error rates
Physical structure	Poor	Good
Logical structure	Uncertain	Uncertain

3-3 Evaluation matrix for error rates.

Networks with high error rates usually indicate physical problems with the network installation or the actual network hardware (about 60 percent of the time). Networks that experience low error rates are preferable. This tends to indicate that the LAN physical infrastructure is designed, installed, and maintained satisfactorily. Suboptimal performance is such cases usually indicates traffic volume, traffic loading peaks, and overloaded stations. Since the physical structure itself is satisfactory, a poor network track record suggests an inadequate logical configuration.

Networks that sustain high error rates conversely indicate a poorly designed, installed, or maintained physical infrastructure. The cable, connectors, NICs, and network devices are installed and perform inadequately. Before embarking upon sophisticated network tuning, consider, instead, evaluating the basic wiring and network hardware. Also, check for improper memory configurations and buffer sizes for network packets and protocols.

Although deferrals indicate the lack of an opportunity to transmit and are a normal element of LAN protocols, errors reflect a failure of the LAN to perform correctly. Although it is difficult to collect deferral data, most LAN protocols maintain error statistics at both station and aggregate levels. Transmission errors usually provide a one-for-one match with LAN specification, installation, or hardware failures. Because error statistics are so narrowly meaningful, they are excellent benchmarks for assessing proper network operation. Error statistics are useful for performance evaluation when they show extreme error levels. In those cases they indicate severe failures. Statistics that show normal error levels while users complain of sluggish network performance tend to suggest that poor network performance is not a network transmission problem. Rather, poor performance results from traffic overloading, suboptimal device performance, or overloaded stations.

Jitter or the *jitter budget*, though principally indigenous to Token-Ring, affects all protocols. It represents variance from the acceptable signal characteristics. Signal frequency variability, strength, stability, deficiency in the square form signal, and a lack of differentiation between "0" and "1" all are characteristic of jitter. Jitter is most pronounced at 16-Mbits/s Token-Ring protocols. It is important to note that, although all computer logic is based upon discrete values, ultimately all network traffic is based upon analog waves. Figure 3-4 shows how signals lack differentiation or decay and become unstable.

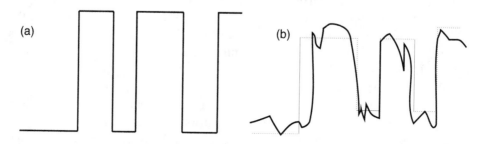

3-4 A comparison between (a) analog and, (b) the optimal digital signals.

This instability is important when signals are regenerated and repeated at each Token-Ring station or regenerated by repeaters, bridges, routers, and gateways. Since the repeating stations cannot interpret the meaning of the signal—only the CRC checksum bits can decay. This might force frequent retransmissions. When a jitter error occurs, the obvious test is to capture and compare the same frames at different parts of the network. When there are obvious differences, tighten the gap between protocol analyzers until the offending repeating device is localized. Although this is not an infrastucture error per se, it is a hardware error that should be resolved. Of note, newer Token-Ring cards often contain a chip designed and produced by Texas Instruments and IBM with a "ringing tank," which is designed to filter signal instability.

Token rotational time

The token rotational time (TRT) is the time it takes for the token to make a complete circuit of the LAN. This is true for a physical circuit or a logical circuit of a star-configured structure, such as IBM Token-Ring. This statistic is difficult to acquire without special equipment since a ring without stations inserted means that there are no tokens on the loop. This value represents the time for a signal to propagate around the LAN and is solely a function of the network length.

As stations are actually activated and inserted into the LAN, TRT slows because of the delay imposed by the electronics in each NIC unit. This also explains why some networks perform well with nodes activated and badly with fewer live nodes. The token signal decays with distance and is routed through a MAU and extensive ring cabling. Realistically, this represents the minimum TRT time most network managers will see. When all stations are quiet and the token circulates, TRT is signal propagation time plus approximately 2 μs (20 bit times) electronics delay at each station's NIC unit. The absolute minimum TRT represents the time it takes for the token to complete a rotation on the LAN with no stations inserted. It must exceed 7 μs by specification. The active monitor will artificially increase the TRT to that level if the network is too short or poses no load.

Under an ultimate load—when every station wants to transmit full-sized packets and exercises that right when it acquires the token—TRT degrades to signal propagation time, approximately 4 to 5 μs electronics delay at each station, and the bit times for the data in the packet, preamble and delay. For example, a 16-Mbits/s Token-Ring with 250 stations (the maximum) will show a minimum TRT of about 7 μs (7x16 bit times), and a maximum TRT of about 253 μs.

Token-Ring networks are controlled by the token passing protocol. Token errors include a lost token and duplicate tokens. While it is functionally difficult to see these problems, the approximate method is to count claim tokens. The *claim token* is a station's attempt to claim access to the network in lieu of a token passing within two average token rotation time (TRT) units. The protocol for *asserting* authority, the claim token, to issue a new token might require four or five average TRT units. When stations insert into the network (usually when they are powered on and the passive bypass in the network NIC becomes active and now repeats signals), the sudden signal noise or disruption might corrupt a few packets or tokens during that brief interval. An excessive number and continuing incidence of purge and claim tokens usually indicates protocol errors, faulty NIC units, or other basic hardware problems.

When collecting and evaluating Token-Ring data, recognize that the token rotational time becomes an inaccurate and irrelevant statistic when the network employs ETR. What was an important value for evaluating Token-Ring performance and stability has no validity under ETR. Under ETR, the protocol is persistent like Ethernet. Hence packets per period, average packet size, channel utilization, and latency form better statistics. Note that these correspond to the most potent statistics for Ethernet. The TRT measures the time duration for the token to make a complete circuit of the ring. Just as collision rate is useful for measuring the health of an Ethernet, the TRT is a useful statistic for measuring the performance of a physical or logical Token-Ring, including ARCnet, IBM Token-Ring, and FDDI.

A token circulates on a ring until captured by a station that wants to transmit data. The data packet makes a complete circuit on the ring (beginning from the source station). The packet is "stripped" from the network using the specification language; in reality, the token portion of the packet is transmitted and the data portion is simply not repeated. The TRT consists of the six components. These include transmission time and signal propagation time. The list on page 59 shows the six components.

The actual TRT times vary by protocol, media, and network length. The example in this section is based upon calculations on the fixed-sized IBM Token-Ring token of 24 bits. Furthermore, the target TRT (TTRT) varies by network load. Therefore,

- Token bits
- Jitter
- Station signal repeater electronic delays
- Signal propagation time
- Data bits
- Overhead bits

it is useful as input for utilization and network length calculations.[5] Specifically, the TRT can be extrapolated to network load and channel bandwidth utilization, as well as *total* network cabling lengths.

$$\text{Utilization} = \frac{\text{Number tokens/second}}{\text{Maximum number of tokens/second}}$$

Since the tokens indicate a token revolution:

Number tokens/second = 1 /Token Rotation Time (TRT)

These two equations reduce to the following useful formula:

Utilization = 1 - Ring latency/TRT

Additionally, the basic latency and utilization equations can be rewritten in another format to solve for the overall network length (when latency, TRT, and utilization values are available):

Ring delay = TRT (1 - Utilization)

where

Ring delay = latency +
    number of stations * (jitter and electronic delay) +
    network sections * 5µs/k

or

L = 8(TRT)(1-U)-7-5/8N) * 82'

where

L = Length of the network wiring
U = Network utilization
N = Number of network ring nodes

The ring latency represents the minimum time for the token and all data packets to go around the ring. Think of this value as the waiting time for a station that wants to transmit. For a Token-Ring running at 4 Mbits/s, the minimum latency is the TRT for an unloaded network. Thus, the minimum latency is the sum of all token rotation components. Figure 3-5 charts these values.

The following two charts were generated by the Lotus spreadsheets included on the companion distribution disk. These files can also be readily converted into MS Excel. TR4MB.WK1 illustrates a 4-Mbits/s IBM Token-Ring. TR16MB.WK1 illustrates a 16-Mbits/s Token-Ring. FDDIRING.WK1 illustrates a 100-Mbits/s

5   Novell Inc. LANalyzer Support Group.

Latency Component	4 Mbits/s	16 Mbits/s
Token	24 bits	24 bits
Jitter per station	3 to 10 bit times	3 to 30 bit times
Electronic delay per station	2.5 to 40 bit times	8 to 45 bit times
Network wiring	5 μs/k	5 μs/k

3-5   Minimum ring latency (minimum TRT).

FDDI. The basic formulas are the same for each spreadsheet; the values differ to reflect network transmission speed. These models are simple and accessible. Modify the transmission and propagation speeds, and set the appropriate number of nodes. Figure 3-6 shows a 4-Mbits/s IBM Token-Ring, and Fig. 3-7 plots a 16-Mbits/s IBM Token-Ring. Both plots were generated with the Lotus graph option.

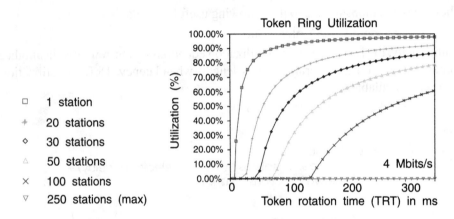

3-6   Utilization based upon TRT for a 4-Mbits/s Token Ring.

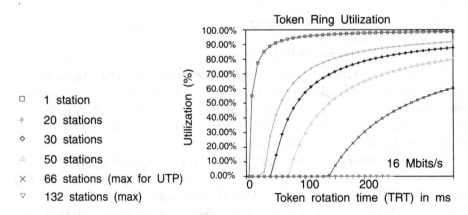

3-7   Utilization based upon TRT for a 16-Mbits/s Token Ring.

These two graphs illustrate two important points. First, a Token-Ring very rarely saturates at a network channel utilization level. It is virtually impossible to use the full channel bandwidth at either 4 Mbits/s or 16 Mbits/s. Second, additional stations on a Token-Ring increase the base latency time by adding to the jitter loss and electronic signal repetition, but do not necessarily affect the average latency time. On the other hand, Ethernet latency is unaffected by the number of stations on the network, but is very sensitive to the channel utilization in the ranges of 20 to 40 percent.

Collision levels

Although an Ethernet collision is not an error an error as previously explained, high collision rates (above 8 percent) typically indicate LAN overloading. Excessive collision rates are considered an error condition, and for this reason collision rates are described in this section. A collision is a normal method for handling simultaneous attempts to transmit. The probability for a collision is the chance that two or more stations transmit within the same idle period. This probability is independent of packet sizes since collisions must occur within the first 468 bit times, while the maximum slot time for an Ethernet is 512. The collision rate is dependent upon the load rate per station, the number of stations on a network segment, the LAN length, and the number of repeaters connecting the LAN. Collisions occurring after 512 bit times, termed *late collisions,* indicate specification, installation, or hardware problems. Figure 3-8 charts the statistical chance for collisions based upon station counts, Fig. 3-9 charts collisions based upon station load levels, and Fig. 3-10 shows how collision rates vary as slot time increases.

Background, overhead, and runaway bunnies

LANs, as well as enterprise-wide networks, experience traffic loading unrelated to the actual anticipated "work" throughput. This unrelated load comprises background, overhead, runaway processes, and perhaps even unauthorized and undesired network usage. These activities normally do not enhance or improve real network projects; they merely support or protect that network activity.

As such, background, overhead, and runaway processes usually represent an unwelcome network load that is best analyzed as part of LAN optimization. When this unrelated load is nonessential on a overloaded network, consider minimizing that activity. These nonessential and runaway activities are not bottlenecks per se, although they usually contribute to an already suboptimal situation.

In some extreme cases (such as a computer virus infestation), however, these activities can cripple the network. They represent anomalies and surprises, and mismanagement or misapplication of network resources. Often, they are invisible except under the watchful trace of a protocol analyzer. It is important to differentiate between a monitor that captures only statistics and a true protocol decoder. More

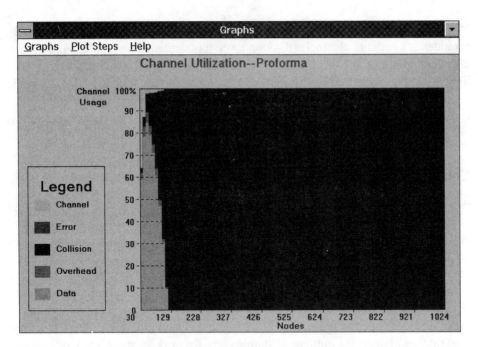

3-8 Collision rates as a function of station counts (3% load per station).

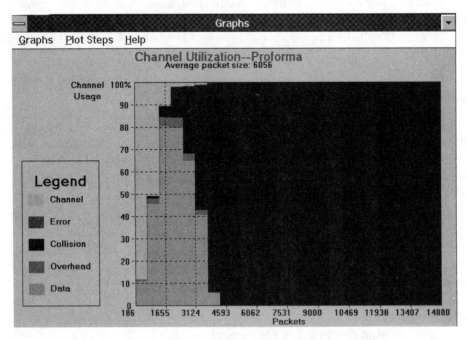

3-9 Collision rates as a function of station load (30 stations).

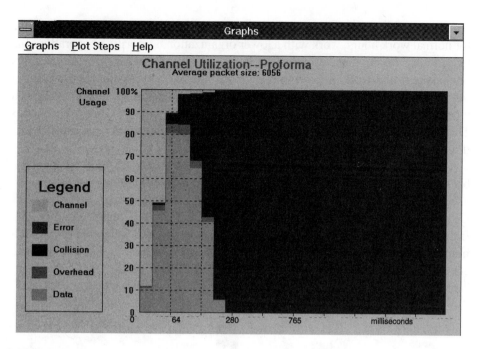

3-10 Collision rates as a function of transmission slot time.

mismanagement or misapplication of network resources. Often, they are invisible except under the watchful trace of a protocol analyzer. It is important to differentiate between a monitor that captures only statistics and a true protocol decoder. More often, unanticipated traffic constitutes greater network bandwidth than expected, and thus a more significant burden to the network than expected. The next several paragraphs describe where nonessential processes might affect network performance and the operations they comprise.

Background processes include network management protocols (SNMP, CMIP, or active proprietary alarms, analysis, and load tracking tools), user access monitoring, security, shared disk partitions, network printing, resource access and management, and disk file mirroring. Overhead processes include access control, accounting and network usage billing, resource usage monitoring, and security. Novell Netware includes such extras as checking each network station for recent activity and automatically logging off inactive users as well as active users who exceed the allowable hours for network access. The Token-Ring active monitor polls all "active" nodes exactly every seven seconds; this is protocol, not an error. More or less frequent polling does constitute a timing and operational problem. Runaway processes include spawned tasks that do not terminate, programs out of control, a user request waiting for a response that never comes but nonetheless continues to poll for a response, and occasionally a token packet or fragment artifact that continues to circulate.

Unauthorized or undesired network usage includes personal work inappropriate for normal work hours, work with a lower organizational priority, or operations that require disproportionate resources during peak network loads. In addition to the obvious personal work, undesirable loads include all activities that could occur at off-peak times. Examples comprise file maintenance activities, device backup to tape, and any active noncrucial although server-bound or network-intensive queries. These are nonessential activities that could be rescheduled from peak traffic times, if not entirely prohibited from the network.

A protocol analyzer makes it possible to assess the network load comprised of background, overhead, runaway processes, unauthorized, and undesired network usage. The tool will count packets by source, destination, protocols (TCP, IP, IPX, OSI, XNS, MAC, NetBEUI, NetBIOS, and others), packet contents, and specific frame bit patterns. While this magnifying glass, if you will, seems to provide too much focus, it is possible to intelligently view network use by exploring packet contents. A map of packet transmission by source and destination is useful for

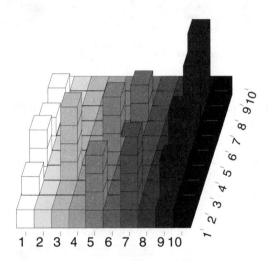

3-11 Network usage mapped by a source and destination matrix.

analyzing network usage by station (and user), as Fig. 3-11 illustrates with a three-dimensional format, while a map of packet transmission by contents or protocols might provide insight into the purpose for network usage, as Fig. 3-12 shows by listing channel usage by protocol.

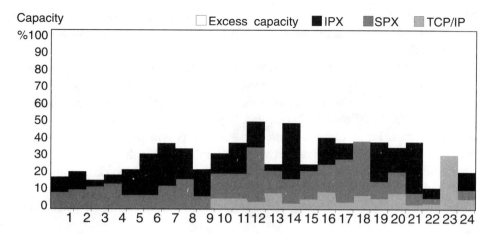

3-12 Network usage listed by protocol and content.

Transmission times

One technique to trace suboptimal LAN performance is to poll or "ping" (a Unix command) stations. A request packet is sent to the target station requesting an "echo" to the simple question, "Are you there?" This will indicate whether a station is attached to the LAN, and the transit times provide a benchmark for assessing the performance of the LAN.

It is important to view this data within perspective. First, a ping, poll, or ARCnet request for transmission is a two-way trip to the target station, from the polling station to the target station and back again. Second, the ping and its "echo" merely confirm that the station is physically connected to the network; the echo is often generated within hardware or at the physical level of the protocol stack. Third, overhead for the echo is minimal.

Rather than perceiving the limitations of this simple technique, analyze the value of this information. The poll echo confirms that a station is physically attached to the network and at least minimally operative. A station that responds to a ping or poll but not to more complex requests might be indicating firmware or hardware inconsistencies, operating system, NOS, application-level software incompatibilities, or incomplete software configuration.

The poll transit time measured in µs by a protocol analyzer provides a benchmark for physical network performance levels. This transit time in conjunction with application-level request response times provides the means to ascertain the causes for suboptimal network performance. A relatively quick time for the poll indicates a network that is not experiencing a channel transmission bottleneck, while slow response might indicate channel saturation. In comparison, workstation or server application-level response times that greatly exceed poll times indicate some sort of obstacle at the station itself. Poll transit times during peak network operation and off-hours. Similar peak versus off-peak transit times indicate bottlenecks caused by insufficient channel capacity, while lower off-peak transit times indicate station or server overloading.

Poll transit times are very useful when assessing performance on WAN inter-connected LANs. When endpoint-remote LANs are connected through multiple midmost remote LANs with wide area links (for example, T-1), progressive meas-urements of poll times at each intermediate hop should indicate progressively longer response times. Large discrepancies between points will point to an overloaded segment. To localize these internetworking bottlenecks, poll stations across the intermediate hops as well. Poll transit times during peak network operation and off-hours. Similar peak versus off-peak transit times indicate bottlenecks caused by insufficient LAN-to-LAN linkage channel capacity, while lower off-peak transit times indicate station routing overloading.

Station performance bottlenecks

Often LANs perform badly because individual stations perform poorly. Those stations create global LAN bottlenecks. This is particularly true for any global LAN resources such as file servers, bridges, routers, gateways, networks trucks in a box, print servers, and printers. Printers that are merely output devices become perform-ance bottlenecks when queued requests saturate the printer server or back up onto bridges, routers, and file servers. High-speed printers, those with capacities greater than 75,000 characters/s, are often faster than the most powerful printer servers. This is particularly relevant for raster and graphic print jobs. As such, the print server is the performance bottleneck. View this problem as a chain reaction traffic jam that spreads well beyond the localized cause.

One of the best data gathering techniques is to replace suspected stations with one with a higher performance rating. Use the network to create a mirror copy of all files and structures from the original onto the replacement station. Activate the new replacement. Collect benchmark data on traffic levels, processing times, and other local and global statistics. If LAN performance improvements warrant it, leave that new station there; otherwise, repeat this performance test for another suspected bottleneck. This same technique can be applied when the hypothesis is that a station component is mismatched and is causing a performance bottleneck. Component examples might include hard drives, memory levels, controller cards, NICs, video drivers, and free available station resources. Try it and test the performance.

Data acquisition techniques

Tools acquire data. The tool set includes physical media testers, hardware protocol analyzers and software-based protocol analysis, network management protocols, utility software, network performance simulators, and suites of benchmarks. Additionally, one of the most potent network management tools is the performance log.

Physical media testers

There are three basic types of media testers. There are voltmeters and multitesters, which check for electrical continuity of electrical wiring and cables, TDRs, which perform the same function as multimeters with more precision, and cable and pair scanners, which have some of the features of TDRs and packet protocol analysis. Basically, voltmeters, multimeters, pair scanners, and TDRs indicate whether the physical medium has shorts, breaks, or open lines. TDRs with optical capabilities perform a corresponding function for optical fiber.

Information gathered from these tools is necessary to qualify the basic integrity of the network plant. The process of tuning LAN performance is imperfect without a sound electrical or optical infrastructure. As previously stated, fundamental infrastructure analysis is not the focus of this book. However, such analysis should *precede* the more complex tuning methods presented in this book.

Protocol analysis and network management protocols

Protocol analysis hardware, software, and network management protocols perform virtually the same functions. They are designed to gather statistics relevant to evaluating LAN performance and operation. The differences among these tools is basically a packaging issue; in some cases, difference among the tools can be seen in their ability to gather accurate data in multivendor, multiprotocol, and large interconnected LANs.

Hardware-based protocol analyzers tend to be single-purpose tools with an ability to capture almost all packets on even the most saturated network channel. In fact, most of the Token-Ring data presented within this book was captured by a Network General Watchdog. This is a representative low-end (low-cost) unit sufficient to gather LAN performance optimization data. It is certainly sufficient for LANModel inputs. Software-based tools piggyback on existing NIC units, whether integrated motherboard controllers or bus card units. As such, they are less expensive and prone to hide protocol discrepancies and vendor implementation oversights, and function best within the confines of a small LAN site. Network management protocols, essentially protocol analysis software designed by committees over many years, provide a robust and general-purpose toolkit. Protocols, to wit, CMIP and SNMP, are unlikely to be completely implemented as part of any network operating system since the database definitions and toolkits are so large, since they are likely to impose significant traffic overhead, and since their very size and capabilities is so overwhelming. However, these tools provide transmission traffic levels, error rates, and all the simple numbers included in most relevant benchmarks. These tools also gather the fundamental statistics necessary for input to simulation models.

Network utility software

Network utility software is usually special-purpose software for network control, remote viewing of a user's screen for technical support or help, control of print queue redirection, automated reboot of slave servers, and various other specialized assignments not provided directly by the network operating system. Most of these tools are indeed very convenient and functional; they provide services otherwise unavailable or poorly implemented within the NOS, or wonderfully inventive concepts previously unknown. However, most of these tools provide operational support and network maintenance. As such, most are not designed for gathering information relevant to LAN performance optimization. Those that do generally provide partial protocol analysis functionality and are appropriate within the needed context. Verify the accuracy and reliable of the utility softwares. Use them to collect data for network tuning.

Benchmark suites

Benchmarks are performance evaluation tests that are formalized, iterative, and highly reproducible. They are compiled into *suites* since reliance upon any single test would be biased and insufficient to accurately assess workstation or network performance. The suites often incorporate timing for complex calculations such as sieves, factorials, transformations, Pascal's Triangle, repetitive memory and disk reads/write operations, and network data requests.

Vendors, independent testing organizations, and many magazines have designed benchmark performance software. They are useful to application developers and hardware designers for optimizing poorly performing components, software modules, and functions in applications that perform poorly. Many benchmarks are published so that they can be evaluated for accuracy and efficacy. They are published so that vendors can see that the tests are fair and reproducible. Benchmarks are also published so that vendors can improve software and hardware.

In fact, many benchmarks suites are available upon request; some can be downloaded from computer bulletin board systems and Compuserve. *Unix Review* has many benchmarks for evaluating workstations, *Byte Magazine* periodically updates their published benchmark series, and *PC Magazine* renews its networking performance BENCH software on Compuserve. Acquire a suite of formal benchmarks. Just as they are useful for software and hardware designers, they are useful for network designers and network managers. Particularly, these provide repeatable and reproducible results useful for assessing the effects of network recabling, hardware repairs and component substitutions, and logical reconfigurations.

```
BUSPERF -- PC Bus Performance Analyser
    (C) Copyright PC TECH Journal 1986

          Timer Count  MilliSeconds
Base PC      54001       45.258
This Run      3191        2.674

Bus Performance index: 16.92
```

3-13 Benchmark report of a Token-Ring Novell NetWare network.

The major limitation of formal network benchmarks is that they fail to qualify the installation, adequacy, or performance of a specific network. In other words, a benchmark will not show if a particular network installation is optimal, how it can be improved, or what is wrong with it. This is not to indicate that benchmarks are useless. They are useful and can be applied as follows: Run the benchmark. Note the results. Effect network changes—repairs, reconfiguration, and component substitution are just a few examples. Rerun the benchmark. Compare results between the two runs. Figure 3-13 lists some sample results. The conclusion after substitution of FDDI fiber, NICs, and an FDDI-compliant NOS in place of the Ethernet hardware and protocols Novell NetWare shows a two-fold performance gain (200 percent).

Network performance log

Even with the best conditions, LAN performance optimization is an iterative process. It is nearly impossible to correct basic network defects, improve the

Network Performance Log

Node	Date	Packets	Rating	Notes
34	4/6/91	525,687	50%	server overloaded?
108	4/6/91	34,580	10%	
183	4/6/91	57,820	3%	disk bottleneck

3-14 Network performance log.

transmission channel efficiency, tune system and network drivers, and improve station performance on the first try. As often as not, attempts to tune a network will fail or diminish network performance below par. Clearly, the idea is to improve network performance, not make it worse. When benchmarks show a degradation, reverse the changes. Rerun the benchmarks to verify restoration to the initial state. Then try something else.

The performance log, as illustrated in Fig. 3-14, provides an *audit trail* of performance-related transactions, that is the changes to the network, as well as before and after pictures. The log minimizes the number of iterations, helps prevent repeating the wrong steps, and shows what actually worked. Since performance bottlenecks tend to reappear again, a formal journal provides the exact steps of what worked well. The log and its history shows how problems were resolved. The log also recalls the misleading sub-par "solutions." Consider maintaining the log or journal in database format. Search, sort, and text-matching commands increase the convenience of the log data. Additionally, the benchmark tools should be stored— not upgraded or completely replaced by newer tools. Although the benchmarks provide no absolute measures, they do provide relative measurements of a particular LAN configuration—those represented by the log entries. As such, even several years thereafter, those old benchmark tools retain value. Because the log contains reference data, it provides a reference point for any new results.

4

Chapter

Network software model

Many network evaluation tools and most types of data are becoming more component-specific to the problems they address. This often represents too narrow a view just as networks are becoming more complicated and incorporate a wider assortment of components. Tools must facilitate a more methodical and system-wide analysis rather than specific. LAN modeling and simulation represent a remarkable aid to analyze or qualify a LAN, design and build a new one, and extend an existing network. There are three basic times such tools are imperative: when designing a LAN, expanding a LAN, or assessing performance bottlenecks. Modeling and simulation tools eliminate the need to understand probability theory and statistical analysis; they bypass the need for such specialized knowledge and the tedium required by complex calculations. Such tools are neither unreliable nor confusing.

LANModel is such a tool. A LAN architect, consultant, or manager can simulate different network scenarios without actually building or reconfiguring a LAN. It provides a means to model the complex interactions of different infrastructures, protocols, or configurations. LANModel specifically provides the means to test complex scenarios without committing any money to physical construction and testing. Furthermore, it is an effective method to assess a current situation and validate conformance to protocol specification and the expected achievable level of traffic and network performance.

For example, a simulation tool is useful for determining whether Ethernet or Token-Ring is the better protocol for a particular requirement, or whether a single channel will be sufficient to carry the anticipated load. Additionally, LAN simulation is pertinent for estimating workload. Actually installing and testing two (or more) configurations would not only be costly and time-consuming, but benchmarking the load imposed by users, operating systems, NOSes, and software applications is extraordinarily difficult, as Chapter 3 explained. Assessing subtle configuration changes would also entail repeating the complex and lengthy testing process.

This chapter describes the theory of the network performance model, *LANModel*. *LANModel* provides performance modeling for ARCnet, Ethernet, FDDI, and both 4-Mbits/s and 16-Mbits/s IBM Token-Ring. This chapter shows how the software tools compute basic usage and describes the requisite data needed as input. This chapter also demonstrates how to benefit from network modeling. Network performance simulation modeling provides a cost-efficient approach to test various physical configurations. A model contrasts LAN protocols, traffic loading levels, anticipated error conditions, and station densities. Further, it simulates proposed changes and any effects upon LAN performance. Below is a list of some common situations that are useful to model with a performance simulation tool. This chapter describes *LANModel* in detail, including software requirements, installation, and usage.

- Physical LAN configuration
  Number of stations
  Traffic load per station
  Application overhead on each station
- LAN protocol
- LAN protocol upgrades
- Operating system alterations
- Network operation system upgrades
- Client-server loads
- Server component speeds
- Workstation component speeds
- Networked groups
- Application performance tuning
- Addition of new applications
  E-mail
  Distributed databases
  GIS
  Optical storage and retrieve (online filing)
- Error conditions
- Poor LAN performance
- Absolute performance benchmarks

LANModel provides a performance measurement capability usually unavailable to most LAN administrators, managers, planners, and consultants. This software runs within a convenient environment, Microsoft Windows (MS Windows), and needs only simple and readily accessible information. In general, LAN performance analysis requires complex mathematics and this makes analysis relatively inaccessible. Furthermore, most people lack the math tools, the time, and the skill or practice to assess performance. LANModel decreases that complexity.

Performance simulation models

Computerized performance simulation is a technology that is at least fifty years old. Early use of the Mark-series computers at Harvard University helped simulate ballistic trajectories for aiming artillery in warfare. The quasi-mechanical *Link* trainers allowed inexperienced pilots to try risky maneuvers in the safety of an earth-bound simulator. This technology has become increasingly important for training commercial pilots and astronauts, and testing concepts for new technology before committing fantastic sums for prototype development. It is certainly pertinent for testing a network design before committing resources for installation.

Performance and routing simulation matured with the computer and telecommunications industry. Basic economic requirements to optimize resources and overcome fixed limitations encouraged managers to apply simulation techniques. Examples include maximizing phone circuit utilization; minimizing distance for connection paths; accounting for downtimes, outage extents, and repair costs for circuit failures; matching traffic volumes with channel speeds, and generating the most efficient routes from among the alternates.

These are complex requirements to optimize spurred development in probability and statistics, Monte Carlo simulation (iteration based upon randomized factors), and queueing analysis modeling. In fact, computerized simulation found acceptance as commercially available products for optimizing mainframe computer capacity and performance. Examples include operating system utilities such as IBM's System Measurement Facility (SMF) and SOS/3000 for HP systems, and commercial products such as *Best/F* from BGS Systems.

With the growing importance and complexity of WANs, LANs, and LAN-to-LAN interconnectivity, there is an increased urgency to design sufficient networking infrastructures, account for loading and burst factors, and resolve network traffic problems. To meet these needs, networking specialists have designed and built network performance simulation software. Examples include BONES from Comdisco, LANSIM from Internetix, and LANModel, which is included with this book.

Theory of LAN modeling

Recall the analogy presented in Chapter 1 that compared a LAN to a highway system. Data packets are the vehicles. They enter the highway (that is, *arrive*, in queueing terminology), according to some random or pseudo-random process, proceed to a random, pseudo-random, or fixed destination, and encounter obstacles and mishaps. Packets maintain various speeds (0 or the fixed LAN transmission speed) as allowed by the existing traffic volume. This information can be modeled within the framework of applied mathematics, probability theory, and statistics. More specifically, three areas are particularly relevant: combinatorics (lottery theory), Markov Chains, and queueing systems. Other methods include Monte Carlo simulation, which is an event-driven model; iterations are performed with different parameters to reflect network conditions. There is also a finite state machine, a good model for simple processes. Some models even apply Petri nets.

Complex branches of mathematics are required in order to accurately represent the arrival process, the mix of destinations, as well as the cost incurred through mishaps and collisions. This includes Operations Research, which encompasses probability theory, simplex reduction techniques, and heuristic modeling. These models have been developed and amplified since the 1950s as an outgrowth of formalized operations research.

The queueing model

The *queueing* (or "queuing") *model* describes waiting lines (hence queues), service response times, and throughput. It is an appropriate LAN model because nodes wait in line for slot time to transmit. Queueing theory provides a large number of alternative mathematical models for predicting different real-world events, such as metropolitan highway traffic jams, toll booth effects, supermarket checkout lines, mean time before failure (MTBF), and ticket dispensing at rock concerts. The queueing model defines process steps, waiting times, service times, service fulfillments, and service request denials (e.g., collisions, lost tokens, and network errors). The three features of any LAN mechanism are the arrival process, the waiting queue, and the service mechanism, as shown by Fig. 4-1.

This waiting line design illustrates the major mathematical groupings, which include the source distribution, the waiting queue, and throughput as represented by serviced requests. Because interconnection of LANs is an important data communications issue, expansion of this model is particularly effective for mixed-protocol networks, networks of LANs, and enterprise-wide networks. However, the software included with this book models only single-protocol local area networks, and single-segment networks (i.e. LANs); this version of LANModel will simulate compound networks by modeling each subnet as an independent LAN.

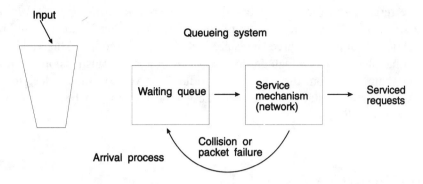

4-1 The queueing model has three key features.

The Markov model

The Markov chain defines transition states for an environment. In the case of any LAN, a transition is the change from a quiet network to a network in collision or in error, or from a network in the *state* of transmission to a network in the *state* of idle. There are many more *transition* states. Markov modeling, sometimes used as part of Monte Carlo calculations, is particularly effective at representing games of chance. In fact, most of these algorithms were developed to increase the personal odds at the card tables of Europe in the eighteenth and nineteenth centuries, as the Monte Carlo designation implies. Gambling provided the major impetus to the development of mathematics and calculus as we know it. Markovian models are appropriate tools to describe LAN request behavior since the transmittal process includes the random arrival of transmission service requests. The state transitions described by the Markov model are presented by the flow diagram in Fig. 4-2.

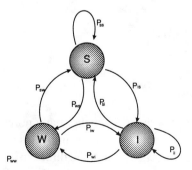

4-2 The state transitions are described by flow diagrams to and from model states (conditions).

The three states for a token-based protocol are *idle, waiting for token*, and *successful transmission*. (Other states might include error, ring failure, or shutdown; for practical reasons only three states are included in the model.) This yields nine transitional phases, which include the change from idle to transmission, from idle to await state, and from the wait state to idle. The Markov model designates a probability for each state change, and these nine factors can be solved in the steady-state equilibrium.

The simulation model

Figure 4-3 shows the single-server mechanisms of transmission fulfillment. All local area networks are single servers; it is important to recognize that the mathematical term *server* refers to the structure that transports data—not to database, print, or file servers. One mechanism services all requests for transmission throughout a network—and this designation is independent of the node or machine count, or the actual network configuration. Only one packet request can be serviced at a time. The alternative is either a ring protocol violation or an Ethernet collision. There are no exceptions on a network (this true for persistent and nonpersistent protocols). Even a 16-Mbits/s Token-Ring with ETR cannot support multiple packets simultaneously. This illustration is a Markovian model because it represents the process rather than the waiting times, lines, and throughput, as previously shown in Fig. 4-2.

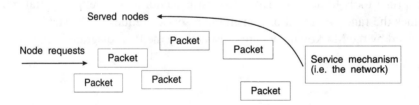

4-3 The queueing model single server mechanism.

The next representation, shown in Fig. 4-4, condenses the many nodes into an organized and elegant model with a single server. This design simplifies the mathematical rendering into a queueing model architecture where the three basic statistics are introduced: successful throughput, error or collision, and traffic, which is the sum of throughput and other events.

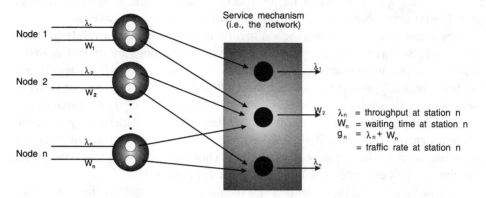

4-4   The network illustrated as a queueing model with a single server.

The Poisson model

The classic queueing model assumes an infinite number of nodes and a fixed arrival time. This needs to be modified to represent the mechanisms of protocol limits. ARCnet supports a maximum of 8 stations per subnet and 255 per installation. Ethernet has a finite number of nodes (maximum 1024). Token-Ring supports a maximum of 250 stations per single LAN at 4 Mbits/s, yet only 136 at 16 Mbits/s, although this number can be increased when long addresses and bridges or routers interconnect *separate* LANs. FDDI supports a maximum of 500 DAS devices and a virtually unlimited number of SAS stations. LANs represent *limited source models* because the calling population is finite. Therefore, transmission request arrivals can be estimated with the Poisson process. Although poisson might aptle model low traffic levels, it is effective and accurate at peak LAN traffic levels.[1]

$$P(t) = \frac{\varepsilon^{-\lambda} \lambda^{\tau}}{T!} \quad \text{for any positive } t = 0, 1, 2, \ldots n$$

i. $N(t)$ has $P(\lambda t)$ for each t
ii. $N(t + h) - N(t)$ is independent of $N(s)$
    for all $s \le t$, $h > 0$, and has $P(\lambda t)$

4-5   The Poisson process.

---

1   *LAN Traffic Analysis and Workload Characterization,* K.M. Khalil, K.Q. Luc, D.V. Wilson, Bell Communication Research, 1990, IEEE 0742-1303/90/0000/0112.

The *Poisson process*, which defines the mean arrival time, is described in Fig. 4-5. The Poisson process models the *interarrival* time, the time between consecutive requests, and describes a phenomenon involving events that occur rarely in small time intervals. It is frequently applied when event distributions are studied, as in the case of transmission service requests. Transmission requests are fulfilled based upon a *birth-and-death process* in queueing theory. "Births" refer to requests for network service, and "deaths" refer to the abandonment of fulfillment of the communication request. Births and deaths occur randomly where the rates depend only upon the current state of the system. The crucial assumption for a Poisson distribution is that only one birth or death can occur at a time. This coincides with token protocols (excluding ETR enhancements), but is not true for Ethernet.

Given these arrival (birth) and service (death) time assumptions, the mathematical architecture can be reduced to a set of queueing equations. In fact, the equations are necessary in order to answer questions posed at the beginning of this chapter; as a by-product, other important statistics can be derived. The waiting queue itself is a quasi-random process that is not useful to model independently since the queue is determined by the controller buffer space, timeout parameters, and token rotation times. Standard queueing equations[2] are listed in Figure 4-6. LAN packet transmission requests (arrivals) are not really Poisson since deferrals and Ethernet collisions place the network in a known "state" (not memory less). Token-Ring is not stateless since requests initiate a formal sequence. Nonetheless, a Poisson probability distribution represents a close match to observations.

$$\rho = \lambda/\mu \qquad \text{network utilization factor} \qquad \qquad 1$$

$$P_0 = 1 - \rho \qquad \text{network initial state} \qquad \qquad 2$$

$$L_n = \frac{\rho^2}{2(1 - \rho)} \qquad \text{expected transmission queue length} \qquad \qquad 3$$

$$L = \frac{\rho}{1 - \rho} = \frac{\lambda}{\mu - \lambda} \qquad \text{number of requests in queue} \qquad \qquad 4$$

$$W_n = \frac{L_n}{\lambda} \qquad \text{waiting time in transmission queue} \qquad \qquad 5$$

$$W = \dot{W}_n + 1/\mu \qquad \text{waiting time in total system} \qquad \qquad 6$$

λ_n = mean packet arrival time
μ_n = mean transmission service rate
$P_n(t)$ = probability of N transmissions at time t

4-6 Standard queueing equations.

2   Frederich S. H. and Lieberman, J.G. *Operations Research*, Holden Day, San Francisco, CA., 1974.

For example, if packets arrive every 16,000 μs and contain 1024 bytes (or 8192 bits), the utilization level will approximate 50 percent by equation (1). Likewise, the length of the queue will be 0.25 packet requests by equation (3) and (4), and wait time will average 16,000 μs by equation (5); this is solved by plugging the resulting values of .25 and 16,000 μs into the formula. The total system time will logically include the 16,000 μs wait time plus the transmission time of 8192 μs by equation (6). Despite the appearance of simplicity and linearity (and some very logical equations), many nonlinear assumptions support these estimates.

It is interesting that, as service times increase, all waiting times increase. Therefore, the key conclusion is that consistency of node service has as important a bearing on network performance as average service speed. In other words, if the network is erratic, performance will be that much worse. In fact, much of the statistical research referenced in this book does support such an assertion. Networks with high *burst* rates are difficult to optimize.

When traffic bursts occur, the traffic load often exceeds the bandwidths of *all* protocols for the duration of the burst. The bottleneck might not clear for a period that approaches 20 times the volume of the burst. Since bursts are random, they often create a deadlock that lingers until the traffic on the network and all backlogged traffic is serviced. Frequent or continuous bursts that overlap cause a gridlock that cannot clear. A key result of these queueing equations shows that, as arrival times approach service times, LAN service failures increase in frequency. When they equal, saturation is inevitable. Also, it is interesting to note that the queueing model does not predict collision frequency; the combinatorial Markov model does.

Dissimilar arrivals

A Markovian model modified to handle a finite number of nodes can explain how peak load periods generate dissimilar arrival rates. "Random" has a special meaning in probability mathematics. It refers to a process with a predictable outcome but stochastic events. Random does not mean "erratic." There is rarely a microscale pattern to network loading, and thus networks display a very "random" and erratic transmission arrival process. In keeping with the practical bent of this book, the reader will be spared the tediousness of this mathematical expansion. However, the preceding solutions assumed a Poisson arrival rate of uniform distribution. In point of fact, arrival rates are not mathematically random or uniform, but either erratic or directly correlated. This is true because of the coordinated nature of most transaction processing; arrival rates correlate. The reasons that network traffic is not random are listed below. Statisticians are realizing that fractile mathematics might be pertinent for modeling and more robust than statistical methods. It is excellent for representing random events and potentially useful for modeling LANs.

- Requests require a NAK or ACK response
- Workload varies with time of day
- People interact and:
  Share work
  Cooperate
  Apply similar work habits
  Perform similar work
  Use the same computer tools and applications
- File services directly involves at least two stations
- Overloads and errors initiate station responses

Two major Poisson distribution assumptions fail with most LAN protocols because there are variations in service times and requests are not random. Packets clearly have different lengths and require varying transmission service times. Protocols remove the randomness of transmissions from the system by providing resolution of transmission contentions and failures. Often, too, arrivals are correlated (not random) as with client-server requests. Additionally, a minimum interarrival time is imposed (96 µs for Ethernet or a fraction of the TRT time for token protocols). *Interarrival time* is the transmission slot time, or the time between consecutive transmissions. Poisson's limited source distribution is not heuristically matched, and for these reasons an Erhlang distribution is sometimes used to approximate collision statistics despite its assumption of random interarrival times. This completes the mathematical modeling.

For all protocols, larger numbers of nodes will halt efficient use of the network as the sheer number of transmitting nodes raises the traffic probability (and actuality) to unacceptable levels. Performance degrades as the channel saturates. Despite the fact that the channel is a single server and the multiple node requests from a single node appear to correspond to single requests from multiple nodes, multiple nodes more readily degrade LAN performance.

This is akin to the familiar highway crawl not merely because too many cars use the highway during the day, but because there is too much traffic during selected intervals and the bottleneck never clears; every automobile is different and can't be likened to a network transmission bus even though a bus logically provides a similar distribution service. Mathematically, the reason for this observable phenomenon is that the variance for transmissions (or packet arrivals) increases as the number of nodes increase. The variability in interpacket spacing increases the odds for simultaneous transmissions. Additionally, more nodes generally provide a proxy for a longer physical network, hence this yields longer delays for token access—*latency* or for the binomial Ethernet collision backup—*collision overhead*. More nodes degrade network throughput substantially.

LANModel software

LANModel is a software application designed for Microsoft Windows (MS Windows). This version is a shareware edition strictly for *LAN Performance Optimization*. It capitalizes upon the Windows graphical user interface (GUI) with its intuitive user interface; the window metaphors, keyboard, mouse, and pen input extensions. LANModel simulates the performance of LANs without wiring a network, testing different configurations, or committing any funds to a prolonged construction project and evaluation process.

LANModel is an enhancement of a consulting tool originally created in a mainframe programming language called APL. While APL is particularly well-suited for statistical experiments, Monte Carlo simulation, queueing analysis, vector and matrix manipulation, and graphical display, MS Windows provides a superior platform. Many LANs support Windows clients and it is a growing choice for user-level applications. IBM OS/2 2.0 also runs LANModel as a Windows client. LANModel executes combinatorial and queueing models. The implementation provided with this book does not include a Monte Carlo simulation. CPU requirements and the slight increases in accuracy (about 2.3% on 3 standard deviation confidence intervals) are not warranted. Also, note, that this shareware version does not include the "expert system" data tables, which interpret model results and provide suggestions for action.

Model system requirements

MS Windows 3.*x* is a basic environment requirement. LANModel will not run otherwise (or without the OS/2 2.0 Windows emulation). At least 650,000 bytes of disk space are required to install one network protocol, with an additional 150,000 bytes per additional protocol. Four protocols are available: ARCnet, Ethernet, FDDI, and Token-Ring. System memory requirements are 2Mb of RAM. More memory allows multiple models to run simultaneously, or duplicate protocols to be invoked concurrently. In other words, more memory makes it possible to model a planned network with the four different protocols at the same time. LANModel runs faster with more RAM, more cache, buffers, or a temporary RAM disk, all of which are typical of a tuned Windows environment. Note that online help is not available due to the distribution disk size limitations. LANModel is activated by selecting its MS Windows icon. At least EGA video resolution is required. A color video display is not required. The software will automatically configure itself for the video resolution (480 x 640, 640 x 800, and 780 x 1024 pixels) and the color mode. Additionally, the black-and-white mode can be optionally enabled to override system attributes. LANModel is therefore functional and easy to view on a monochrome laptop computer.

LANModel installation

The 5 1/4" distribution disk that is packaged with *LAN Performance Optimization* contains LANModel, other optional performance tools, and selected documentation. Installation is streamlined with an automated installation routine. Insert the diskette in a suitable floppy disk drive (usually designated as A: or B:). While running within MS Windows (version 3.0, version 3.1, and future releases subject to compatibility), select File from the Program Manager. Choose the Run option. Type A:SETUP, or B:SETUP if that is the designation for the 5 1/4" floppy drive. Figure 4-7 shows these steps. Note: to achieve the best results and to minimize the potential for conflicts, halt all background operations and end all tasks running as icons. Only the Program Manager should be active during application software installations.

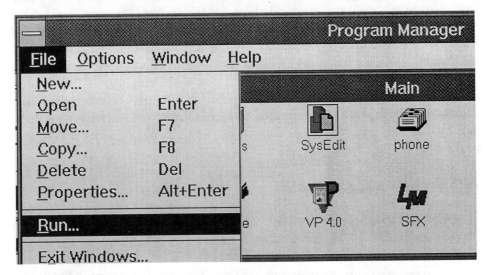

4-7   *LANModel* installation starts from the File/Run option of Windows program manager.

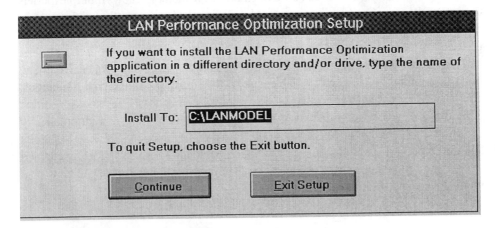

4-8   Alternate path for *LANModel* installation.

Indicate the designation of the floppy drive where the installation disk is inserted. Next, indicate where the LANModel software should reside. The default (and recommended) installation is C:\LANModel. Users that run MS Windows over a network from diskless workstations should indicate an alternate drive and path (e.g., F:\NETWORK\SOFTWARE\TOOLS\LANMODEL), as Fig. 4-8 indicates. The software locates key MS Windows directory paths and installs two necessary files within those paths. Note that LANModel provides two useful features. First, installation can be customized for current LAN environments or current disk space limitations *and* later revised for new protocols or increased disk space.

The SETUP routine is installed along with LANModel for future reconfiguration. Second, a LANModel removal routine is provided to remove the software and all associated files completely. Due to MS Windows automatic desktop save and backup features, it might be necessary on some versions to manually remove the LANModel icon group from Program Manager; while the group is iconized, highlight it, and then use the delete key to remove it. No other references to LANModel will remain on the computer.

Optional installation procedures

The distribution disk contains modeling software for ARCnet, Ethernet, FDDI, and Token-Ring. At least one protocol must be installed as part of the installation process. Additionally, optional software and documentation can be installed during the installation process. This optional software includes several LAN block transfer (i.e., component) benchmark tests and CPU benchmark performance measuring tools. The optional documentation includes three Lotus 1-2-3 spreadsheets, as described in Chapter 3, for computing Token-Ring and FDDI wiring lengths and token rotation times. Click to enable those options desired, as Fig. 4-9 displays.

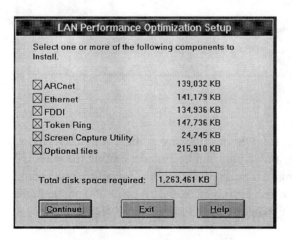

4-9 *LANModel* installation options.

These optional spreadsheets files are compressed and can be extracted for use by running the executable file from MS Windows File Manager or from the DOS prompt (type RING_WK1.EXE).

A screen capture utility is also *optionally* installed. SCRNCAP loads into windows as an icon. When you enable it by clicking on the icon (a camera), a window pops up and asks for a filename in which to save the current screen image. This utility is supplied to capture graphs and results for inclusion within presentations or desktop publishing documents.

The installation routine will check the target path and directory for sufficient disk space. Note that the installation routine does not search for a currently installed version of LANModel, so that subsequent installations will actually require less net disk space than indicated by the options menu.

The installation routine creates and copies files to the designated directories and paths, creates a Program Manager group folder; and creates four icons. The first icon (i.e., the stopwatch) is the LANModel icon. The second icon invokes the Windows Notepad with online documentation. The third icon represents the LANModel Setup (and optional reinstallation). The fourth icon provides a swift means to remove all of LANModel from the disk. Figure 4-10 shows the default-sized LANModel icon group.

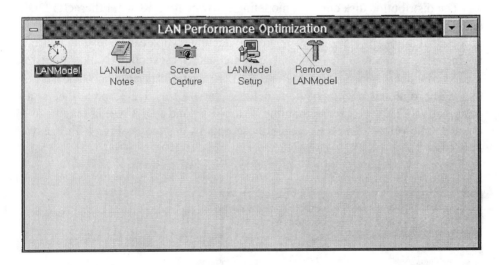

4-10 *LANModel* icon group.

Users with a monochrome laptop who have trouble differentiating Windows Help standard text from keywords and popups might consider editing the WIN.INI file. It is highly recommended to make a backup copy of this file before proceeding since MS Windows will not work with a corrupted one. Keywords and popup items are usually a light green. Add these two lines after the [Windows Help] section:

and replace the zeroes with RGB colors that are visible on the two-color monitor. 130 000 000, for example, represents red. Different colors for these options are best. This change is activated after Windows is restarted.

Model application

The bottom line for network modeling is that network performance modelers and network designers do not need to understand applied mathematics, statistics, probability theory, or queueing models. Users need only to understand how to use LAN simulation tools. LANModel is simple in use. Any complexity materializes from data collection efforts and understanding how to utilize the data. For each LAN protocol, the model requires specification information about the LAN architecture. This information describes the physical infrastructure of the current LAN or proposed (planned) LAN. Typically, the required parameters include the length of the LAN, the number of nodes, the type of wiring or cabling, the LAN transmission speed, and perhaps even the protocol. Figure 4-11 illustrates how to invoke the protocol models with the model configured for ARCnet, Ethernet, FDDI, and Token-Ring.

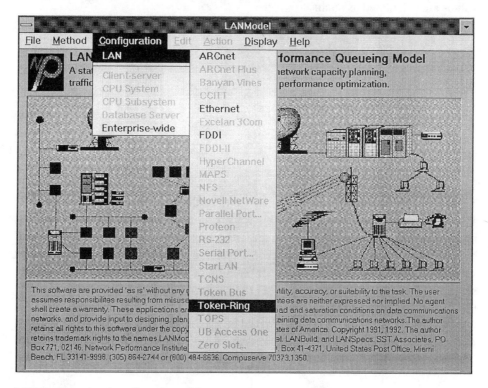

4-11 Use the network configuration pulldown menu to invoke *LANModel*.

The combinatorial model is computed based upon this rudimentary information and forms the basis for the more complex queueing mathematics. Actual performance data are represented by a small number of parameters, and therefore easily collected. Performance data are represented by traffic information: counts, timings, collision rates, error rates, observed, proposed, or estimated workloads, traffic composition, and cyclical loading, as the following list specifies.

- Arrival times (packets or frames per time period)
- Arrival variability
- Average packet or frame sizes
- The mode of the packet size
- The variance of the packet size
- The observed or anticipated error rate

Realize that average (mean), mode and variance have very specific definitions. The *average* is the predicted value most likely to occur in the sample; it is a statistical construction and might not even represent observed values. The *mode* is the value most likely to occur in the sample. The *variance* is the sum of the squares of difference between all sample values and the average value. Mathematically, these values are calculated as such:

$$\text{Mean} = \sum_{i=1}^{n} \frac{x_i}{n}$$

$$\text{Mode} = \text{Maximizefor } F(x), \text{ or set } F'(x)=0$$

$$\text{Variance} = \sum_{i=1}^{n} (x_i - x)$$

Since a picture is often highly informative, the following illustration in Fig. 4-12 shows these concepts. In practice, this information is captured with the aid of a protocol analyzer or monitor. Much of the data represented in this book was collected by a Network General product called a Watchdog. Comparable tools from other vendors are sufficient subject to the limitations raised in Chapter 3, namely, they should be fast enough to collect most of the packets and accurately size and collate them. There are other alternatives that might not entail financial outlays.

For example, many NOSes track packet sizes and transmission rates for both outgoing and incoming traffic on a per-station basis. Sun Microsystems provides NETSTAT and PERFORM utilities, as well as a few newer ones for X-Windows.

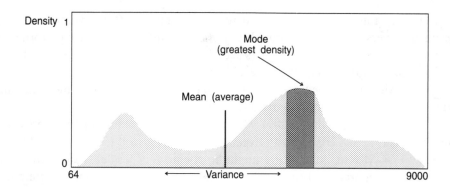

4-12 Traffic sample set (a) mean, (b) mode, and (c) variance.

LAN Manager, LAN Server, FTP, and Netware (at the server level) track and capture network traffic counts. SNMP and CMIP monitoring stations gather packet size, error rate, and traffic rates from stations and network devices. If operative, accumulate the relevant values. Realize that data acquired on a per-station basis will double-count actual traffic volumes and error rates, since this information would include counts for both outgoing and incoming traffic. An outgoing packet to one machine represents an incoming packet to at least one another machine. (Broadcasts and multicasts potentially represent multiple incoming packets.) Packet size, however, is unaffected by double counting.

Proforma modeling samples

The samples that follow are useful for exploring some typical network performance problems and the methodology for solving them with performance simulation software. The first one explores the problems inherent in planning and building a new LAN. While it is expensive to build a new network with overcapacity to meet actual traffic, it is even more expensive to misjudge the traffic load and overload the new network. LANModel provides an efficient means to model network size and traffic loading. The second example shows how to estimate traffic as a network grows in size, and plan how to break the sections into subnets. The third example illustrates the effects of bursts and peaks on network performance.

Planning a new network

In lieu of hard and firm rules for designing a network, most consultants and network experts overdesign a LAN. Nothing undermines the perceived success of a designer more than a brand new LAN that underestimates initial traffic requirements. As a result, designers opt instead to provide anywhere from 10 to 50 percent performance overcapacity—that is, if the designers actually forecasts performance correctly and understand how to estimate traffic levels. Overcapacity is expensive and unnecessary. LANModel provides a means to define capacity and scope the minimum capacity and LAN performance requirements.

Consider that installing FDDI where any other protocol will serve presently increases wiring and connectivity expenses by a factor of three of four; 3-Mbits/s ARCnet or 4-Mbits/s Token-Ring might be adequate at less cost and with lower service and support complications. Faster and newer protocols impose a premium. Because they are newer, vendor alternatives are fewer. Support is harder since the knowledge is not as yet disseminated. Furthermore, early in the product lifecycle, costs are higher and have not yet begun to be pressured from competition and other options. LANModel provides a proforma feature for viewing the effects of station counts and traffic levels on LAN performance.

For example, consider the need to design a LAN to support mission-critical processing for 30 accountants, a 60-person software design team, and 50 other various support staff. Here are some key questions for proforma analysis:

- How will they be using the network?
- What applications will they be using?
- What applications are mission-critical?
- What happens when an error occurs or key component fails?
- What are the hours of operation?
- What are the workloads?
- Where are these people located?
- Who supports the network (are they included in headcount)?

Answers must be quantified. Thus, the first item to note is that the total user count is 140. Unless the network is peer-to-peer, station count is apt to be 154 units (10 percent overhead). A single 16-Mbits/s Token-Ring will be a specification violation. Second, determine what operations are mission-critical. Is it the accounting or the software development, or rather, are the support activities (as in customer support) the aspect that is mission-critical? Third, accounting and software design usually mix painfully. Software developers tend to push performance, traffic, and stability to the design envelope.

Hence, the LAN begins to look best if it is separated into at least two LANs; one for accounting and one for software development. It is prudent to also consider subdividing critical operations onto separate LANs so that some fraction of their activity will be available at all times. Therefore, the network environment might consist of two or more separate LANs, perhaps interconnected by a bridge, router, or gateway. Now, each LAN can be optimized for performance as a separate entity.

Also, note again that the headcount (140) might not necessarily equal the network device counts. Add to that number file servers, support machines, network printers, and the interconnectivity devices. The table in Fig. 4-13 lists LANModel inputs for this theoretical organization.

The simulation results for Ethernet show that software development will require subnetted Ethernet LANs or carefully configured FDDI DAS and SAS configuration. The requirements for support and accounting are fairly minor in terms of LAN performance. When the source numbers above are plugged into the simulation, the model indicates that any protocol is sufficient. Figure 4-14 illustrates this conclusion.

	Accounting	Development	Support
Node counts	34	82	53
Packets/s	550	2500	750
Packet variance/s	135	450	350
Packet size	735	128	128
Packet size mode	500	285	460
Packet size variance	20	720	60

4-13 Model inputs for a new network infrastructure for an example organization.

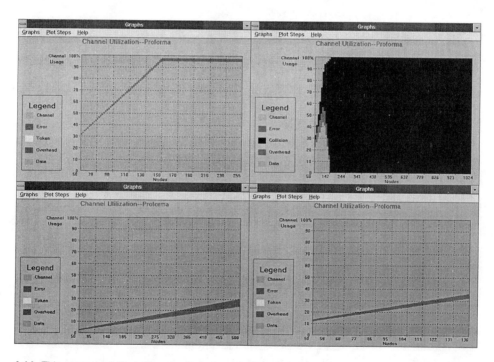

4-14 This compound illustration shows that most networks bottlenecks result from factors other than network channel saturation.

A careful investigation might entail a sensitivity analysis to see where ARCnet or 4-Mbits/s Token-Ring might be insufficient for accounting and support. Adjust the inputs and rerun LANModel. Note that it is probably sensible to install the same networking protocols for all groups in order to minimize knowledge requirements, increase purchasing power, and simplify installation, management, and expansion. If some aspect of software development can be isolated strictly in terms of the high traffic (i.e., graphics design or a data repository) and that group is expected to grow, perhaps a second protocol is reasonable.

Proposed changes to network size

Networks tend to grow. Most companies install PC-based LANs on a department or group basis. These isolated LANs become connected and eventually essential to daily operations. Furthermore, new users are added to the growing infrastructure. Typically, performance becomes erratic or poor. All current users realize that adding more users to the network will adversely affect performance. At that point, management is perceived as essential. The LANModel graph in Fig. 4-15 dramatically shows what will happen to traffic with more Token-Ring users.

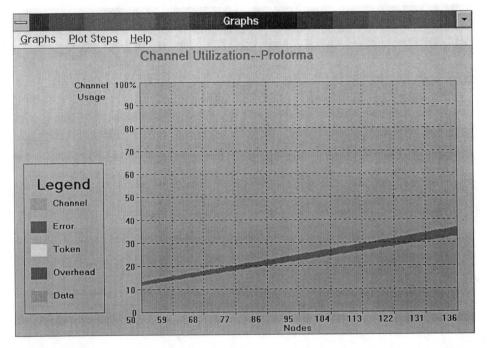

4-15 Proposed changes in network size.

Mixed transmission speeds

Some LANs include sections with a different transmission speed. This includes LANs with some wireless nodes or with a wireless interbuilding link. Since wireless, both infrared and radio frequency, usually transmit at 1.5 Mbits/s to 3.6 Mbit/s, these linkages are slower than those of standard protocols. Sections with slower transmission speeds will increase TRT on networks with token-passing protocols and increase the slot time on Ethernet. When these links or node subsets are not isolated by routers or gateways, model the network at the slowest effective transmission speed on the LAN. LANModel will not show degraded performance even with the decreased transmission for most LANs; the channel is rarely the LAN constraint. TRT, slot time, collision rates, and channel utilization will however be greater.

Changes in loading levels

Network loading levels usually increase over time because networks are rarely consolidated and made smaller. The performance model easily shows the waiting time effects and traffic levels for increases. However, an important question is often, what happens to traffic levels when a LAN is subdivided? Will performance improve on the subnets? Figure 4-16 illustrates the proforma charting feature of LANModel.

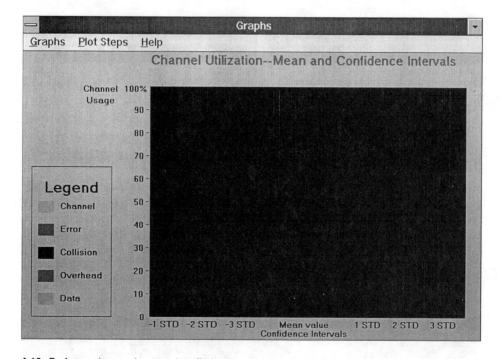

4-16 Proforma changes in network traffic levels.

Changes in load variance

Network performance is more sensitive to variance in packet rates and packet sizes than it is to protocol speed. Sudden bursts of traffic and peak volumes saturate the transmission channel; latency and slot times are very sensitive to variances. Note that network response time will be far worse with volatile-sized packets than with fixed-sized packets with the same average length. Sudden bursts also tend to increase the latency for access to the network. This means that the waiting time until transmission increases substantially. And most users quickly perceive these slowdowns.

With token-based protocols, this often happens when all users arrive in the morning and start reading their mail. Performance will slow but remain consistent; each mail request will require at least the token rotation. On Ethernet, sudden bursts and packet storms create a bottleneck that is hard to clear. Operation might even cease because of station-level timeouts. *Drift* is a measure of stability[3] that measures backlogged packets and retransmission rates. These settings are often a feature of LAN configurations and are sometimes adjustable, as Chapter 5 discusses. Figure 4-17 illustrates how transmission waiting times increase with variance. Note that only the LANModel confidence level intervals and confidence level graph truly show the effects of increased variance on channel usage.

3   Coyle and Lui

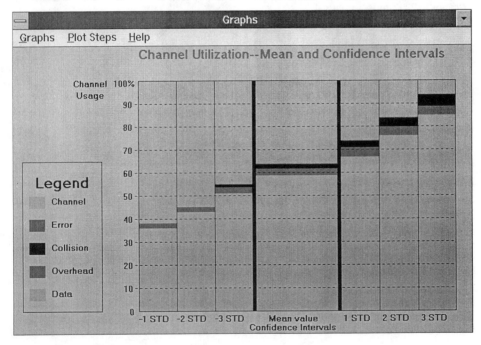

4-17 Changes to traffic load variance.

How to interpret results

The most important information reported by LANModel for the nonpersistent token-based protocols is waiting time. Note that waiting times are provided in this version of LANModel in terms of bittimes. A bit time is the time it nominally takes to transmit one bit at the speed of the protocol. For example, 10 bits at 10 Mbits/s is equivalent to 1 μs. A Token-Ring TRT of 28 μs is equivalent to 448 bits on a 16-Mbits/s Token-Ring. Only in extreme loading will channel bandwidth be fully committed. When LAN traffic bottlenecks are transmission based, explore the station, transmission, and total system waiting times. The channel utilization graph is interesting, though only marginally pertinent for token protocols. It is interesting to note that as Token-Ring utilization curves approach the asymptotic limits, as illustrated in Fig. 3-7 and 3-8, channel utilization is below full saturation.

As the number of nodes or the packet arrival volume increases, waiting time will increase to the detriment of LAN performance. The reasonable assumption in instances where LANModel indicates very low loads and reasonable waiting times while a live network exhibits poor performance is that the bottleneck is caused by high error levels, poor server performance, or an overall situation where stations are suboptimally configured at the hardware or software level. LANModel thus provides valuable new information to confirm the source of the bottlenecks. In general, LANModel can challenge the notion that network channel is the bottleneck, or substantiate that the the bottleneck is caused by faulty installation, maintenance, and basic network configuration.

Note, however, that NOS, application, network management protocol, or OSI overheads can affect LAN performance. If channel bandwidth is fully utilized and true workload is low, investigate traffic packet composition and congestion with a protocol analyzer that can disassemble packets by protocol layers. Similarly, when traffic levels, error rates, application loads are low, yet performance is poor, investigate how the protocol is implemented. Compare local workstation processing with remote processing. Dramatic differences in timings should signal high overheads or perhaps even poor disk performance.

The most important information provided by LANModel for the persistent CSMA/CD-based protocols is collision rates and channel loading rates. Only in extreme loading will channel bandwidth be fully committed. Saturation will occur when the collision and the frequency of the "silent" collision backoffs dissipate the channel bandwidth. LANModel shows that Ethernet saturates near the critical traffic rate of 37 percent (1/e), as predicted in 1979 by Metcalf and Biggs[4]. Of significant note, protocol analyzers do not track how long a channel is "crowded" by the silent

---

4   Metcalf and Briggs

backoff gaps; there is no signal, and thus it will not count that time. While Ethernet (a one-persistent protocol) saturates below full channel utilization, Token-Ring performance remains consistent but increasingly sluggish. The waiting time (i.e., slot or latency) becomes increasingly larger and less acceptable. Waiting time values are calculated by the queueing models.

Ethernet rarely experiences dramatic degradation in transmission waiting times unless the collision rate increases beyond 8 percent. The graphs and the built-in proforma capability are very useful for establishing transmission channel bottlenecks or evaluating the effects of network growth. Ethernet performs well until the slope of the collision curve begins to flatten; waiting time will increase to the detriment of LAN performance. That information is an extra confirmation that the collision rate is increasing.

As with token-based networks, the reasonable assumption in instances where LANModel indicates very low Ethernet loads and reasonable collision rates, while a live network exhibits poor performance, is that the bottleneck is caused by high error levels, poor server performance, or an overall situation where stations are suboptimally configured at the hardware or software level. LANModel thus provides valuable new information to confirm the source of the bottlenecks. In general, LANModel can challenge the notion that the network channel is the bottleneck, or substantiate that the bottleneck is caused by basic network specification violations, poor installation, maintenance flaws, or complex constraints such as I/O bottlenecks, maximized disk access, 100 percent server CPU utilization, and inefficient client-server applications.

5
Chapter

Optimization techniques

Optimizing the performance of a LAN rarely means replacing the network cable with faster optical fiber and substituting a different transmission protocol. Successful network tuning encompasses more than just the transmission channel. It requires revaluation of configuration, LAN architecture, and station performance. In fact, substituting a crosspoint matrix switch (a telephone PBX-like technology), or 100-bits/s network such as TCNS and FDDI for a constricted 10-Mbits/s Ethernet rarely provides the 1000 percent gains imagined.

Likely improvements to transmission throughput by applying faster LAN protocols might yield about 45 percent at best—about a 200 to 300 percent overall LAN performance improvement at best. By comparison, "unlikely" changes such as providing larger server disks, installing bus mastering controllers for disks and NICs on a file server, establishing local disk caches, purging dead files and records, adding more memory or larger buffers, and substituting faster CPUs, video controllers, or buses with integrated high-resolution video could improve server response and workstation throughout by a factor of 2000 percent or more. Usually, merely reconciling the network configuration with the formal specifications and improving the quality of all electrical connections enhances performance by as much as 100 percent.[1]

Establish file search priorities so that client requests search the local drives first. Review network routing requests for spurious activity and unnecessary subnet or routing addresses (as in Netware "hops"). Establish local swap or temporary files.

Setting NIC buffer sizes to the maximum tends to strengthen performance. Check that bridge and router packet forward legal packets of all sizes. *Remove* inferior devices from the network; many devices will *ignore* packets that exceed 512 bytes. Combining these changes together often provides throughput improvements of at least 400 percent, to performance gains of 4000 or 5000 percent for GUI front ends interconnecting into client-server databases.

Optimize what you tune. If you tune the wrong component, that component is likely to perform better in the vacuum of a stand-alone setting, and perhaps no better at all within the LAN setting. If you tune the wrong component, any performance effect is likely to be less than anticipated, or the reverse of the hoped-for results, as the table in Fig. 5-16 shows at the end of this chapter. Improper optimization, therefore, tends to be self-limiting. Consider this key recommendation: maintain a careful log of network performance, the exact steps taken to alter performance, and the consequences resulting from *each* step. You might have to reverse any perform-ance dilution and diminishment.

Tuning network performance is a complex process since the network is not a single device. Tuning could represent optimization of a single station's performance, that of a single server's, a network segment that performs poorly, or aggregate LAN performance. It could also represent the stepwise evaluation and enhancement of each subset. Correspondingly, this book espouses this stepwise refinement. Recall a basic message of this book, that the LAN is a system representing the aggregate of network devices and processes. Frequently, attempts to optimize the performance of a single device performing poorly fail since that device is already performing at its peak within the context of the network. That device's performance is conditional upon its own attributes and configurations while subordinated to the limitations imposed by servers, hosts, and other stations, as Fig. 5-1 illustrates. Within that setting, actual tuning proceeds first with elemental components such as stand-alone PCs and workstations, and progresses to more complicated and intertwined LAN

Tune\Results	Single station	Server	Segment	Network
Single station	Optimum	No effect	Unknown	Unknown
Server	Better	Optimum	Unknown	Unknown
Segment	Qualified	Qualified	Optimum	Qualified
Network	Unknown	Unknown	Unknown	Optimum
Interconnectivity	Qualified	Qualified	Qualified	Optimum

5-1 LAN performance optimization goals and resulting performance improvements.

1   Haller, Ted, *Cookbook approach to troubleshooting in the Token-Ring environment*, 1992 Communication Test Symposium, Hewlett-Packard.

stations and processes. Realize that even seemingly elemental and stand-alone components might impose limitations when optimizing performance of servers, segments, and the aggregate network. In spite of these complex interactions—while LAN performance optimization is elusive and iterative—it is certainly worthwhile to master the bottlenecks and assess how performance on a LAN can be enhanced.

Physical infrastructure

The physical infrastructure of any network must be sound to achieve optimal performance. All transmission components—the cable, fiber, or wire, connectors, transceivers, MAUs, interconnectivity devices, lobe or drop cables, NICs, and NIC drivers—can be tested for conformance to specification and proper installation. Basic network installation, infrastructure that matches specification, maintenance, or acceptable installation and careful maintenance do improve LAN performance but this basic technique is outside the scope of this book.

A good infrastructure minimizes the effects of signal decay and distortion, timing errors, false signals, crosstalk, and random noise. Even networks that are poorly designed and improperly configured or balanced to match task workloads can realize 15 percent throughput gains through remedial physical infrastructure adjustments. Recall that a list from Chapter 3 showed that at least 80 percent of all LANs have physical defects contributing to suboptimal performance. Do a quick visual inspection for loose cables, broken connectors, transceivers, or other devices with error indicator lights. Replace suspected components. Test the infrastructure with voltmeters, TDRs, OTDRs, cable scanners, and signal injectors, but correct any deficiencies as the initial step in the LAN performance optimization cycle.

Do not intermix components from different manufacturers. While this seems a small point, consider traffic rated at 16,000,000 characters per second on a 16-Mbits/s Token-Ring with a network length of 2100 m. At a signal failure rate of 0.01 percent per 100 ft, the error rate will grow to 2.1 percent, or 42,000 characters each second at an average traffic load. On a saturated network, the immediate problem is to lower network demands, or rechannel that load. The list on the next page outlines the steps necessary to alleviate compatibility problem.

Network configuration

The actual physical layout of a network has a significant effect on network performance. This broad assertion is most relevant for LANs that are extended beyond the simple bus or ring structure; it is also relevant for LANs unequally balanced in terms of workload. This represents client-server and distributed computing environments and LANs that have grown beyond small workgroups and now service the needs of departments, larger divisions, and entire organizations.

- Support LAN with a single protocol
- Do not run multiple protocols on same channel
- Segregate unique entities on subnets
- Ascertain and match BIOS versions
- Maintain uniform operating system releases
- Check NIC crystal clock rates for uniformity
- Set uniform packet address sizes (ARCnet, Token-Ring)

For these flourishing LANs, optimal performance is crucially dependent upon sufficient design. The physical infrastructure must incorporate adequate file and application servers to match the workload and a cabling configuration to equal transmission channel throughputs, as Fig. 5-2 illustrates. Divide overloaded LANs to balance workload since the contention for each segment is less than the original combined LAN. This is particularly relevant for Ethernet, although also pertinent for other protocols too, as fewer stations compete for a token.

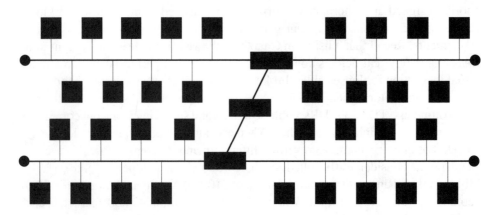

5-2   Divide overloaded LANs to balance workload.

Station placement tends to carry significant effects on some LANs, chiefly persistent protocols such as Ethernet. This effect is called *position-dependent unfairness.*[2] Busy nodes that are centralized on the coaxial bus, or logically positioned together in a twisted-pair star initiate collision detection and resolve the collisions sooner than they would if placed at extreme ends of the LAN. Similarly, minimizing cable and wire runs shortens the contention interval. Less cable means less time

2   Gonsalves, Timothy A., and Tobagi, Fouad A., "On the performance effects of station locations," *IEEE Transactions on Communications,* pp. 441-449, April 1988.

required to traverse the Token-Ring, a rate of 5 µs per K at 4 Mbits/s and 16 Mbits/s. This time is relevant on FDDI rings only when segments approach the 100K maximum. Ethernet defines the maximum slot time as 512 bit times, the collision contention interval as a maximum of 448 bit times. This provides sufficient time delay for multiple-hop LANs to receive all signals and respond properly.

However, the slot time and contention intervals can be *shorter* Ethernet performance is better with smaller networks. This is also true for ARCnet, FDDI, and Token-Ring, though to a lesser degree. Since the data signal travels at nearly the speed of light (in a vacuum, 3×10^{10}) for all protocols, cable lengths are not as much an issue as the number of nodes. Each Token-Ring node repeats data signals and the electronics delay the reiteratation of those signals by 2 to 40 µs. Cumulatively, excess wiring and node repeater delays can increase minimum token rotational times by 400 percent. Therefore, commensurate with the protocol and architecture, minimize LAN path lengths, adjusted ring lengths (ARLs), lobe lengths, and node counts to provide faster response.

Processing configuration

Peer-to-peer networks tend toward low volume utilization of global resources, such as the LAN transmission channel. Any perceived slowdowns are usually caused by station-level bottlenecks. Performance bottlenecks tend to be isolated and local problems best solved by optimizing the performance of those local resources. In other words, tune each peer-to-peer station in turn to best meet the requirements of individual users. Later sections in this chapter address the process for tuning individual stations.

Client-server and distributed processing networks represent more complex LAN configurations. Performance is influenced by server loads, workstation loads, channel capacity, and loading—including traffic burst loads, where the intensive CPU work is processed. *File* servers exporting entire database files for remote processing might not only clog the transmission channel but create backlogs when many stations request files simultaneously. Additionally, the overhead for fetching the files and creating intermediate views might overwhelm the local workstation as well. This is not a true client-server architecture; rather, this merely represents a dispersed file service application.

True client-server database servers export views (processed subsets of data from a transaction database, GIS images, CAD displays, or scientific data sets) and partially processed client requests. Client-server file servers optimize those requests to generate significantly better performance given the same hardware configuration and network transmission capacities than within a file server environment. Distributed processing applications supposedly represent a step further advanced in that server versus remote processing is optimized on the fly to maximize available free resources and alleviate bottlenecks.

Consider software upgrades

When LAN bottlenecks have definitively been traced to software, more server and workstation horsepower is usually the best recourse. Migration to Unix or Unix-derivatives which support parallel processing and multiple processors might overcome the software contraints. However, when the dispersed application has other serious flaws, consider upgrading that dispersed application software with something supporting client-server optimization. Slow client-server applications can be upgraded to a distributed computing version. In some (few) cases, the software upgrade might be more straightforward, particularly when the applications are based upon a generic standard such as ANSI C or SQL. However, note that bottlenecks attributed to slow applications actually could be precipitated by slow disk searches through large data sets, poor index selections, lack of indexes (instead, relying upon sequential lookups), as well as many dead files and deleted records (but not removed). In some instances, poor software execution can be improved by moving the application to a local disk on a network workstation.

LAN growth configuration

Massive LANs—LANs started as test projects or as ad hoc resources to bypass the traditional MIS department that have since grown explosively—might actually saturate the transmission channel. They are best optimized by a process sometimes termed "load leveling" and by segregating workgroups on linked segments. This effectively amounts to identifying workgroup units and constructing separate LAN segments adequate to match the requirements for each individual unit. Since E-mail, shared resources, shared access, and communication are fundamental to the success of the LAN, each subnet needs a central connecting backbone.

This subnet approach has the advantage of simplicity, immediacy, and control. Subnetworking also provides isolation from LAN failures in other workgroups and a global failure in the central backbone. Ideally, each subnet could function adequately without the central backbone. This is a traditional and acceptable approach that has proven effective for overloaded Token-Ring and Ethernet LANs. These "firebreaks" increase reliability while isolating traffic to the subnets for improved performance. Bridges, routers, and gateways actually interconnect the workgroup LANs. There are three shortcomings to this approach.

The first of these shortcomings includes the overhead and bottlenecks imposed by the routing software (traditionally at servers) or the stand-alone connectivity devices. When stations perform double duty as file servers, mail servers, print servers, and gateways, the usual performance bottlenecks tend to occur at these CPU choke points.

The second shortcoming is that stand-alone connectivity devices might not match the traffic requirements. A repeater is not the appropriate device to interconnect high-traffic subnets; a repeater is best used to extend signals for servicing physically dispersed areas. Repeaters increase the collision and dropped packet rate on Ethernet while increasing the TRT on token-based networks. Bridges, in the traditional definition of course, merely repeat LLC-layer protocol and filter signals to connect LANs with different media. As such, they are signal repeaters for different media. MAC bridges that filter packets are protocol dependent. Routers are complex to install, configure, and maintain. They are frequently slow. Gateways performing routing, or protocol encapsulation or translation tend to be slower still.

The third shortcoming is that internetwork traffic—that is, the traffic originating on one subnet and routed to another subnet—often traverses many other subnets, as Fig. 5-3 illustrates. These other subnets are used merely as links; the local traffic increases significantly, sometimes to the saturation point.

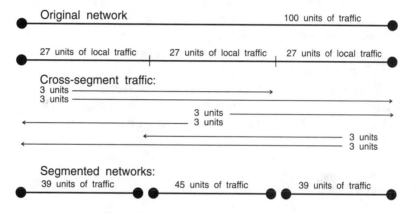

5-3 Improper network division increases internetwork traffic.

The solution to these network configuration flaws is three-fold. First, subnets should be intelligently designed with some other purpose than merely cable length minimization or convenience of installation. Each subnet should be balanced for load as an individual resource. Servers, when overloaded, can be partitioned to distribute their processing loads to other subordinated devices. Standard PCs or Unix workstations can provide the same or better performance than specialized, single-purpose bridging and routing hardware—in some cases. Moreover, standard station hardware obviates the need for learning how to operate another type of device, or stocking specialized replacement parts.

Second, bridges, routers, and gateways should replace repeaters for enhancing performance. The MAC-layer packet forwarding and filtering capability of bridges, routers, and gateways reduces transient and irrelevant traffic. Note, however, that bridges, routers, and gateways from various manufacturers differ in performance characteristics. Some can handle high-volume traffic without loosing packet header bits or completely dropping packets. Some optimize routing. Some also create their own traffic as they maintain and update routing tables or distribute management information and performance statistics. When typical routers and gateways become LAN subnet bottlenecks, there are two solutions. Reassess configuration and install bridges, or install higher performance device called "cross-point switch matrixes." These switches are specialized computers with high-performance data buses; they route packets from multiple subnetworks at traffic volumes up to 340 Mbits/s.

Remove repeaters

Repeaters generally create performance problems by extending the transmission slot time. This increases the likelihood of collisions on the network, or increased latency and TRT. A repeater simply increases the potential for too-large, too-busy network configurations by extending the network architecture to the statistical breaking point. In situations where a network is grossly overloaded, disconnection of repeater units might solve the traffic bottleneck, as shown in Fig. 5-4. This obviously defeats the purpose of the network by cutting intercommunication channels. There are other alternatives, but this iconoclastic solution is quickly implemented to solve short-term overloading until more reasonable (and expensive) options can be implemented. A router with a filtering technology, a high-speed packet switch, a spanning tree, or a backbone in a bus represent superior alternatives.

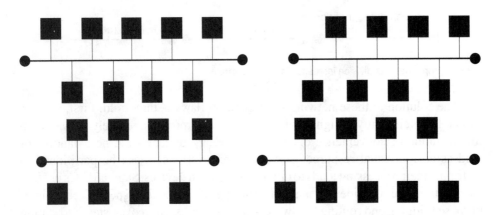

5-4   Split multiple subnet linkage.

Some newer-model bridges can be configured through software as routers; similarly, some routers can be configured as bridges for faster execution. Bridges tend to be faster than routers by several times. 3Com, Retix, and Synernetics provide these configurable devices. Forwarding throughput can reach 95 percent or more of full channel capacities. One point is that vendors are aware of subnetwork interconnectivity bottlenecks and requirements, and seek to redress these needs. The other point is that older model bridging and routing equipment might be insufficient to match current LAN performance needs. The technology has improved; unit for unit replacement of substandard components might resolve the obstruction.

Third, design a configuration so that all stand-alone subnets connect to a hub (backbone) rather than chain into other LAN segments. In other words, set up parallel channels for segmenting traffic, or establish single-purpose router-to-router links. Servers or mainframe hosts that must communicate with every subnet can reside on the hub or else connect into each LAN segment where these stations can support multiple NICs. In this configuration the hub serves no other purpose than to facilitate communication among the various LAN segments. Physically, the hub could be a segment of coax, a Token-Ring intelligent concentrator, an FDDI DAS segment or device, a single workstation, a LAN-in-a-box device, or the previously mentioned specialty hubs.

Load balancing

Excessive loads on any single LAN component will undermine performance. Providing additional parallel capacity is one solution to these bottlenecks. Bottlenecks best solved with this technique include network file servers, overloaded LAN output devices, transmission channels, and internetworking devices such as bridges, routers, and gateways.

As previously stated, work from an overloaded server can be allocated among several other subordinated stations. Overloaded departmental file servers often simultaneously and concurrently provide file services, mail, print service, routing to other subnetworks, user login, and security functions. When the network operating system supports backup and secondary networks servers, one or more of these fundamental services can be moved to another server. Output devices such as printers and network fax servers place a significant load upon their file server and the print server. When the file and print server are the same, the CPU overhead is significant for supporting the spooling, network output redirection, temporary storage of the output to disk, and control of the output devices; see Fig. 5-5.

Provide alternative channels

When a network carries a traffic volume in excess of design capacity, performance deteriorates nonlinearly for Ethernet and linearly for token protocols; this is a function of persistence, as previously explained. If performance is already degraded, new loads degrade performance disproportionately, as illustrated mathematically in Chapter 4. Alternative channels provide additional communication paths, much as local side roads and highway "shoulders" relieve a highway bottleneck after a traffic accident. While the same volume of traffic is transported, waiting time is decreased. An alternative channel might provide specialized high-speed disk-to-disk file transfers, imaging information transfer, or terminal services.

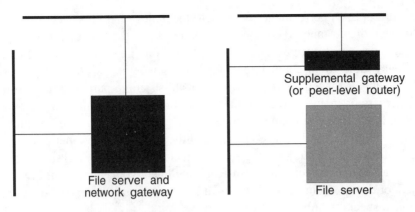

5-5 A supplemental gateway provides dedicated service to reduce a bottleneck.

Terminals (DTE) require full packet transmission for each keystroke and are an overlooked resource hog. A fast typist on a networked word processing terminal can create 480 packets per minute, and another 2560 with every screen page (requests, keystrokes, display echo, and ack/nak). Terminal equipment transmissions reveal efficiencies of less than 2 percent when most network traffic will experience 60 percent efficiencies or higher. RS-232 lines—twisted-pair serial connections, for example— yield a better match than LAN protocols for such low-speed transmission. Conversely, an imaging camera or scanner often digitizes upward of a megabyte of information from a single picture. At LAN speeds, 1000 or more packets will need to be built and transmitted. Such a load could jam an unloaded network completely for 4 s, or a network at capacity for several minutes. Direct device-to-node bus connection improves transfer rates and transfer success rates. Many managers recommend hybrid networks and tune performance in just this manner. Figure 5-6 lists local workstation tuning points.

Buffer networks with store-and-forward gateways

The store-and-forward mechanism duplicates some of the filtration functionality of the router. It will store a message packet for an unlimited amount of time until network slot time is available; it might save the message packet until off-peak hours. This store-and-forward technology is used for long-haul optical fiber networks, microwave, and VSAT links. Store-and-forward mechanisms require that network protocols be decoupled from a return receipt message (ack/nak) so as to free applications from timing out.

This is an expensive technology, usually installed as an ISO gateway. It is, however, suitable for low-volume, low-priority transmission. It is dependent upon the robustness of the network software, since the typical TCP/ IP or IPX transmission confirmation is not supported in real time. In fact, receipt confirmation might not be supported except at the mechanical level of the store-and-forward gateway. The

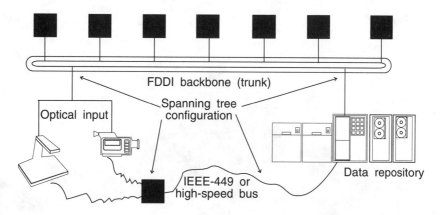

5-6 Alternate channels and spanning-trees bridges balance network loads

concept is akin to a receptionist taking a message when the telephoned party is already busy; no message receipt confirmation is provided to the caller and the intended recipient of the call never knows he was wanted until a message is received, or until a follow-up call is accepted.

Distribute load

The most economically available method of lowering network usage is to charge for network service at graduated rates and offer users incentives to avoid prime-time network access. This is what telephone companies do to reduce daytime traffic and encourage off-peak usage. Since any network is built to handle a peak load, and since a peak load might be several times larger than off-hour usage, there is a built-in network excess capacity. Unfortunately, that extra capacity is available during nonworking hours. Figure 5-7 illustrates this principle by graphing the network load during the progress of a normal day. Harried users often implicitly understand this principle and reorient their work schedules to reduce the impact on the overloaded network. Publish a graph of daily network loads to encourage off-peak usage if financial incentives are impractical.

When this last option is unavailable, the next-easiest method to reduce traffic levels is to filter the traffic and not allow certain vehicles on the network during peak usage. The network administration group, for example, doesn't need to perform data backups when the network is overloaded. Electronic mail can be stored and forwarded when the network shows a lull, or else saved for distribution during off-peak hours. Other processes can be hogs of network resources. Curtail such processes. Figure 5-8 illustrates a typical distribution of network traffic. Note that this display represents volume percentages each hour of a typical day. Collision traffic parallels the peaks of the last figure, but most traffic is disk access. Mail and graphics paging is a minor component in this sample.

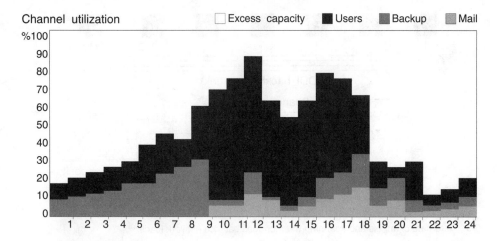

5-7 Network workload during a typical workday.

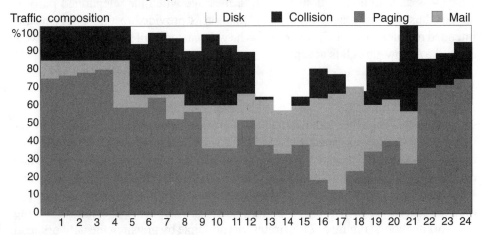

5-8 Network traffic composition by application.

Electronic mail often starts as a 10-line memo containing 1000 characters, but is then directed to 150 users. Since each user receives a separate copy, 150,000 characters plus the mail addressing information and Ethernet packet information must be included. That simple mail message therefore requires upward of 300,000 characters of network transmission. A bulletin board with a single posting reduces this "junk mail" load almost fully. Side benefits include a reduction of "temporary" mail disk storage; temporary because each day's new mail will require that old space.

Data backup could be banned from the network and performed exclusively from the node bus. Such a policy might entail additional backup devices; it shifts financial costs from network communication channel improvements (infrastructure) to node-specific upgrades (depreciable usage-specific equipment).

Component consistency

Another common cause for degraded network performance is noncompliance with a single LAN protocol standard. Ethernet 1.0 does not work well in conjunction with Ethernet 2.0 because of collision detection differences, nor will IEEE 802.3 standard systems work efficiently with either Ethernet. All are similar. Token-Ring products designed primarily for 4 Mbits/s are not always consistent with 16 Mbits/s de facto standards. Hardware control of jitter and signal decay do not conform with the "ringing tank" advances made by Texas Instruments and IBM in 1989. Likewise, since Token-Ring ETR is implemented in software, drivers must conform to NOS demands. The NIC hardware must be able to support the software; minor differences in EPROM or design could render the board incapable to recognize the continuous flow of valid packets.

Timing differences are the primary cause of traffic inconsistency. The same argument can be made with XNS, AIX, Novell IPX, DECnet, and HPnet TCP/ IP derivatives. When multiple system software architectures must interface on the same network, the different systems can be isolated on separate network segments, as a previous section outlined. At a minimum, monitor mixed networks specifically for transmission deficiencies. Other specialized interfacing equipment such as routers, gateways, or bridges can adequately protect network users from performance degradation due to mismatched standards and minor operational or component variations.

LAN components, too, can create intractable problems. Different vendors might supply transceivers or controllers with transmission rate clocks with subtle timing differences, or marginal signal quality. This equipment, while tuned for single-vendor usage, might communicate with other vendors' equipment unpredictably. Therefore, maintain consistent network node configurations for best performance.

Protocol selections

Protocol selection provides few degrees of freedom for optimizing network performance. Many PCs and engineering workstations (Sun and NeXt, for example) incorporate built-in and optimized network adapters; changing to other protocols represents a commitment. The political powers-that-be in most organizations mandate certain hardware and software brandnames and vendors. This in turn limits the range of available networking protocols. Most network application software mandate certain hardware computing platforms and network operating systems. Network operating systems, in turn, mandate the LAN protocol. Few networks can benefit from substitution of another protocol. Furthermore, when a hardware platform or network operating system can support multiple protocols (concurrently or interchangeably), end-user applications might not work with a desired protocol. Some protocol implementations are not as well debugged, as stable, nor as robust. Improving performance by changing protocols is usually a red herring. Ethernet provides no protocol upgrade path; ARCnet and Token-Ring might.

LAN protocols are fundamentally similar. Differences are represented by implementations; these include ETR, address field sizes, data payload size, token hold times, and support levels (ARCnet). In rare instances, protocols can be substituted. The most readily successful upgrade is a 16-Mbits/s Token-Ring in place of 4 Mbits/s. Drivers, software, and hardware are the same. Packet and protocol buffer space should increase 400 percent, while NIC reconfiguration is minor. Verify that the wiring plant will support the faster protocol; failure to verify this crucial requirement generates high error rates, lost tokens, and a new type of performance problem.

Similarly, TCNS and ARCnet *plus* function with the same software drivers as the original 2.5-Mbits/s ARCnet. NIC hardware is new. Wiring requirements are more stringent, although similar in specification to other high-performance copper-based LAN wiring plants (data-quality twisted-pair, perhaps shielded). Users report network file transfer times that exceed local disk performance typical of most end-user workstations.

FDDI (and CDDI) represent cost-effective protocol upgrades for specialized needs. This works best when FDDI provides only internetworking backbone connectivity. Stack protocols require 30 to 55 percent overhead when applications and network do not agree; evaluate FDDI LAN to the desktop carefully. It is a daunting challenge to integrate new software drivers, and new and as yet unproven hardware interfaces, install fiber or adequate (shielded) twisted-pair cable, and test end-user applications. It is worthwhile for specialized needs, *or* when planning LAN expansions.

A NOS refinement optimized for a large data block is available from Novell for the NetWare networking software. The new upper-level protocol sits above ARCnet, Ethernet, or Token-Ring and improves performance for large file transfers to 300 percent. The enhancement is called "burst mode protocol" and is effective for file server operations, GIS, and some types of database activities when the BURST.NLM version 1.0 does not destabilize the disk file system. Environments supporting intensive file transfer operations might benefit from the NOS upgrade. LIPX.NLM is effective for boosting the packet size across networks connected by routers and other server-based hops.

However, NOS performance can frequently be tuned for improved LAN performance. Cumulative effects of small adjustments can improve station performance, memory utilization, and disk thrashing. Memory, location in memory, order of loading modules, or overlays into memory can be adjusted. There are so many adjustable setup parameters for each different NOS—cache sizes; the number of buffers; the size of buffers; the numbers of concurrent processes allowed; the numbers of concurrent users, "superusers," or network supervisors; the sizes of routing tables; security settings; network accounting overheads; network management controls and performance tracking; mountable and cross-mountable partitions; user accounts—that optimizing parameters is a topic beyond the scope of this book. However, realize that poor network performance depends dramatically upon these NOS setup parameters, as can all underlying OS parameters. While Unix (and derivatives) are fairly open, there are many adjustable DOS parameters. OS/2 provides an enormous number of changeable operating system parameters; they are generally located in STARTUP.CMD, CONFIG.SYS, AUTOEXEC.BAT, and several other key memory management and network configuration files. MS Windows, while perhaps not an operating system per se but rather an OS shell, for example, provides enormous leeway to establish disk and memory cache, memory range exclusions, optimal utilization of the CPU instruction-set (enhanced and linear memory mapping on 80386 chips), diskless and networked application support, and reallocation of memory for video paging.

Workstation configuration

Performance of a LAN workstation is not only dependent upon the traffic performance of the LAN and the loading and speed of any LAN server resources, but is also governed by its own performance. Network tuning encompasses more than remedial repairs. Most Ethernet controllers provide average transmission throughput of about 1 Mbits/s, or 10 percent of the channel capacity. (Note that the Ethernet transceiver always sends signals at 10 Mbits/s as per Ethernet specification, but that few personal computers or even engineering workstations can sustain that transmission rate for more than a few seconds per minute. A time delay exists for gathering the data, assembling it into packets, transmitting the frames, and verifying acceptance by the recipient.) Additionally, few file servers have hard disks that can transfer 1.2-Mb of information from disk into memory per second, let alone buffer a significant portion of that full image in memory at any one time while waiting for the controller to construct packets at its capacity. Most personal computers (with ISA disk controllers) can achieve the slow disk transfer speed of 256K (or 0.25 Mbyte) per second. Even if the file server with a SCSI-2 disk drive and controller were to sustain the data transfer speed of 4.4 Mbytes/s, the receiving PC might not be able to handle more than 256 Kbytes/s. Although this might seem like a bottleneck, this data transfer rate is faster than most Ethernet controllers. Floppy drives might create bottlenecks due to their slower transfer speeds.

Consider the following example: transfer of a 10Mb graphics file on a two-node Ethernet network nominally requires 8.165 s across the communications channel. The time is derived by dividing 10,000,000 by 1500 to find the number of packets required, and multiplying this figure by the full frame size of 1518. This figure is then multiplied by 8 (bits per byte) and divided by the channel speed. This assumes Ethernet packets with the maximum data field size of 1500 bytes, while ignoring stack or protocol overheads. The fractional seconds indicate frame address overhead and the mandatory 96 µs interpacket delay. Besides, higher-level protocols expect a one-for-one acknowledgment of each packet sent. This could increase the transmission time by 0.40 s, assuming 6667 minimum-sized Ethernet frames (and the interpacket delay). If collisions result, both nodes will send the jam signal and try to transmit again, thereby increasing the transmission time. Recall, however, that the Ethernet controller can sustain only 10 percent of channel capacity. This will suggest a transfer time around 60 s.

In reality, upper-layer protocols are not that efficient. The application software will need to monitor transmission if only to count packets received and administer the sequence of data parsing and transmission. The graphic image in this example is a complex delivery, and the packets must be reassembled like a puzzle. Failure to reassemble the graphics data in sequence at this application level will result in unhappy users with a processing problem, as illustrated by the jigsaw puzzle in Fig. 5-9.

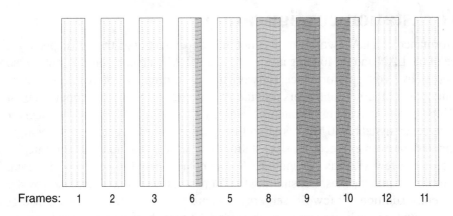

Frames: 1   2   3   6   5   8   9   10   12   11

5-9   Graphic image transmission broadcast sequence error.

Furthermore, recall that the TCP/ IP MAC and LLC protocols require space within the data buffer of each packet. This is easily overlooked since these bits and meager bytes are hidden at the lowest levels. Since they are encoded as bit information, decoding the MAC and LLC parameters requires some effort. However, the point is that each OSI, IPX, or TCP/ IP protocol layer adds control blocks and bytes to the network frame, thus decreasing throughput efficiency. Transmission of the 10Mb image might require 90 s regardless of the protocol. Despite this apparent inefficiency, Seybold has documented that transmission is dependent upon the protocol overhead.[3]

Few networks consist of a mere two nodes. Most have many nodes. Nonetheless, the controller transfer limitation implies that about 10 nodes (ignoring collisions) could probably transmit at constant capacity to 10 other receiving nodes before saturating the Ethernet channel. A bottleneck at the server level might masquerade as poor Ethernet channel performance. Bottlenecks will occur when multiple nodes

---

3   *The Seybold Report on Publishing Systems*, Vol. 20, No. 10/11, Autumn 1990.

send to or request information from a single node at once. The single node becomes a bottleneck despite excess channel capacity. This occurs not because this node simultaneously receives 10 packets at once, but because it cannot. Recall that only one packet can exist on Ethernet at a single time by definition, or a collision will result. The bottleneck occurs because this node must process the requests associated with each transmission.

For example, a file server handles user (or application) requests for data from files, while an application server overlays sequential or program overlays for client users. Each request requires the server to interpret and process this. A client requesting an SQL view wants the server to extract specific information from a database and formulate that view for transmission to the client. That processing is not simple and is usually CPU-intensive. Similar multiple requests from clients will cause a performance bottleneck at the server. This contrasts the issue of maximum network performance against maximum server performance. While these requests might necessitate some higher-level protocol transmission, network load might reach only 15 percent of capacity. By comparison, the file or application server has reached 100 percent of CPU, controller transmission, disk access, or bus capacity. In fact, improving local resources might yield the most significant global performance improvements for many environments. Below are some pertinent tuning steps that are independent of most operating systems and network protocols. The following sections present these tuning points in detail. They outline the methodology for implementing them for enhance station and LAN performance.

- Optimize system configurations
- Optimize software locally
- Optimize CPU-intensive activities
- Minimize accounting overheads
- Remove TSRs and background processes
- Increase CPU and memory speeds
- Increase local disk speeds
- Establish optimal sector interleave
- Low level format
- Defragment disks
- Maintain free disk Space
- Reorganize file placement
- Caching, buffering, and RAM disks
- Software optimization

Optimize system configurations

A general truism is that all computer systems perform better when adequately configured. This holds true independent of the operating system, the application software, and other details specific to a LAN installation. Adequate configuration includes coordinating versions of operating systems with system firmware, hardware, and device drivers. Note, however, that there initially exists some major contra-indications to tuning and optimizating NOS, operating system, and software configurations for multiple application and networked environments. While these limitations mostly burden MS-DOS, they do affect OS/2, Unix, VMS, and other OS environments to a lesser degree. Specifically, some applications require device drivers, memory allocations, open file buffers, and disk record buffers. These values might conflict with the requirements for other software applications.

For example, Lotus 1-2-3, release 3.0 for MS-DOS, wants expanded memory (mapped in 16Kb blocks) while MS-Windows 3. x maps extended memory in contiguous ranges. Optimal configuration for one application is insufficient for the other. As a further example, while RAM disks or caches dramatically enhance workstation performance, some software will not work. As such, "optimal" workstation performance might comprise *any* configuration for which all needed user applications function. The effort required to obtain 10 percent improvements might not warrant the time or financial costs. New software upgrades—as a likely and seductive example—might precipitate a direction of workstation modification, which creates havoc. In such a situation, any functional configuration is suitable.

Workstation configuration represents issues other than software compatibility. Although there is a trend toward hardware with software-configurable drivers or automatic switch settings, most hardware contains physical switches. Computers generally have physical microswitches or jumpers for establishing amounts of memory, wait states, interrupt conditions, response priorities, and physical device address resolution. Figure 5-10 illustrates these jumpers and microswitches.

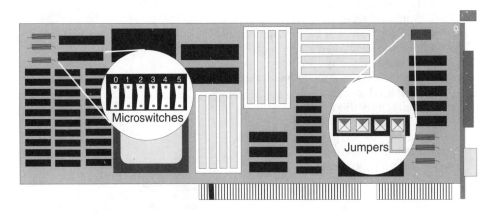

5-10 Illustration of NIC jumpers and microswitches.

Additionally, as PC-based workstations and servers (whether for DOS, OS/2, or Unix) grow more complex and more varied, it is critical to match CPU cycle and refresh times with static and dynamic memory chip speeds. Install hardware interface cards that connect properly with the system, and apply the correct settings for those units. Improving both local station performance and distributed processing might involve nothing more magical than resolving memory conflicts, wait state discrepancies, interrupt contention, and overlapping system priorities.

Unfortunately, most workstations represent a hodgepodge of components. Only in rare cases do vendors promote and qualify a workstation or server as a "tuned" system. Another issue is the ROM BIOS (basic input/output services) chip—the low-level software code governing basic computer functionality—that controls and configures low-level PC operation. Various manufacturers produce these chips. Some contain outright defects or minor variations from the "IBM PC AT or compatible" standard. In fact, most BIOS chips must contain significant variations from the standard so as not to infringe upon software code and (EPROM and BIOS microcode) copyrights. For example, a BIOS might function improperly with a particular hard drive controller or network interface card. A BIOS function call might reference memory that conflicts with high memory drivers, cache memory, or basic system function calls. Increasingly, conflicts with Unix OS derivatives, OS/2, DEC, client-server applications, and complex GUIs such as MS Windows are common as well. This is also true for Sun Microsystem SPARCstation knockoffs.

As another concern, software adds a far-reaching complexity to the component equation. Device drivers and OS settings are most often at odds with the hardware. More specifically, MS DOS 5-0 was distributed as an *update* only, not as a replacement operating system for PCs. The reason for this policy is that all PC manufacturers provide DOS with a BIOS software driver specifically designed to match the ROM BIOS firmware (PROM, EPROM, or EEPROM) provided with that computer. Note that only IBM computers can be installed with PC-DOS 5-0 as a newly installed operating system. To minimize conflicts and perhaps improve the processing speed of disk read/write, memory access, and video operations, install the operating system that corresponds to ROM BIOS.

Network administrators and managers who believe that their LAN is optimally tuned should re-evaluate that conceited belief. A Network General *Sniffer* running the latest expert system technology uncovered three hidden inefficiencies on a Novell network that appeared well optimized. First, due to the network administrator's oversight, the network Saber menu system increased the network load by invoking all executable files without the DOS file extension. Since Saber conforms to MS-DOS rules, it correctly generated repetitive network loading requests that fail for .EXE files, then for .COM files, before matching the actual .BAT file. Since DOS tries to match (by implicit wild-cards) in that priority, the nonspecific request was repeated across the network until matched. The efficient solution is to invoke executable files specifically with *full* path and complete filename extents.

Second, the Sniffer identified two logical networks within what was actually one Token-Ring. A search through the captured packets resolved the mystery; an access server supporting external dial-in traffic was installed with a network number different from all other network nodes. While this discrepancy actually increased the network traffic load, it more importantly increased the workload on the network server. The network server, already the bottleneck, was performing address translation and routing for the incorrect network address. While most networks might not support mixed addresses, the maxim is to check a network for uniform configuration.

Third, the protocol analyzer indicated that the Token-Ring active monitor was initiating the specified network *ping* every six and a fraction seconds. Since the specifications indicate that this should occur at seven-second intervals, the active monitor was showing that its crystal clock was fast. This caused no profound problems, although network traffic load was increased (marginally). If one inactive station has a bad NIC, perhaps others do as well and with more intrusive flaws than active monitor clock error. Fast clocks cause signal interpretation problems. Likewise, smart tools or well-trained personnel can use an analyzer to resolve other performance flaws. Consider this common example: ARCnet broadcasting 507-byte packets, regardless of contents represents a bug easily fixed with software patches from NIC vendors; many older components incorporate this hidden flaw. Small packets are incorrectly padded to 507 bytes for 12-byte transmission requests, ACK, and NAK. Larger packets, too, would be improperly segmented into multiple broadcasts resulting in less efficiency.

As a final word for this section, configuration parameters can be tuned for significant compatibility and performance improvements. The order in invoking system drivers, settings for those drivers, placement within memory, allocation of memory or buffer space, and activation of supplemental drivers or system-level software can provide wide latitude—good and bad—in workstation and server performance. Specifically, OS/2 provides many types of memory buffers and supports an enhanced file directory structure; DOS can load device drivers and part of the operating system into high memory areas to overcome the inherent 640Kb memory limitation and frequent EMS memory paging, and Unix can run many concurrent operations that are sometimes to the detriment of LAN performance. All of these operating systems benefit from larger disk (fixed and removable) caches, temporary file space on RAM disks, and a judicious installation of utility tools, background tasks, extra device drivers, shorter search paths, and directories with fewer files. Another example of system settings that will affect station performance is disk block size settings, and disk block transfer sizes (256 bits to 16Mb contingent upon the OS and configurations). This issue is discussed again.

Optimize software locally

A useful LAN enhancement is to lower the need to access the server and network channels. Increase read to write ratios. Lower the LAN traffic component. While this might appear to be a contradiction for LAN and client-server applications, increased performance on traffic-bound or server-bound LANs results from localizing some procedures. For example, service for diskless workstations, which normally have no local resources, can be improved with "flash cards" and larger cache buffers. Flash cards provide the operating system and overlays on a ROM card. Larger cache buffers statistically increase the odds that information is already in local memory. This strategy does not defeat the security or financial reasons for installing diskless workstations.

Since network traffic often consists of paging information, graphics display, or mail transmissions throughout a facility, a solution is to install local resources. Network printing can be relegated to local nodes, as can file storage. Determine the composition of the network traffic and rebuild the network to optimize for local solutions. Local disks and segregated backup channels might be an appropriate step to improve the performance of the sample networks, as illustrated in Figures 5-11

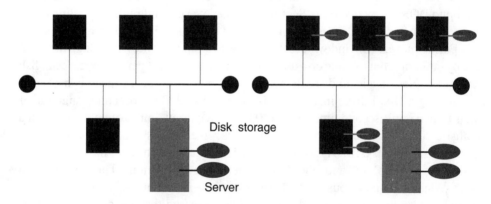

5-11 Improve network performance by installing local disk resources for individual network nodes.

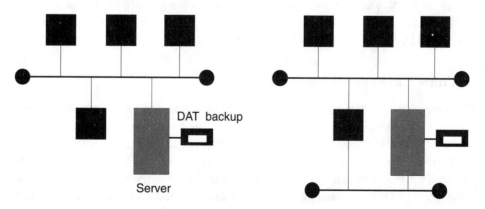

5-12 Provide separate network channels for network backups when backups overload the LAN.

and 5-12. This type of analysis is ideal before embarking on any network reconfiguration. The down side to partitioning a network into clusters of local resources is that the concentration of resources originally available through networking is reversed and shifts financial costs. Management load increases, and costs increase with additional local resources because local units are generally more expensive than the public "bulk" versions. This reverses the economies of scale available through network resources. While this alternative might be more expensive, or take too long a time to install, it is an option.

A similar strategy works for nodes with local disks. Operating systems, application software, and configuration files that are frequently read and/or rewritten are best installed locally. The LAN file server thus serves as a repository of multiuser data, current and globally accessed data, and specialty items. GUIs are network performance hogs because of code and data paging. A typical example is MS Windows, which requires about 2Mb of disk space, plus another 4Mb for utilities; it is about 10Mb for a server installation. Obviously, all of MS Windows does not load into DOS at any one time. Sections of code overlay and replace existing code. These sections of code (.EXEs and .DLLs) and user-specific files can reside locally.

Furthermore, MS Windows creates swap and temporary files. Although the swap file by definition must reside on a local disk partition, for best performance, establish temporary files on a local disk. Better yet, temporary file access speed is increased by creating a RAM disk since access is in the 44 to 200 nanosecond range rather than 16 to 65 millisecond time frame (40,000 percent raw improvement, although a realistic 200 to 300 percent throughput improvement). Diskless workstations can have local RAM disks; this is not a paradox. The same holds true for most significant Unix, OS/2, MicroVAX, and other LAN system user applications. This is also useful for X-Windows, a notorious hog of LAN resources. The technology and demand for more complex and sophisticated software has increased the size of the code. Very few "modern" programs fit into memory in their entirety; pieces are switched in and out of memory. This memory paging (data and code), particularly for diskless workstations, places an inordinate strain upon a LAN, a strain which can be minimized by increasing available RAM disk space.

Optimize CPU-intensive activities

CPU-intensive activities represent disk access, device access, number manipulation, and memory access. These activities can be optimized individually. Specifically, disk operations benefit from hardware device caches built into hard drive controllers; RAM-based memory caches are almost as efficient. Also, bus mastering controllers reduce the CPU overhead by incorporating a sophisticated secondary CPU on the controller card and by channeling data requests to specific parts of workstation memory.

Bus-mastering is essentially a technique used by adapters (primarily disk, network, and video adapters) to gain control of the system I/O bus. Bus-master adapters bypass system CPU to effectively manipulate data, address, and control signals to deliver blocks of data directly between peripheral devices and system memory or other peripheral devices. This mastering technique relieves the system CPU for other tasks. Special bus mastering modes, burst mode and streaming mode, minimize bus signaling but hog the bus and block out other access. Conflicts over the bus in real-time applications require careful analysis. Generally, this does improve workstation performance, and is most beneficial for high-demand servers supporting intensive transaction processing applications.

Similarly, access to the network itself can be improved through bus-mastering technology. Bus-mastering NICs apply the same technology as bus-mastering disk controllers, and yield corresponding benefits. Note that workstations rarely experience bottlenecks at the NIC unless there are configuration problems, hardware problems, or an astounding LAN demand at that machine. This is usually most beneficial for servers. It is likely that any NIC bottlenecks on workstations with a single NIC card and servers with multiple NIC cards will be displaced somewhere else when the original problem is resolved. That is merely logical.

Access to other devices such as printers, graphic screens, and the NIC itself profit from similar hardware. Printing performance and return to the application after a print request can be improved by hardware printer buffers, larger data buffers in printers, and spooling software. Graphics accelerators boost performance dramatically (when the hardware is well matched to the software application and the basic workstation hardware, ROM BIOS included) by offloading video processing. This is pertinent for scientific applications, graphic-intensive software such as CAD, CAP, image preparation, graphic presentation software, and GUIs. X-Windows, OS/2, and MS Windows are graphic-intensive GUI applications that benefit from graphic accelerators and local bus video included on the motherboard.

Servers functioning as routers or gateways might not fully exploit the expected benefit of bus-mastering NICs. Since this technology usurps control of the workstation data bus, multiple cards might clash over access to the data bus. Test the configuration under true workstation load to see if the extra cost and difficulty in configuring the workstation are warranted. The first bus-mastering card, whether a NIC or disk controller, might boost performance about 20 percent. The second and subsequent units might advance station performance 2 percent each. Some requirements might demand that marginal 2 percent.

Minimize accounting overheads

LAN accounting operations include actual Account Billing, time and usage tracking, user login security, file access security, read-after-write verification, file deletion recovery support (UNDELETE), transmission security, data encryption, watchdog features, and any network management activities. The list on the following page shows some nonproductive overhead and LAN accounting activities.

- Account billing
- Time and usage log
- Login security
- File access (ring rights) security
- Read-after-write verification
- Job tracking log
- Files marked for deletion (but still accessible)
- Network management tracking
- Network management alarms
- Network watchdog
- Data encryption
- User help

Such activities are background support activities that apply a load to many LAN components, whether these are LAN channel, server CPU time, server disk space, server memory, remote devices, or individual workstations. Some of these activities yield no work accomplished, just accounting results. Obviously, some of these features are crucial for some LANs. Some are imposed by zealous system administrators. Strike a balance. Evaluate the need for the management overhead.

Network management software frequently creates a worse situation when there is already a bad situation. Typically, a system administrator will set alarms, capture traffic data, and request remote devices to transmit local management data to a key server in order to analyze that self-same bad performance. This results in an even higher load on network resources. Turn them off. Resort to other devices. Passive network-management external devices, such as a stand-alone protocol analyzer, can perform these same functions without degrading performance.

Some "secure" systems incorporate encryption for all packet transmissions. Data encryption exacts a high toll in terms of performance, even when the encryption is accomplished in hardware. The toll is more pronounced when each workstation or server encodes (and decodes) packets with software in memory. Security overhead is mostly CPU processing time; the actual packet traffic volume is not affected. Sometimes traffic can be reduced when encryption also compresses the data payload.

However, when security is so implemented on a LAN, reducing the overhead imposed by the security measures is clearly not an option. Security is the *primary* concern. Performance can be improved by other methods. Since the bottleneck is at the LAN nodes, more horsepower is the most viable option for improving global LAN performance. Adjusting other station configurations as described in this chapter, nonetheless, will improve local performance.

Remove TSRs and background processes

TSRs (terminate and stay resident) are background processes that require system resources. Examples include print spoolers and redirecters, autosaves, applications loaded into MS Windows at the start, or the many quasi-active or idled processes that are iconized in a GUI screen. As such, both TSRs and other background processes are undesirable on overloaded stations.

Patently, all background processes are not useless or a waste of resources. Many TSRs extend vital services, others are labor savers, and some are merely activated as a convenience and might not be used at all. Window processes loaded as icons often fall into that last category. In the final analysis, all these processes encumber memory, interrupt and process keystrokes, require occasional shared time from the CPU, use specialized memory heaps, and slow performance. The CPU has to poll devices and check the status of background operations periodically. The stack space required in memory subtracts from total available memory, and the polling time lowers CPU availability. Reassess which should be memory-resident and active processes—and which are best omitted.

Increase CPU and memory speeds

Station performance increases with faster CPUs and memory matched to that speed. This often involves replacing system motherboards, or effectively replacing an entire station with a more powerful one. Achievable performance improvements are not linear with CPU and memory speed increases. Performance might improve 100 percent for processor-bound tasks, or not at all if the CPU is not the bottleneck.

For example, early PCs (XT) run at 5 Mhz with memory rated at 220 ns. The current generation of PCs (AT based upon 486) run at 50 Mhz with memory speeds at 60 ns. While the processor is now ten times as fast, memory is about three times faster. Some applications run 4000 percent faster. Some perform only 1000 faster. This is not a linear relationship.

Significant performance enhancements can be achieved by substituting a more powerful station. The data bus (typically 8 bits, 16 bits, or 32 bits) is also a factor. The bus is analogous to the transmission channel. Wider data bus paths accommodate a greater transfer bandwidth. When the operating system, device drivers, and bus devices utilize the full bus bandwidth, performance improves dramatically. Major software vendors are redesigning, recoding, and using more powerful programming compilers to take advantage of the 32-bit data buses. IBM OS/2 2.0 and MS Windows NT represent crucial efforts to optimize the software performance of inherently LAN-based and data access-bound applications.

However, direct substitution of a slow CPU with a faster CPU might not always yield such dramatic improvements. The station bottleneck might be caused by slow video speeds, bus data transfer limitations, and slow disk access speeds. This limitation is best assessed on a case by case basis. In general, though, upgrade any station that is a bottleneck for a user, and especially any station that creates a bottleneck for the network as a whole.

Install specialty controllers

There are more sophisticated and expensive methods to resolve LAN bottlenecks. It is possible—but unlikely for most network users—to modify TCP/ IP or build a new operating system to provide for priority transmissions. There are also specialized hardware implementations that can improve Ethernet performance. Controllers with more buffer space increase throughput for slow workstations by caching large transmissions. Specifically, Ethernet controllers are a growing tuning option. As an example, the *interphase controller* provides better node performance at the link level by providing three times the normal Ethernet clock rate, thereby timing transmissions to overlap; it is unlikely to become a commodity item. Other controllers that compress data achieve more efficient network utilization, while some vendors are designing hardware that will provide optimized protocol translations faster than software. Below is a list of some common methods for improving disk access on server-based bottlenecks.

- Faster disks
- 16-bit and 32-bit controller cards
- Caching controller cards
- Bus-mastering controller cards
- Local bus services or integrated controllers
- Fewer disks with larger capacities
- Avoid disk daisy chains
- Install a CPU with a wider and faster data bus

Increase local disk speeds

Hard disks storage devices represent a major network bottleneck. Hard drive performance becomes crucial for file-intensive applications and for any LANs that support transmission speeds exceeding disk data transfer speeds (Ethernet, 16-Mbits/s Token-Ring, TCNS, 100-Mbits/s Token-Ring, and FDDI). Note that all LAN protocols are faster than 8-bit and 16-bit disk controllers such as RLL, MFM, and the persistent AT ST-506 standards. Since MFM disk controllers support sustained disk transfer speeds of 512 Kbits/s, SCSI supports about 4 Mbits/s, and ESDI controllers about 6 Mbits/s, local disk speeds are very relevant bottlenecks. These transfer speeds are all slower than the network channel. For example, consider the transfer of a 10Mb graphic image or GIS vector data file.

Systems bootstrap from disks, applications are loaded from disks, overlays page to disk, temporary files are created on disks, databases are stored on disks and views are built there, and queued network print jobs are temporarily stored in disk files. Typically, poor file and disk performance results from many factors, as explained in Chapter 2. Disk access speed is measured in milliseconds and is a composite of disk rotational speed, head access speed, sector interleave, alignment error rates, and data bus widths. Faster disks improve server performance dramatically. If at all in doubt, substitute a network disk with a faster model and test the new configuration.

A second factor in physical disk performance is the disk controller. Wider data buses increase data transfer speeds by increasing the number of bits that can be transferred in parallel. Controllers (with suitable software drivers) supporting a wider data bus might enhance performance. Alternatively, wider buses provide data transfer in parallel with simultaneous disk control commands; this yields a two-way conversation between CPU and disk instead of slower sequential control. Note that all software and hardware timing parameters must support the wider bus in order to achieve performance boosts. Bus-mastering controllers offload the CPU and move files through memory without CPU resources. Caching disk controllers increase performance for read-intensive operations (database and transaction processing applications) by buffering most frequently read data or most recently read data in fast RAM. Furthermore, daisy-chained disk drives as found on VMEbus, multibus, CMD, and SCSI encourage adding hard drives up to the actual capacity for connecting these components to the controller card. Figure 5-13 lists the number of disks (and other I/O devices in the specific case of SCSI) commonly supported on various controllers.

Interface	Number of devices	Supplemental devices
ST-506	2	2 removable diskette drives
MFM	2	2 removable diskette drives
RLL	2	2 removable diskette drives
ESDI	4	2 removable diskette drives
SCSI	7 I/O devices	
SCSI-II	7 I/O devices	
CMD	2 to 4	
Multibus	Controller specific	
VMEbus	Controller specific	

5-13 Disk controller attachment limitations for commonly-available bus controllers.

Optimize disk device support

Although it is economically sound to "chain" drives up to the controller's capacity, this typifies a common performance mistake. For example, while a SCSI interface physically can support seven devices, including disks, tape units, CD-ROMs, printers, and other global network devices, the management overhead is tremendous. Furthermore, it is difficult to correctly configure the interrupt and priorities switches even for matched devices, let alone a hodge-podge of devices. Enhance high-performance stations by providing one controller card per storage device, or reduce the total number of hard drives by installing the largest drive(s) available to meet the required storage capacity. It is also possible to replace slow storage units with those that have more platters; this often provides data transfer speed enhancements through the parallel efforts of the extra heads.

Establish optimal sector interleave

Hard disk read/write movements often default to factory settings, or controller preferences, or are established by operating system parameters. These settings are called the disk *interleave factor* and establish the order in which the pie-shaped sectors and concentric tracks are accessed. Random interleave values can short-change a good controller and fast disk. Various utilities measure disk rotation speeds, head access times, disk controller capabilities, and file sizes to calculate an optimal interleave factor. Examples include Norton Utilities, Optune, and MACE; such utilities are available for MS-DOS, OS/2, Unix, and specific NOSes. Some tools even repartition, low-level reformat, and move data on the fly. Performance is rarely degraded and disk access can be improved up to 15 percent. Similarly, disk block size—the smallest unit stored on a hard disk—influences disk performance. While smaller blocks are more efficient in terms of disk space utilization efficiency, larger blocks tend to be more efficient from a disk access speed viewpoint. File blocksize, read-ahead record buffering, and disk-to-memory transfer blocksize are usually operating system parameters. Adjust them to match applications, NIC buffer sizes, cache space, and available system memory.

Reformat at a low level

Over time, the strength of the magnetic fields on a hard drive decay. The physical recording substrata expands and contracts with temperature variances, and it also stretches, sags, and warps under its own weight. The same physical changes affect the drive motor and its rotation speed as well as the disk controller motor and disk heads. The read/write head might no longer align precisely with the format tracks on the disk. Dead spots creep into the media from head strikes, dust, and normal wear. As a result, media errors creep into the drive. These might not cause overt system-level disk errors, but might initiate frequent data transfer errors and requests by the disk controller to reread the data again. Repeated reads clearly degrade disk performance and ensuing system performance. Tools such as SpinRite locates and mark bad spots while moving or recovering data on the fly.

A low-level media format reinitializes and realigns the tracks to the head and motor parameters. Furthermore, a low-level format locates and marks defects as areas best not used. It is important to recognize that a low-level format might differ from a system-level format. A system format might partition the disk into usable structures for that operating system. A low-level format is controller-specific and is often initiated from BIOS calls or special diagnostic routines. The Unix DIAG is one such program, as is the MS-DOS DEBUG call to C800:G5 where many disk controller cards and their diagnostic and initialization routines reside in encoded PROM firmware.

Defragment disks

Most operating systems chain files and recycle space from deleted files on an ad hoc basic for disk space efficiency and performance. As files expand in size, grow smaller through deletions, are marked as erased on a disk (files are rarely actually erased from the disk, and marked as free space only for recycling), they fragment into chains of small blocks. As an example, it is easier to link newly added individual records within a database than to rewrite the entire database to account for the new, revised, or deleted records. It is not practical to rewrite a 10Mb database to account for a single new 20-byte record; instead, records are added to chained disk file blocks. Figure 5-14 depicts the inefficiency of chained files.

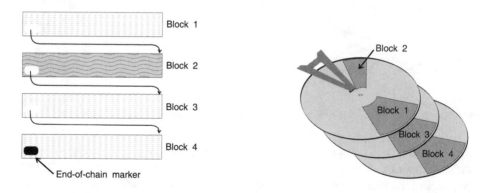

5-14 Chained disk files are inefficient to read, write, and access.

Unchain files

Utilities exist for most operating systems to defragment chained files and create continuous, contiguous disk blocks. This improves disk access performance anywhere from 5 to 20 percent. It is very relevant for files that are read more often than written, such as executable files, configurations, operating system or network software, and databases. It is particularly relevant for file and database servers.

Some operating systems do not provide this defragmenting facility. Unix is an example. Nonetheless, disk performance degrades over time as files fragment into chained minimum-sized blocks. The same defragmentation effect can be achieved by backing up the system to a tape (or other media), reformatting the disk, and restoring the tape to the disk. Unix system administrators avoid this because of the labor.

Contiguous free space speeds the disk writing time. Defragmenting disk space improves not only write times but also read times. Contiguous block reads (and read-ahead disk buffers) improve the access times to files that are read and reread, as are records in a database. When blocks are contiguous, the read heads do not have to seek and reseek for widely scattered blocks or translate the continuation pointers, as Fig. 5-15 illustrates. Contiguous blocks do not have continuation pointers. The next block to read in this case is the next most accessible block.

Maintain free disk space

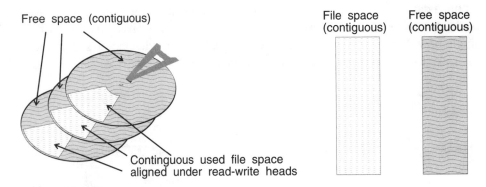

5-15 Contiguous files and free disk space improve server and workstation disk performance.

Disks that approach capacity by definition lack contiguous blocks of free space. Block writes, temporary data swapping, and paging to disk create a situation called "thrashing," where the heads continuously look for enough space to write the data blocks to the disk. This is time-intensive. Disks with less than 10 percent free space impose a significant overhead on the station. Servers with little free space create a bottleneck that can only be solved by adding disk space or by purging files and records.

It is interesting to note that Unix systems measure disk space with an extra margin. A Unix volume is not actually full until file space in use reaches 110 percent of capacity. Because Unix systems recycle free space on the fly, free space tends to fragment into "clusters" of the minimum-sized block (usually 4Kb). Unix systems without that 10 percent margin thrash while establishing the long connected chains required for most significant files. The search is slow. In any event, the largest available contiguous disk space should be sufficient to contain the largest single file on the system with room to spare. Free up disk space, increase disk size, install a disk compression driver (SuperStor or Stacker, for example), and defragment files.

Reorganize file placement

Physical file placement on disks also affects disk transfer rate performance. The read/write heads normally return to a rest position. Additionally, certain sequences of tracks are faster to access than others—usually the inner tracks. Placing key files there will improve system operation about 2-3%. The best files to place in this area are files that are frequently read and never written. The files most frequently read are operating system overlays, network software overlays, and application overlays. The operating system itself is read and loaded into memory only once; in some cases, the operating system is loaded into memory only once a month or so when the system crashes. Unix and OS/2 operating systems and network file servers are rarely rebooted; the general consensus is that this leads to the least file system damage and wear and tear on station components. The operating system kernel is low priority; the overlays and linkage files are high priority.

However, extended support files are loaded or called frequently. Examples include dynamic link libraries (.DLLs), code overlays, and subroutines for large applications. This is true for .DLL files (MS Windows and OS/2), .OVR files (Unix and DOS), and the nonresident portion of DOS TSRs and Netware NLM routines. Even simple MS-DOS benefits from positioning MSDOS.SYS and IO.SYS as the first entries on hard drive. Position data reference files, databases, and other files that are more frequently read than written in outer tracks. Dead files and infrequently invoked executable code should be placed to the edges of the drive. Although any performance gain is slight, this technique is a one time event with no cost but some maintenance time. Utilities, such as Norton SPEEDISK, help optimize such file and directory access.

Use caches, buffers, and RAM disks

Memory buffers and caches improve performance by providing a temporary place to keep data that is fast to access and process. Buffers and caches are much alike in that they are RAM memory spaces; they vary in usage. Buffers are memory areas with fixed structures. They usually contain file pointers, path names, memory addresses, memory pointers, and space for blocks of data. Typical applications for buffers are assembling a packet for transmission, storing a sequence of packets for translation or disassembly, or placing a block of data just read from the disk. Caches contain transient memory blocks, a holding area if you will. A physical analogy of the computer cache is a water tower. The usual application for caches is to store the most recently read or most frequently read blocks of data in case they are requested again. Disk cache contents that are frequently read contain directory structures and addresses for the actual files; stations running database applications might retain keys or records in the cache.

Larger buffer and caches improve station performance since memory access requires from 2 to 40 machine cycles versus several thousand for disk access. It is generally a thousand times faster. A large buffer space minimizes the need for temporary file space or disk swapping. A good cache program can improve performance 300 percent.

For these same reasons, a RAM disk performs better than a mechanical disk, as previously stated. A RAM disk mirrors the structures of a physical disk but stores and retrieves data (until the station is powered off or a catastrophe happens) at memory access speeds. RAM disks are ideal for swap files, temporary files space, key database files, overlays, and frequently accessed .DLLs. MS Windows performance improves remarkably even for diskless stations when some local memory is set aside for RAM disks. This configuration reduces the thrashing typical with multiprocessing and user windowing while lowering network traffic and improving local performance.

Software optimization

Programmers optimize software to various constraints. Code is optimized so as to minimize the application code size, distribution media size, memory requirements, types of memory required (cache, file buffers, buffers, RAM, high memory, or extended and expanded memory), disk space, loading time, processing time, or perceptual performance (as the user sees it). Network software is optimized to redistribute the client-server load, server overheads, network channel utilization, and perceptual performance. Often, these optimization objectives are mutually exclusive; in order words, an application can be designed and coded to run faster, use less disk space, use less memory, or require less of the user's time—but not all of them. Optimization represents a compromise. The following page has a list of typical application optimization objectives.

Typical application optimization objectives

Older applications revised for new platforms usually represent performance problems. They might have been recoded in a newer language, partially rewritten, optimized with assembly code, and updated with new features that increase overhead, disk space requirements, memory needs, and processing time. Often, mainframe applications are converted with an intact structure, or run within a pseudo-code or interpreted runtime language. The basic tradeoffs made to optimize the application for the initial platform have not been reassessed or revised for the newer one.

For instance, DOS applications written for early-model PCs and Unix applications were created to function within the strictures imposed by expensive memory

- Code size distribution
- RAM requirements
- Platform environment overhead
- Distribution media size
- Disk space
- Disk data file space
- Data file access times
- Application loading time
- User perceptual performance
- Interoperation, cooperation, multitasking, multiprocessing
- Server overhead
- Server cache performance
- Network traffic utilization
- Server disk utilization

and disk space; the user's time was cheaper. Now the cost of memory and disk space is factored less; accelerated processor speeds, expanded memory ranges available now under DOS, MS Windows, OS/2, and greater bus widths and memory ranges under Unix hardware are cheaper than time to most organizations. As these early applications have been upgraded every eighteen months for the last ten years, some of the original optimization compromises remain intact.

While vendors and programmers tend to upgrade software and optimize it within the new environment, the original decisions and program structures will adversely affect station and network performance. More recent applications—designed specifically for the target platform perform—perform faster. However, evaluate whether they perform *better* and warrant the difficult transition and retraining.

Software optimization techniques

Optimize software applications by installing them per instructions, configuring per vendor instructions, and providing them with at least the minimal resources they require. This often translates in terms of providing sufficient disk space, setting buffer and file spaces (for example in DOS, BUFFERS = 99, FILES = 99, MAX-PAGINGFILESIZE = 512 in the MS Windows SYSTEM.INI file, or MAXFILE-SOPEN = 99 in OS/2), file path statements, library assignments, and directory paths or file associations to temporary variable names. GUI interfaces have an enormous range of configurable values. MS Windows, for instance, can exchange or exclude memory ranges, perform direct disk block reads, activate IRQs, establish the frequency of paging, and even remap the keyboard. Some applications require supporting tools, such as disk managers or device drivers. Review application documentation and reconfigure the workstation as instructed. This tends to optimize application performance.

The solution is either ad hoc, or through the efforts of software technical support from a vendor of an affected software. Minor conflicts can prevent multiprotocol stacks (NDIS, and ODI), network operating systems, and device drivers from functioning correctly on the LAN. Such bottlenecks adversely affect LAN performance. Documentation for tuning these complex interactions is usually nonexistent.

Software optimization tends to fail when multiple applications work at cross purposes. In order to assure proper installation of their applications, vendors create complex and "foolproof" scripts to load *their* software and optimally configure the workstation for reliability and optimal performance for that software. These scripts modify system configuration files that include AUTOEXEC.BAT and CONFIG.SYS in DOS, COMMAND.CMD and various .INI files in OS/2, WIN.INI, and SYSTEM.INI for MS Windows, as well as the Unix system bootstrap file. Frequently, many different software applications share executable and initialization filenames or support facilities. Identical or similar environmental variables can disrupt optimum system and network performance. Recall that EXE and COM executable files assert priority before BAT in DOS and OS/2, but that executable files may have almost any name in Unix. There are some general naming conventions but no rules for guaranteeing uniqueness of filenames or environment variables. It is best to install applications with virgin system configuration files and then copy these key files (modified or not) for safekeeping. Note changes and apply sequentially to optimize configuration files. This information is sometimes important merely to get new software to load, let alone function with the complex environment of the station.

In-house software

Software built in-house provides more degrees of freedom than commercial software. Code developed in-house can be tailored and optimized; the source code exists as does the knowledge of how the application works. Typical performance improvements include establishing better memory management (RAM, paging, buffers, and disk), *force reduction* in the code, and shifting interactive processing to batch modes.

Other ideas include utilizing existing (already loaded into memory) .DLL code rather than creating new MS Windows code or using kernel functions where applicable. Similarly, common functions can be modularized to not only reduce the code and disk space, but also run faster. Some programming environments and operating systems provide a tool called *profiler* which will track, report, and perhaps even chart where most of the time is spent in an application. The primary benefit in improving performance is to optimize these code obstructions.

Database applications sink under poor record and file structures and overfilled disks. Purge dead files. Purge old, dead, marked (as deleted) records from the indexed data files. Also, consider better indexes, faster lookup or search methods, and fewer active indexes. Sorts require less committed overhead although compensate by requiring more CPU time; however, frequent sorts might be best replaced by permanent indexing.

Similarly, purge historical records from databases. Sort, search, lookup, and index routines run faster without the chaff. The disk access will improve as well. Graphic applications are notorious resource hogs. Like databases, graphic manipulation represents massive amounts of data. When images can be represented by vector notation, object embedding, and primitives rather than by bit-mapped data streams, station, disk, and network performance will improve. Catalogs of graphic images and the overhead required to select a specific item are often improved by creating thumbnail views of complex graphics. Note that this is a tradeoff in terms of improved speed provided by increases in disk storage. Optimization often is a compromise.

Data entry and retrieval operations

Data entry operations impose relatively light loads on the network. Terminals attached to a host (multiplexers and serial ports) are the most cost-effective solution, and terminal servers provide a convenient means to connect them. Terminal servers are adaptable since they provide the physical freedom to place the terminals anywhere. Terminal servers are not like file servers; they are router-like devices attached to file servers that encapsulate keyboard characters into network packets and parse them for the attached terminals.

Local echo is a host implementation. However, the duplex (two-way echo) method is inefficient. An individual keystroke is captured across a network and then each keystroke is transmitted back across the network. The packets, even if minimum-sized, are padded for that single character. NETBIOS or TCP/IP overhead is enormous, and the packet load for a moderate data entry operation can quickly overwhelm the transmission channel. Segregate—build a unique subnet—for terminal services to improve performance.

Database data entry and retrieval operations stress file server disks. Poor performance most likely results from server overloads, fragmented files, and slow disk transfer speeds rather than for any other reasons. Some databases (the actual software) are, however, notoriously inefficient. Careful tuning of system parameters, buffer spaces, and caches can yield better LAN database throughput. In some rarer cases, the gain achieved by replacing a poor database with better software surpasses the cost, time, training, and difficulty in making that transition.

Another effective LAN database tuning procedure is to purge excess records from the databases, pack and recover deleted although still-available records, and archive noncurrent but historical data offline. Duplicate files with backup data, test data, and historical data slow database record access. Slimmer data files, fewer column or tabular search keys, and indexed file structures improve seek operations. It is important to realize that record read operations outnumber write operations from 1000 to 10,000 percent. Optimize for that by trimming bloated databases. The database server will run faster and provide better throughput for more requests, and the disk will be less likely to thrash when new records must be written to disk.

Graphic-oriented databases do challenge the limits of the transmission channel. GIS, satellite and weather data, CAD graphics, and image data storage and retrieval (that is, microfiche on a network) create bursty traffic. This technology is increasingly cost-effective for the organization although a serious challenge for network administrators. Relevant performance solutions include installing crosspoint matrix switches, TCNS, FDDI, or other high-speed transmission backbones. Moreover, subnet isolation is pragmatic.

Tuning recommendations

The last section in this chapter includes a table of tuning recommendations for the four protocols presented in this book. While many suggestions are presented as specific to a protocol, consider also that a suggestion might be pertinent to other protocols as well.

Ethernet

- Check that the binary backoff algorithm for collision resolution is implemented rather than a straight binomial backoff algorithm. The linear backoff drives a highly loaded network into instability. Ensure proper collision detection and binary backoff implementation (and not fixed 96 µs backoffs).
- Configure deferral timout settings and collision failures, if possible. Higher settings should be proportional to priority. Sun Microsystems provides configurable settings for their Unix. Set higher values or longer intervals for servers and priority stations before they are disconnected from the network. Set lower values for clients and nonpriority stations. Reset timeouts and collision-retry counters to lower values for nonpriority stations, increase the number for key stations such as servers.
- Check for transient site failures.
- Use bridges and routers which filter errors, collisions, and packets by source and destination.
- Use crosspoint matrix switches as concentrating hubs.
- Minimize broadcast packets (they tend to be captured and rebroadcast back onto the network by routers)... these packets multiply until the channel bandwidth is saturated.
- Provide wide channel interconnects (switches, FDDI, busses, TCNS).
- Do not double-load servers; establish secondary slave servers for printing, user security, modem sharing, external access, and gateway support services.
- Minimize the number of multiple protocols and protocol translation or encapsulation on a single LAN or network site. Stick to one protocol (either, LAT, NFS, XNS, TCP, DECNET, or IPX).
- Establish separate subnets for terminal services or rewire for serial terminals. Although it is convenient to create one master network for a unified wiring scheme, it represents a potential performance disaster.
- Realize that there is a position-dependent unfairness (particularly for real-time applications) on Ethernet. Hosts in large clusters get better service because collisions are resolved more quickly within subnets than between

subnets. The LAN is not fair, since collisions resolve faster in the middle of a bus than toward the ends of coaxial cable. The same holds true for the star structure of 10BASE-T, which is nonetheless a logical bus configuration.
- Do not install long cables. This increases the collision slot and resolution time. Keep the network, bus or star, as short as possible.

ARCnet

- Upgrade to 20 Mbits *plus* or install TCNS.
- Do not mix speeds on the same LAN.
- Shift to a double-byte addressing scheme and large-packet format for file-intensive operations.
- Shift to one byte addressing scheme and use short packet format for terminal servers and IPX protocols.
- Do not install long cables to mimize the latency and token rotational time. Keep the network, bus or star, as short as possible.
- Replace the 8-bit with 16-bit controller cards in those systems that can benefit. Ensure that software drivers for those devices profit from the wider communication channel; some operating systems, stations, and NOSes are oblivious to ARCnet controller performance enhancements.
- Replace standard controller cards in those systems that can benefit from bus-mastering technology. Systems that are bus-bound or CPU-bound are likely candidates. However, some operating systems, stations, and NOSes are too slow to benefit because of the bus architecture.
- Install faster server disks.
- Add server memory.
- Increase either the number of packet buffers or the packet buffer sizes.
- Break large networks into smaller subnets that are carefully focused to represent workgroups and workloads. Configure to minimize internetwork traffic.
- Install no repeaters and first generation bridges.

Token-Ring

- Move active monitor to the least-used node rather than a random node. The active monitor is typically a domain or primary server, the station that has the highest load on the network.
- Install NIC controllers with the newest TI chipset with the ringing tank technology. It lowers the jitter budget, increases signal strength and reception, and increases station throughout.
- Upgrade from a 4-Mbits/s operation to 16 Mbits/s.
- Verify that the overhead of secondary domain servers does not generate excessive backup and redundancy traffic.
- Minimize current overlap of token traffic oblivious to each other.
- Replace the 8-bit and 16-bit with 32-bit controller cards in those systems that can benefit. Ensure that software drivers for those devices profit from the wider communication channel; some operating systems, stations, and NOSes are oblivious to 32-bit computing. Pertinent controller cards include disk controllers and NICs, or video for graphic-bound applications.

- Replace standard controller cards in those systems that can benefit from bus-mastering technology. Systems that are bus-bound or CPU-bound are likely candidates. However, Some operating systems, stations, and NOSes are too slow to benefit because of the bus architecture.
- Install faster server disks.
- Install more server memory.
- Increase either the number of packet buffers or the packet buffer sizes.
- Break large networks into smaller subnets that are carefully focused to represent workgroups and workloads.
- Install no repeaters and first generation bridges.

16 Mbits/s Token-Ring

- Move active monitor to the least used node rather than a random node.
- Check wiring conformity to STP standards (not UTP).
- Activate ETR. This is effective for TCP and IPX with nak, ack, and LLC small-packet requests, although irrelevant for networks transmitting packets with average sizes over 2000 bytes.
- Install a burst mode protocol, large packet protocol, or spanning-tree bridges (specification IEEE 802.1d) when routing to multiple interconnected subnets.
- Qualify NIC device drivers for 16-Mbits/s operation.
- Link servers and key stations with Ethernet, FDDI, or a crosspoint matrix hub.

FDDI

- Do not encapsulate or translate other protocols; maintain the native protocol.
- Test the clarity of optical cable.
- Check reception sensitivity and transmitter strengths, as well as timing.
- Minimize DAS ring length.
- Minimize SAS connection length.
- Establish priority support.
- Test FDDI NICs and drivers for efficiency.

Optimization Target	Result
Optimize server	Greater LAN throughout
	Faster LAN response time
Optimize workstation (node)	Faster application processing
	Greater work throughput
Optimize transmission channel	No LAN improvements
	Greater server and node CPU overhead
	Greater protocol overhead
	Unstable environment
	Routing bottlenecks

5-16 LAN bottlenecks tend to migrate as component bottlenecks are optimized.

6
Chapter

LAN performance reference tables

This chapter presents four individual sections that cross-reference practical diagnostic information. They are useful both to provide diagnostic clues and to confirm that a hypothetical diagnosis does explain the observed performance bottlenecks on a LAN.

The first section lists typical network bottlenecks. The first column is a common name to describe the bottleneck. The second column shows just how common these network flaws are, while column three details the frequency that these bottlenecks become serious performance problems. It is very common for a network to have many of these flaws. But performance bottlenecks might represent an accumulation of multiple flaws, although none is, in itself, serious enough to cause the observed problems.

The second section lists common failures with each failure's characteristic symptoms. This table provides feedback as to whether a performance optimization process has correctly addressed the situation. Use it to confirm a diagnosis.

The third section matches characteristic symptoms with the possible causes, therefore providing valuable ideas when a bottleneck defies solution and has stumped the administration team. This section is a reorganization of the second section. If the causes or symptoms that your network is exhibiting are not listed, look at related items. These lists are not exhaustive, but rather sufficiently comprehensive to provide insight into most network trouble.

The fourth section offers possible solutions for the typical performance bottlenecks listed in the prior sections.

Typical network bottlenecks	Incidence	Serious
Software application is slow	92.00	55.00
Installation errors	60.00	47.00
Specification violation(s)	80.00	36.00
Wrong connectors	80.00	36.00
Server (or workstation) overloaded	57.00	36.00
Network misspecified	75.00	24.00
Network too long	35.00	23.00
Suboptimal hardware configuration	78.00	23.00
Resource-bound server	76.00	22.00
Insufficient memory	65.00	21.00
Resource-bound application	92.00	20.00
Misallocated memory space	40.00	18.00
Lobe/node cable too long	25.00	15.00
Suboptimal logical configuration	95.00	9.00
Slow disk access time	95.00	9.00
Slow workstations	29.00	9.00
Overloaded with requests	45.00	9.00
Transmission errors	14.00	7.00
Overloaded internetwork linkage	41.00	7.00
Network devices overloaded	25.00	6.00
Resource-bound NOS	53.00	6.00
Suboptimal physical configuration	85.00	6.00
Wrong medium	25.00	5.00
Slow protocol	36.00	4.00
Suboptimal memory configuration	25.00	4.00
Significant burst transmissions	7.00	3.00
Slow internet protocol translation	33.00	3.00
Slow bus	22.00	3.00
Disk fragmented	28.00	3.00
Overloaded channel capacity	8.00	3.00
Incompatible software	39.00	3.00
Heterogeneous protocols	37.00	3.00
Too many nodes	15.00	2.00
Sporadic peak loads	5.00	2.00
Too many disks	43.00	2.00
Software configuration error	45.00	2.00
Network device incompatibilities	11.00	2.00
Not enough packet buffers	25.00	2.00
Heterogeneous environment	24.00	2.00
Software installation error	100.0	2.00
Bridge inconsistent with design	32.00	2.00
Gateway bottleneck	34.00	2.00

Typical network bottlenecks	Incidence	Serious
Protocol interpretation discrepancy	2.00	2.00
Signal speed jitter	15.00	1.75
Modem bottleneck	18.00	1.00
Slow internetwork encapsulation	21.00	1.00
Radio-frequency interference (RFI)	26.00	1.00
Repeater errors	17.00	1.00
Transmission timing errors	4.00	1.00
Electro-magnetic interference (EMI)	17.00	1.00
Router errors	7.00	1.00
Undesired processes	15.00	1.00
Slow memory paging/swapping	38.00	1.00
Disk full (or too full)	15.00	1.00
Excessive LAN management overhead	10.00	1.00
Protocol errors	8.00	1.00
Slow memory	38.00	1.00
Runaway processes	10.00	1.00
Improper interrupt settings	9.00	1.00
Packet address errors	0.50	0.50
Memory parity errors	0.50	0.50
RAM/CPU refresh time discrepancy	0.25	0.25
IEEE 802.3 heartbeat (SQE) error	2.00	0.25
Other channel bandwidth uses	10.00	0.00
Discrepancies	14.00	0.00
Low cache hit rate	32.00	0.00
Bus master incompatibilities	2.00	0.00
Corrupted files	16.00	0.00
Frame relay bottleneck	1.00	0.00
Signal propagation speed error	3.50	0.00
ETR interoperability	0.00	0.00
Incorrect network subaddresses	4.00	0.00

Common performance failures (causes)
characteristic symptoms

Application running across bridge
Bridge overloaded
Excessive collisions
File server jammed
Network jammed

Overloaded network
Poor performance
Slow file service
Slow response
Software problems

Application running across gateway
Excessive collisions
File server jammed
Gateway overloaded
Network jammed

Overloaded network
Poor performance
Slow file service
Slow response
Software problems

Application running across router
Excessive collisions
File server jammed
Overloaded network
Poor performance

Router overloaded
Slow file service
Slow response
Software problems

Application running on server
Excessive collisions
File server jammed
Network jammed
Overloaded network

Poor performance
Slow file service
Slow response
Software problems

ARCnet hub in overloaded PC
Bad packets
Intermittent slowdowns
Network jammed
No file space

No free disk space
Overloaded network
Poor performance
Slow file service
Slow response

ARL too long
Bad packets
Excessive collisions
High error rate
Intermittent slowdowns
Network jammed

No file space
No free disk space
Overloaded network
Poor performance
Slow file service
Slow response

Bad address
Bridge overloaded
Node dead

Protocol error
Router overloaded

Bad interrupt request (DOS IRQ)
Bad packets
Bridge overloaded
Disk space fragmented
Encapsulation error
Excessive collisions
File server jammed
Gateway overloaded
High error rate

Network jammed
No disk space
Poor performance
Repeater overloaded
Retransmissions
Slow file service
Slow response
Software problems
Workstation jammed

Common performance failures (causes)
characteristic symptoms

Bad tap
Bad packets
Excessive collisions

Files corrupted
High error rate
Poor performance

Bridge overloaded
Bad packets
Bridge overloaded
Encapsulation routing overloaded
Excessive collisions
File server jammed
Network jammed

Poor performance
Retransmissions
Slow file service
Slow response
Software problems
Workstation jammed

Broadcast storm
Bridge overloaded

Excessive network management alarms
Intermittent slowdowns

Broadcast storm
Management software overload

Router overloaded

Brouter overloaded
Node dead
Nodes missing

Poor performance
Retransmissions

Brouter routing error
Excessive collisions
Network jammed
Node dead
Nodes missing

Poor performance
Retransmissions
Slow file service
Slow response
Workstation jammed

CMIP messages saturating network
Bad packets
Excessive collisions
File server jammed
Network jammed
Poor performance

Retransmissions
Slow file service
Slow response
Software problems
Workstation jammed

Coaxial cable metal fatigue
Bad packets
Excessive collisions
Network jammed

No file service
Slow response
Workstation jammed

Corrupted database
Bad packets
Encapsulation error
Excessive collisions
File server jammed
Files corrupted
Network jammed
No file space
No free disk space

Nodes missing
Overloaded network
Poor performance
Protocol error
Retransmissions
Slow file service
Slow response
Workstation jammed

Common performance failures (causes)
characteristic symptoms

Corrupted distributed database
Bad packets	Nodes missing
Encapsulation error	Overloaded network
Excessive collisions	Poor performance
File server jammed	Protocol error
Files corrupted	Retransmissions
Network jammed	Slow file service
No file space	Slow response
No free disk space	Workstation jammed

CPU too slow
File server jammed	No free disk space
Intermittent slowdowns	Overloaded network
Network jammed	Poor performance
No file space	Slow file service
	Slow response

Defective lobe/drop cable
Bad packets	No free disk space
Excessive collisions	Overloaded network
Files corrupted	Poor performance
High error rate	Retransmissions
Network jammed	Slow file service
Network jammed	Slow response
No file space	Workstation jammed

Defective system software
High error rate	Slow file service
No file service	Slow response
	Workstation jammed

Device creating broadcast storm
Excessive collisions	Retransmissions
File server jammed	Slow file service
Network jammed	Slow response
Poor performance	Software problems
	Workstation jammed

Disk space fragmented
Bridge overloaded	No free disk space
File server jammed	Poor performance
Gateway overloaded	Retransmissions
High error rate	Slow file service
Network jammed	Slow response
No disk space	Software problems
	Workstation jammed

Disk too slow
Slow file service	Slow response

Disk too small
No disk space

Common performance failures (causes)
characteristic symptoms

Driver configuration error
Bad packets
Bridge overloaded
Disk space fragmented
Encapsulation error
Excessive collisions
File server jammed
Gateway overloaded
High error rate

Network jammed
No disk space
Poor performance
Repeater overloaded
Retransmissions
Slow file service
Slow response
Software problems
Workstation jammed

Drop cable not properly connected
Bad packets
Excessive collisions
Files corrupted

High error rate
Network jammed
Retransmissions
Workstation jammed

Drop cable polarity error
Network jammed

Workstation jammed

Encapsulation error
Protocol error

Encapsulation protocol error
Bad packets
Bridge overloaded
Encapsulation routing overloaded
Excessive collisions
File server jammed
Gateway overloaded
Network jammed

No disk space
Poor performance
Repeater overloaded
Retransmissions
Slow file service
Slow response
Software problems
Workstation jammed

Excessive collisions
Poor performance

Repeater overloaded
Retransmissions

Fan-out jammed
High error rate

Network jammed

Fan-out jammed
Server jammed

Workstation jammed

Faulty transceiver
Bad packets
Excessive collisions

Files corrupted
High error rate
Workstation jammed

File server disk too slow
Bad packets
Excessive collisions
File server jammed
Network jammed
Poor performance

Retransmissions
Slow file service
Slow response
Software problems
Workstation jammed

File server down
File server jammed
High error rate

No file service
Slow file service
Slow response

Common performance failures (causes)
characteristic symptoms

File server jammed
Bad packets
Bridge overloaded
Disk space fragmented
Encapsulation routing overloaded
Excessive collisions
File server jammed
Gateway overloaded
Network jammed

No disk space
Poor performance
Repeater overloaded
Retransmissions
Slow file service
Slow response
Software problems
Workstation jammed

File server memory error
Bad packets
Bridge overloaded
Disk space fragmented
Encapsulation routing overloaded
Excessive collisions
File server jammed
Gateway overloaded
High error rate

Network jammed
No disk space
Poor performance
Repeater overloaded
Retransmissions
Slow file service
Slow response
Software problems
Workstation jammed

File server overloaded
High error rate
No file service

Slow file service
Slow response

Files marked deleted not purged
No disk space

Gateway overloaded
Bad packets
Bridge overloaded
Encapsulation routing overloaded
Excessive collisions
File server jammed
Gateway overloaded
Network jammed

No disk space
Poor performance
Retransmissions
Slow file service
Slow response
Software problems
Workstation jammed

Improper coaxial grounding
Excessive collisions
High error rate

Network jammed
Slow response

Improper shielding from noise
Bad packets
Excessive collisions
Files corrupted
High error rate

Network jammed
Nodes missing
Poor performance
Software problems

In excess of 100 taps on a coax
Excessive collisions

Network jammed
Slow response

In excess of 100 taps on network
High error rate

Common performance failures (causes)
characteristic symptoms

Inconsistent network software
Bad packets
Bridge overloaded
Disk space fragmented
Encapsulation error
Excessive collisions
File server jammed
Gateway overloaded
High error rate

Network jammed
No disk space
Poor performance
Repeater overloaded
Retransmissions
Slow file service
Slow response
Software problems
Workstation jammed

Insufficient buffer size
Protocol error

Insufficient buffer space
Intermittent slowdowns
Network jammed
No file space
No free disk space

Overloaded network
Poor performance
Slow file service
Slow response

Insufficient cache space
Network jammed
No file space
No free disk space

Overloaded network
Poor performance
Slow file service
Slow response

Insufficient free disk space
Network jammed
No file space
No free disk space

Overloaded network
Poor performance
Slow file service
Slow response

Lack of SNMP agent
Incorrect collisions statistics

Incorrect network statistics

Lobe cable too long
Bad packets
Excessive collisions
High error rate
Intermittent slowdowns
Network jammed

No file space
No free disk space
Overloaded network
Poor performance
Slow file service
Slow response

Malfunctioning bridge
High error rate

Malfunctioning gateway
Bad packets
File server jammed

High error rate
Network jammed
Nodes missing

Malfunctioning repeater
Bad packets
File server jammed

High error rate
Network jammed
Nodes missing

Mismatched device drivers
Protocol error

Common performance failures (causes)
characteristic symptoms

Mismatched hardware
Bad packets
Excessive collisions
Files corrupted
High error rate
Network jammed

No file service
Node dead
Slow file service
Slow response
Software problems
Workstation jammed

Multicast storm
Bridge overloaded

Intermittent slowdowns
Router overloaded

Network audit functions enabled
Excessive collisions
File server jammed
Network jammed

Poor performance
Slow file service
Slow response
Software problems

Network configuration error
Bad packets
Bridge overloaded
Disk space fragmented
Encapsulation error
Excessive collisions
File server jammed
Gateway overloaded
Network jammed

No disk space
Poor performance
Repeater overloaded
Retransmissions
Slow file service
Slow response
Software problems
Workstation jammed

Network jammed
High error rate

Network out-of-spec error
Bad packets
Bridge overloaded
Excessive collisions
File server jammed
Gateway overloaded
Network jammed
No disk space

Poor performance
Repeater overloaded
Retransmissions
Slow file service
Slow response
Software problems
Workstation jammed

Network terminator missing
Network jammed

Network tool stressing network
Bad packets
Bridge overloaded
Encapsulation routing overloaded
Excessive collisions
File server jammed
Gateway overloaded
Network jammed

No disk space
Poor performance
Repeater overloaded
Retransmissions
Slow file service
Slow response
Software problems
Workstation jammed

Common performance failures (causes)
characteristic symptoms

Network undergoing maintenance
Bad packets
Bridge overloaded
Disk space fragmented
Encapsulation routing overloaded
Excessive collisions
Gateway overloaded
Network jammed
No disk space

Node dead
Poor performance
Repeater overloaded
Retransmissions
Slow file service
Slow response
Software problems
Workstation jammed

NIC active on disabled node
Bad packets
Network jammed
No file space
No free disk space

Overloaded network
Poor performance
Slow file service
Slow response

NIC configuration error
Excessive collisions
Node dead

Poor performance
Retransmissions

NIC driver problems
Intermittent slowdowns

NIC errors
Intermittent slowdowns

NIC not inserting into ring
Node dead

No disk space
High error rate

No free disk space
Bridge overloaded
Disk space fragmented
File server jammed
Gateway overloaded
Network jammed
No disk space

Poor performance
Repeater overloaded
Retransmissions
Slow file service
Slow response
Software problems
Workstation jammed

No transceiver heartbeat
Intermittent slowdowns
Poor performance

Slow response
Workstation jammed

Nodes missing from address table
Node dead

Nodes missing

Open break on network
Network jammed
No file service

Node dead
Nodes missing
Software problems

Open short on network
Network jammed
No file service

Node dead
Software problems

Common performance failures (causes)
characteristic symptoms

Optical fiber break
Network jammed
No file service

Node dead
Nodes missing
Software problems

Optical fiber clarity degradation
Bad packets
Encapsulation error
Excessive collisions
File server jammed
Files corrupted
Network jammed

No file service
Nodes missing
Poor performance
Protocol error
Retransmissions
Slow response
Workstation jammed

Optical fiber ends not polished
Bad packets
Encapsulation error
Excessive collisions
File server jammed
Files corrupted

Nodes missing
Poor performance
Protocol error
Retransmissions
Slow response
Workstation jammed

Overloaded network
Bad packets
Bridge overloaded
Disk space fragmented
Encapsulation routing overloaded
Excessive collisions
File server jammed
Gateway overloaded
High error rate
Network jammed
Network jammed

No disk space
No file space
No free disk space
Overloaded network
Poor performance
Repeater overloaded
Retransmissions
Slow file service
Slow response
Software problems
Workstation jammed

Parity errors
Bad packets

Parity errors
Excessive collisions

Intermittent slowdowns

Protocol address error
Encapsulation error

Intermittent slowdowns
Router overloaded

Protocol analyzer creating traffic
Bad packets
Excessive collisions
File server jammed
Network jammed
Poor performance

Retransmissions
Slow file service
Slow response
Software problems
Workstation jammed

Protocol analyzer error
Incorrect collision statistics

Protocol analyzer not fast enough
Incorrect collision statistics

Incorrect network statistics

Common performance failures (causes)
characteristic symptoms

Protocol error
Bad packets
Bridge overloaded
Disk space fragmented
Encapsulation error
Excessive collisions
Excessive collisions

File server jammed
Gateway overloaded
Network jammed
No disk space
Node dead
Poor performance
Repeater overloaded

Protocol error
Retransmissions
Slow file service
Slow response
Software problems
Workstation jammed
Incorrect collision statistics

Incorrect network statistics
Incorrect network statistics
No disk space
No disk space
Excessive collisions
File server jammed
Network jammed

Remote query not optimized locally
Overloaded network
Poor performance
Slow file service
Slow response

Software problems
Bad packets
Encapsulation routing overloaded
Excessive collisions

Repeater overloaded
File server jammed
Network jammed
No disk space
Poor performance
Repeater overloaded
Retransmissions

Slow file service
Slow response
Software problems
Workstation jammed
Intermittent slowdowns
Bad packets
Encapsulation routing overloaded

Router overloaded
Excessive collisions
File server jammed
Network jammed
No disk space
Poor performance
Retransmissions

Slow file service
Slow response
Software problems
Workstation jammed
Bad packets
Bridge overloaded

Router table address error
Disk space fragmented
Encapsulation error
Excessive collisions
File server jammed
Gateway overloaded
Network jammed
No disk space
Poor performance

Repeater overloaded
Retransmissions
Slow file service
Slow response
Software problems
Workstation jammed
Excessive collisions
File server jammed

Security functions enabled
Network jammed
Overloaded network
Poor performance
Slow file service

Slow response
Software problems
File server jammed
Bad packets

Common performance failures (causes)
characteristic symptoms

Server bus bandwidth overwhelmed
Excessive collisions
File server jammed
Network jammed
Poor performance
Retransmissions

Slow file service
Slow response
Software problems
Workstation jammed
Bad packets

Server I/O (input/output) bound
Excessive collisions
File server jammed
Network jammed
Poor performance
Retransmissions

Slow file service
Slow response
Software problems
Workstation jammed
Bad packets

Signal injector creating traffic
Excessive collisions
File server jammed
Network jammed
Poor performance
Retransmissions

Slow file service
Slow response
Software problems
Workstation jammed
Protocol error

Signal timing error
Protocol error

Slow NIC
Slow file service

Slow response

SNMP messages saturating network
Bad packets
Excessive collisions
File server jammed
Network jammed
Poor performance

Retransmissions
Slow file service
Slow response
Software problems
Workstation jammed

Software application error
Protocol error

Software incompatibility
Bad packets
Bridge overloaded

High error rate
Intermittent slowdowns
Router overloaded

Static electricity strike
Bad packets
Disk space fragmented
Encapsulation error
File server jammed
Gateway overloaded

Network jammed
No disk space
Poor performance
Slow response
Software problems
Workstation jammed

Store-and-forward message lost
Bad packets
Encapsulation error
Excessive collisions
File server jammed
Files corrupted

Nodes missing
Poor performance
Protocol error
Retransmissions
Slow response
Workstation jammed

Common performance failures (causes)
characteristic symptoms

Stray voltage corrupted memory
- Bad packets
- Disk space fragmented
- Encapsulation error
- File server jammed
- Gateway overloaded

- Network jammed
- No disk space
- Poor performance
- Slow response
- Software problems
- Workstation jammed

Tap probe not in contact with coax
- Network jammed

- Poor performance

Too few buffers on controller
- Excessive collisions

Too many distributed processes
- Excessive collisions
- File server jammed
- Network jammed
- Poor performance

- Retransmissions
- Slow file service
- Slow response
- Software problems
- Workstation jammed

Too many network nodes
- Network jammed
- No file space
- No free disk space

- Overloaded network
- Poor performance
- Slow file service
- Slow response

Too many statistics captured
- Incorrect collition statistics

- Incorrect network statistics

Too many wireless stations
- Bad packets
- Encapsulation error
- Excessive collisions
- File server jammed
- Files corrupted

- Nodes missing
- Poor performance
- Protocol error
- Retransmissions
- Slow response
- Workstation jammed

Too much network traffic
- Excessive collisions
- File server jammed
- Network jammed
- Poor performance

- Retransmissions
- Slow file service
- Slow response
- Software problems
- Workstation jammed

Transceiver edge connector broken
- Bad packets

- Network jammed
- Node dead

Transceiver tap probes broken
- Bad packets

- Node dead

Transceiver with improper frequency
- Network jammed

Transceiver with improper voltage
- Network jammed

Translation error
- Protocol error

Common performance failures (causes)
characteristic symptoms

Translation gateway too slow
Bad packets
Excessive collisions
File server jammed
Network jammed
No disk space

Poor performance
Retransmissions
Slow file service
Slow response
Software problems
Workstation jammed

Translation protocol error
Bad packets
Excessive collisions
File server jammed
Network jammed
No disk space

Poor performance
Retransmissions
Slow file service
Slow response
Software problems
Workstation jammed

Twisted-pair bundle overutilized
Bad packets
Encapsulation error
Excessive collisions
File server jammed
Files corrupted

Nodes missing
Poor performance
Protocol error
Retransmissions
Slow response
Workstation jammed

Twisted-pair crosstalk
Bad packets
Encapsulation error
Excessive collisions
File server jammed
Files corrupted

Nodes missing
Poor performance
Protocol error
Retransmissions
Slow response
Workstation jammed

Twisted-pair intermixed with RS-232
Bad packets
Encapsulation error
Excessive collisions
File server jammed
Files corrupted

Node dead
Nodes missing
Poor performance
Protocol error
Retransmissions
Workstation jammed

Twisted-pair not properly connected
Bad packets
Excessive collisions
Files corrupted

Network jammed
Retransmissions
Workstation jammed

Twisted-pair on live phone lines
Bad packets
Encapsulation error
Excessive collisions
File server jammed
Files corrupted

Node dead
Nodes missing
Poor performance
Protocol error
Retransmissions
Workstation jammed

Twisted-pair pairs reversed
Network jammed

Workstation jammed

Common performance failures (causes)
characteristic symptoms

Twisted-pair polarity error
Network jammed

Workstation jammed

Twisted-pair substandard
Bad packets
Encapsulation error
Excessive collisions
File server jammed
Files corrupted

Nodes missing
Poor performance
Protocol error
Retransmissions
Slow response
Workstation jammed

Twisted-pair wire metal fatigue
Bad packets
Excessive collisions
Network jammed

No file service
Slow response
Workstation jammed

Usage audit functions enabled
Excessive collisions
File server jammed
Network jammed
Overloaded network

Poor performance
Slow file service
Slow response
Software problems

User files corrupted
Retransmissions

Software problems

UTP instead of STP
Bad packets
Excessive collisions
Intermittent slowdowns
Network jammed
No file space

No free disk space
Overloaded network
Poor performance
Slow file service
Slow response

Wireless RF frequency overlap
Bad packets
Encapsulation error
Excessive collisions
File server jammed
Files corrupted
Network jammed
No file space
No free disk space

Nodes missing
Overloaded network
Poor performance
Protocol error
Retransmissions
Slow file service
Slow response
Workstation jammed

Wireless signal conflict
Bad packets
Encapsulation error
Excessive collisions
File server jammed
Files corrupted
Network jammed
No file space
No free disk space

Nodes missing
Overloaded network
Poor performance
Protocol error
Retransmissions
Slow file service
Slow response
Workstation jammed

Common performance failures (causes)
characteristic symptoms

Wireless signal distorted by dust
Bad packets
Encapsulation error
Excessive collisions
File server jammed
Files corrupted
Network jammed
No file space
No free disk space

Nodes missing
Overloaded network
Poor performance
Protocol error
Retransmissions
Slow file service
Slow response
Workstation jammed

Wireless signal too weak
Bad packets
Encapsulation error
Excessive collisions
File server jammed
Files corrupted
Network jammed
No file space
No free disk space

Nodes missing
Overloaded network
Poor performance
Protocol error
Retransmissions
Slow file service
Slow response
Workstation jammed

Wireless stations too far apart
Bad packets
Encapsulation error
Excessive collisions
File server jammed
Files corrupted
Network jammed
No file space
No free disk space

Nodes missing
Overloaded network
Poor performance
Protocol error
Retransmissions
Slow file service
Slow response
Workstation jammed

Workstation undergoing maintenance
Node dead
Nodes missing

Poor performance
Retransmissions
Slow response

Characteristic performance symptoms
Possible causes

Bad packets

ARCnet hub in overloaded PC
ARL too long
Bad interrupt request (DOS IRQ)
Bad tap
Bridge overloaded
CMIP messages saturating network
Coaxial cable metal fatigue
Corrupted database
Corrupted distributed database
Defective lobe/drop cable
Driver configuration error
Drop cable not properly connected
Encapsulation protocol error
Faulty transceiver
File server disk too slow
File server jammed
File server memory error
Gateway overloaded
Improper shielding from noise
Inconsistent network software
Lobe cable too long
Malfunctioning gateway
Malfunctioning repeater
Mismatched hardware
Network configuration error
Network out-of-spec error
Network tool stressing network
Network undergoing maintenance
NIC active on disabled node
Optical fiber clarity degradation
Optical fiber ends not polished
Overloaded network

Parity errors
Protocol analyzer creating traffic
Protocol error
Repeater overloaded
Router overloaded
Router table address error
Server bus bandwidth overwhelmed
Server I/O (input/output) bound
Signal injector creating traffic
SNMP messages saturating network
Software incompatibility
Static electricity strike
Store-and-forward message lost
Stray voltage corrupted memory
Too many wireless stations
Transceiver edge connector broken
Transceiver tap probes broken
Translation gateway too slow
Translation protocol error
Twisted-pair bundle overutilized
Twisted-pair crosstalk
Twisted-pair intermixed with RS-232
Twisted-pair not properly connected
Twisted-pair on live phone lines
Twisted-pair substandard
Twisted-pair wire metal fatigue
UTP instead of STP
Wireless RF frequency overlap
Wireless signal conflict
Wireless signal distorted by dust
Wireless signal too weak
Wireless stations too far apart

Bridge overloaded

Application running across bridge
Bad address
Bad interrupt request (DOS IRQ)
Bridge overloaded
Broadcast storm
Disk space fragmented
Driver configuration error
Encapsulation protocol error
File server jammed
File server memory error
Gateway overloaded

Inconsistent network software
Multicast storm
Network configuration error
Network out-of-spec error
Network tool stressing network
Network undergoing maintenance
No free disk space
Overloaded network
Protocol error
Router table address error
Software incompatibility

Characteristic performance symptoms
Possible causes

Disk space fragmented
Bad interrupt request (DOS IRQ)
Driver configuration error
File server jammed
File server memory error
Inconsistent network software
Network configuration error
Network undergoing maintenance
No free disk space
Overloaded network
Protocol error
Router table address error
Static electricity strike
Stray voltage corrupted memory

Encapsulation error
Bad interrupt request (DOS IRQ)
Corrupted database
Corrupted distributed database
Driver configuration error
Inconsistent network software
Network configuration error
Optical fiber clarity degradation
Optical fiber ends not polished
Protocol address error
Protocol error
Router table address error
Static electricity strike
Store-and-forward message lost
Stray voltage corrupted memory
Too many wireless stations
Twisted-pair bundle overutilized
Twisted-pair crosstalk
Twisted-pair intermixed with RS-232
Twisted-pair on live phone lines
Twisted-pair substandard
Wireless RF frequency overlap
Wireless signal conflict
Wireless signal distorted by dust
Wireless signal too weak
Wireless stations too far apart

Encapsulation routing overloaded
Bridge overloaded
Encapsulation protocol error
File server jammed
File server memory error
Gateway overloaded
Network tool stressing network
Network undergoing maintenance
Overloaded network
Repeater overloaded
Router overloaded

Characteristic performance symptoms
Possible causes

Excessive collisions [Ethernet only]
Application running across bridge
Application running across gateway
Application running across router
Application running on server
ARL too long
Bad interrupt request (DOS IRQ)
Bad tap
Bridge overloaded
Brouter routing error
CMIP messages saturating network
Coaxial cable metal fatigue
Corrupted database
Corrupted distributed database
Defective lobe/drop cable
Device creating broadcast storm
Driver configuration error
Drop cable not properly connected
Encapsulation protocol error
Faulty transceiver
File server disk too slow
File server jammed
File server memory error
Gateway overloaded
Improper coaxial grounding
Improper shielding from noise
In excess of 100 taps on a coax
Inconsistent network software
Lobe cable too long
Mismatched hardware
Network audit functions enabled
Network configuration error
Network out-of-spec error
Network tool stressing network
Network undergoing maintenance
NIC configuration error
Optical fiber clarity degradation

Optical fiber ends not polished
Overloaded network
Parity errors
Protocol analyzer creating traffic
Protocol error
Protocol error
Remote query not optimized locally
Repeater overloaded
Router overloaded
Router table address error
Security functions enabled
Server bus bandwidth overwhelmed
Server I/O (input/output) bound
Signal injector creating traffic
SNMP messages saturating network
Store-and-forward message lost
Too few buffers on controller
Too many distributed processes
Too many wireless stations
Too much network traffic
Translation gateway too slow
Translation protocol error
Twisted-pair bundle overutilized
Twisted-pair crosstalk
Twisted-pair intermixed with RS-232
Twisted-pair not properly connected
Twisted-pair on live phone lines
Twisted-pair substandard
Twisted-pair wire metal fatigue
Usage audit functions enabled
UTP instead of STP
Wireless RF frequency overlap
Wireless signal conflict
Wireless signal distorted by dust
Wireless signal too weak
Wireless stations too far apart

Excessive network management alarms
Broadcast storm

File server jammed

Application running across bridge
Application running across gateway
Application running across router
Application running on server
Bad interrupt request (DOS IRQ)
Bridge overloaded
CMIP messages saturating network
Corrupted database
Corrupted distributed database
CPU too slow
Device creating broadcast storm
Disk space fragmented
Driver configuration error
Encapsulation protocol error
File server disk too slow
File server down
File server jammed
File server memory error
Gateway overloaded
Inconsistent network software
Malfunctioning gateway
Malfunctioning repeater
Network audit functions enabled
Network configuration error
Network out-of-spec error
Network tool stressing network
No free disk space
Optical fiber clarity degradation
Optical fiber ends not polished
Overloaded network

Protocol analyzer creating traffic
Protocol error
Remote query not optimized locally
Repeater overloaded
Router overloaded
Router table address error
Security functions enabled
Server also router or gateway
Server bus bandwidth overwhelmed
Server I/O (input/output) bound
Signal injector creating traffic
SNMP messages saturating network
Static electricity strike
Store-and-forward message lost
Stray voltage corrupted memory
Too many distributed processes
Too many wireless stations
Too much network traffic
Translation gateway too slow
Translation protocol error
Twisted-pair bundle overutilized
Twisted-pair crosstalk
Twisted-pair intermixed with RS-232
Twisted-pair on live phone lines
Twisted-pair substandard
Usage audit functions enabled
Wireless RF frequency overlap
Wireless signal conflict
Wireless signal distorted by dust
Wireless signal too weak
Wireless stations too far apart

Files corrupted

Bad tap
Corrupted database
Corrupted distributed database
Defective lobe/drop cable
Drop cable not properly connected
Faulty transceiver
Improper shielding from noise
Mismatched hardware
Optical fiber clarity degradation
Optical fiber ends not polished
Store-and-forward message lost

Too many wireless stations
Twisted-pair bundle overutilized
Twisted-pair crosstalk
Twisted-pair intermixed with RS-232
Twisted-pair not properly connected
Twisted-pair on live phone lines
Twisted-pair substandard
Wireless RF frequency overlap
Wireless signal conflict
Wireless signal distorted by dust
Wireless signal too weak
Wireless stations too far apart

Characteristic performance symptoms
Possible causes

Gateway overloaded
Application running across gateway
Bad interrupt request (DOS IRQ)
Disk space fragmented
Driver configuration error
Encapsulation protocol error
File server jammed
File server memory error
Gateway overloaded
Inconsistent network software

Network configuration error
Network out-of-spec error
Network tool stressing network
Network undergoing maintenance
No free disk space
Overloaded network
Protocol error
Router table address error
Static electricity strike
Stray voltage corrupted memory

High error rate
ARL too long
Bad interrupt request (DOS IRQ)
Bad tap
Defective lobe/drop cable
Defective system software
Disk space fragmented
Driver configuration error
Drop cable not properly connected
Fan-out jammed
Faulty transceiver
File server down
File server memory error
File server overloaded

Improper coaxial grounding
Improper shielding from noise
In excess of 100 taps on network
Inconsistent network software
Lobe cable too long
Malfunctioning bridge
Malfunctioning gateway
Malfunctioning repeater
Mismatched hardware
Network jammed
No disk space
Overloaded network
Software incompatibility

Incorrect collision statistics
Protocol analyzer error

Protocol analyzer not fast enough
Protocol incompatibilities

Incorrect collisions statistics
Lack of SNMP agent

Incorrect collition statistics
Too many statistics captured

Incorrect network statistics
Lack of SNMP agent
Protocol analyzer not fast enough

Protocol incompatibilities
Protocol incompatibilities
Too many statistics captured

Intermittent slowdowns
ARCnet hub in overloaded PC
ARL too long
Broadcast storm
CPU too slow
Insufficient buffer space
Lobe cable too long
Multicast storm

NIC driver problems
NIC errors
No transceiver heartbeat
Parity errors
Protocol address error
Ring in panic resets
Software incompatibility
UTP instead of STP

Management software overload
Broadcast storm

Characteristic performance symptoms
Possible causes

Network jammed

Application running across bridge
Application running across gateway
Application running on server
ARCnet hub in overloaded PC
ARL too long
Bad interrupt request (DOS IRQ)
Bridge overloaded
Brouter routing error
CMIP messages saturating network
Coaxial cable metal fatigue
Corrupted database
Corrupted distributed database
CPU too slow
Defective drop cable
Defective lobe cable
Device creating broadcast storm
Disk space fragmented
Driver configuration error
Drop cable not properly connected
Drop cable polarity error
Encapsulation protocol error
Fan-out jammed
File server disk too slow
File server jammed
File server memory error
Gateway overloaded
Improper coaxial grounding
Improper shielding from noise
In excess of 100 taps on a coax
Inconsistent network software
Insufficient buffer space
Insufficient cache space
Insufficient free disk space
Lobe cable too long
Malfunctioning gateway
Malfunctioning repeater
Mismatched hardware
Network audit functions enabled
Network configuration error
Network out-of-spec error
Network terminator missing

Network tool stressing network
Network undergoing maintenance
NIC active on disabled node
No free disk space
Open break on network
Open short on network
Optical fiber break
Optical fiber clarity degradation
Overloaded network
Overloaded server
Protocol analyzer creating traffic
Protocol error
Remote query not optimized locally
Repeater overloaded
Router overloaded
Router table address error
Security functions enabled
Server bus bandwidth overwhelmed
Server I/O (input/output) bound
Signal injector creating traffic
SNMP messages saturating network
Static electricity strike
Stray voltage corrupted memory
Tap probe not in contact with coax
Too many distributed processes
Too many network nodes
Too much network traffic
Transceiver edge connector broken
Transceiver with improper frequency
Transceiver with improper voltage
Translation gateway too slow
Translation protocol error
Twisted-pair not properly connected
Twisted-pair pairs reversed
Twisted-pair polarity error
Twisted-pair wire metal fatigue
Usage audit functions enabled
UTP instead of STP
Wireless RF frequency overlap
Wireless signal conflict
Wireless signal distorted by dust
Wireless signal too weak

Network jammed

Wireless stations too far apart
Bad interrupt request (DOS IRQ)
Disk space fragmented
Disk too small
Driver configuration error
Encapsulation protocol error
File server jammed
File server memory error
Files marked deleted not purged
Gateway overloaded
Inconsistent network software
Network configuration error
Network out-of-spec error
Network tool stressing network
Network undergoing maintenance
No free disk space
Overloaded network
Protocol error
RAM disk too small
Records marked deleted not purged
Repeater overloaded
Router overloaded
Router table address error
Static electricity strike
Stray voltage corrupted memory
Translation gateway too slow
Translation protocol error
Coaxial cable metal fatigue
Defective system software
File server down
File server overloaded
Mismatched hardware
Open break on network
Open short on network
Optical fiber break
Optical fiber clarity degradation
Twisted-pair wire metal fatigue
ARCnet hub in overloaded PC
ARL too long
Corrupted database
Corrupted distributed database

CPU too slow
Defective lobe/drop cable
Insufficient buffer space
Insufficient cache space
Insufficient free disk space
Lobe cable too long
NIC active on disabled node
Overloaded network
Too many network nodes
UTP instead of STP
Wireless RF frequency overlap
Wireless signal conflict
Wireless signal distorted by dust
Wireless signal too weak
Wireless stations too far apart
ARCnet hub in overloaded PC
ARL too long
Corrupted database
Corrupted distributed database
CPU too slow
Defective lobe/drop cable
Disk space fragmented
Insufficient buffer space
Insufficient cache space
Insufficient free disk space
Lobe cable too long
NIC active on disabled node
Overloaded network
Too many network nodes
UTP instead of STP
Wireless RF frequency overlap
Wireless signal conflict
Wireless signal distorted by dust
Wireless signal too weak
Wireless stations too far apart
Bad address
Brouter overloaded
Brouter routing error
Mismatched hardware
Network undergoing maintenance
NIC configuration error
NIC not inserting into ring

Characteristic performance symptoms
Possible causes

Node dead
Nodes missing from address table
Open break on network
Open short on network
Optical fiber break
Protocol error
Transceiver edge connector broken
Transceiver tap probes broken
Twisted-pair intermixed with RS-232

Twisted-pair on live phone lines
Workstation undergoing maintenance
Brouter overloaded
Brouter routing error
Corrupted database
Corrupted distributed database
Improper shielding from noise
Malfunctioning gateway
Malfunctioning repeater

Nodes missing
Nodes missing from address table
Open break on network
Optical fiber break
Optical fiber clarity degradation
Optical fiber ends not polished
Store-and-forward message lost
Too many wireless stations
Twisted-pair bundle overutilized
Twisted-pair crosstalk
Twisted-pair intermixed with RS-232
Twisted-pair on live phone lines
Twisted-pair substandard

Wireless RF frequency overlap
Wireless signal conflict
Wireless signal distorted by dust
Wireless signal too weak
Wireless stations too far apart
Workstation undergoing maintenance
Application running across bridge
Application running across gateway
Application running across router
Application running on server
ARCnet hub in overloaded PC
ARL too long
Corrupted database

Overloaded network
Corrupted distributed database
CPU too slow
Defective lobe/drop cable
Insufficient buffer space
Insufficient cache space
Insufficient free disk space
Lobe cable too long
NIC active on disabled node
Overloaded network
Remote query not optimized locally
Security functions enabled
Too many network nodes
Usage audit functions enabled

UTP instead of STP
Wireless RF frequency overlap
Wireless signal conflict
Wireless signal distorted by dust
Wireless signal too weak
Wireless stations too far apart
Application running across bridge
Application running across gateway
Application running across router
Application running on server
ARCnet hub in overloaded PC
ARL too long
Bad interrupt request (DOS IRQ)

Characteristic performance symptoms
Possible causes

Poor performance

Bad tap
Bridge overloaded
Brouter overloaded
Brouter routing error
CMIP messages saturating network
Corrupted database
Corrupted distributed database
CPU too slow
Defective lobe/drop cable
Device creating broadcast storm
Disk space fragmented
Driver configuration error
Encapsulation protocol error
Excessive collisions
File server disk too slow
File server jammed
File server memory error
Gateway overloaded
Improper shielding from noise
Inconsistent network software
Insufficient buffer space
Insufficient cache space
Insufficient free disk space
Lobe cable too long
Network audit functions enabled
Network configuration error
Network out-of-spec error
Network tool stressing network
Network undergoing maintenance
NIC active on disabled node
NIC configuration error
No free disk space
No transceiver heartbeat
Optical fiber clarity degradation
Optical fiber ends not polished
Overloaded network
Protocol analyzer creating traffic
Protocol error

Remote query not optimized locally
Repeater overloaded
Router overloaded
Router table address error
Security functions enabled
Server bus bandwidth overwhelmed
Server I/O (input/output) bound
Signal injector creating traffic
SNMP messages saturating network
Static electricity strike
Store-and-forward message lost
Stray voltage corrupted memory
Tap probe not in contact with coax
Too many distributed processes
Too many network nodes
Too many wireless stations
Too much network traffic
Translation gateway too slow
Translation protocol error
Twisted-pair bundle overutilized
Twisted-pair crosstalk
Twisted-pair intermixed with RS-232
Twisted-pair on live phone lines
Twisted-pair substandard
Usage audit functions enabled
UTP instead of STP
Wireless RF frequency overlap
Wireless signal conflict
Wireless signal distorted by dust
Wireless signal too weak
Wireless stations too far apart
Workstation undergoing maintenance
Bad address
Corrupted database
Corrupted distributed database
Encapsulation error
Insufficient buffer size
Mismatched device drivers
Optical fiber clarity degradation

Characteristic performance symptoms
Possible causes

Protocol error

Optical fiber ends not polished
Signal strength error
Signal timing error
Software application error
Store-and-forward message lost
Too many wireless stations
Translation error
Twisted-pair bundle overutilized
Twisted-pair crosstalk
Twisted-pair intermixed with RS-232
Twisted-pair on live phone lines
Twisted-pair substandard

Wireless RF frequency overlap
Wireless signal conflict
Wireless signal distorted by dust
Wireless signal too weak
Wireless stations too far apart
Bad interrupt request (DOS IRQ)
Driver configuration error
Encapsulation protocol error
Excessive collisions
File server jammed
File server memory error
Inconsistent network software

Repeater overloaded

Network configuration error
Network out-of-spec error
Network tool stressing network
Network undergoing maintenance
No free disk space
Overloaded network
Protocol error
Repeater overloaded

Router table address error
Bad interrupt request (DOS IRQ)
Bridge overloaded
Brouter overloaded
Brouter routing error
CMIP messages saturating network
Corrupted database
Corrupted distributed database

Retransmissions

Defective lobe/drop cable
Device creating broadcast storm
Disk space fragmented
Driver configuration error
Drop cable not properly connected
Encapsulation protocol error
Excessive collisions
File server disk too slow
File server jammed
File server memory error
Gateway overloaded
Inconsistent network software
Network configuration error
Network out-of-spec error
Network tool stressing network
Network undergoing maintenance
NIC configuration error
No free disk space
Optical fiber clarity degradation
Optical fiber ends not polished
Overloaded network
Protocol analyzer creating traffic
Protocol error
Repeater overloaded
Router overloaded
Router table address error
Server bus bandwidth overwhelmed
Server I/O (input/output) bound

Signal injector creating traffic
SNMP messages saturating network
Store-and-forward message lost
Too many distributed processes
Too many wireless stations
Too much network traffic
Translation gateway too slow
Translation protocol error
Twisted-pair bundle overutilized
Twisted-pair crosstalk
Twisted-pair intermixed with RS-232
Twisted-pair not properly connected
Twisted-pair on live phone lines
Twisted-pair substandard
User files corrupted
Wireless RF frequency overlap
Wireless signal conflict
Wireless signal distorted by dust
Wireless signal too weak
Wireless stations too far apart
Workstation undergoing maintenance
Application running across router
Bad address
Broadcast storm
Multicast storm
Protocol address error
Software incompatibility
Fan-out jammed

Characteristic performance symptoms
Possible causes

Slow file service

Application running across bridge
Application running across gateway
Application running across router
Application running on server
ARCnet hub in overloaded PC
ARL too long
Bad interrupt request (DOS IRQ)
Bridge overloaded
Brouter routing error
CMIP messages saturating network
Corrupted database
Corrupted distributed database
CPU too slow
Defective lobe/drop cable
Defective system software
Device creating broadcast storm
Disk space fragmented
Disk too slow
Driver configuration error
Encapsulation protocol error
File server disk too slow
File server down
File server jammed
File server memory error
File server overloaded
Gateway overloaded
Inconsistent network software
Insufficient buffer space
Insufficient cache space
Insufficient free disk space
Lobe cable too long
Mismatched hardware

Network audit functions enabled
Network configuration error
Network out-of-spec error
Network tool stressing network
Network undergoing maintenance
NIC active on disabled node
No free disk space
Overloaded network
Protocol analyzer creating traffic
Protocol error
Remote query not optimized locally
Repeater overloaded
Router overloaded
Router table address error
Security functions enabled
Server bus bandwidth overwhelmed
Server I/O (input/output) bound
Signal injector creating traffic
Slow NIC
SNMP messages saturating network
Too many distributed processes
Too many network nodes
Too much network traffic
Translation gateway too slow
Translation protocol error
Usage audit functions enabled
UTP instead of STP
Wireless RF frequency overlap
Wireless signal conflict
Wireless signal distorted by dust
Wireless signal too weak
Wireless stations too far apart

Characteristic performance symptoms
Possible causes

Slow response

Application running across bridge
Application running across gateway
Application running across router
Application running on server
ARCnet hub in overloaded PC
ARL too long
Bad interrupt request (DOS IRQ)
Bridge overloaded
Brouter routing error
CMIP messages saturating network
Coaxial cable metal fatigue
Corrupted database
Corrupted distributed database
CPU too slow
Defective lobe/drop cable
Defective system software
Device creating broadcast storm
Disk space fragmented
Disk too slow
Driver configuration error
Encapsulation protocol error
File server disk too slow
File server down
File server jammed
File server memory error
File server overloaded
Gateway overloaded
Improper coaxial grounding
In excess of 100 taps on a coax
Inconsistent network software
Insufficient buffer space
Insufficient cache space
Insufficient free disk space
Lobe cable too long
Mismatched hardware
Network audit functions enabled
Network configuration error
Network out-of-spec error
Network tool stressing network

Network undergoing maintenance
NIC active on disabled node
No free disk space
No transceiver heartbeat
Optical fiber clarity degradation
Optical fiber ends not polished
Overloaded network
Protocol analyzer creating traffic
Protocol error
Remote query not optimized locally
Repeater overloaded
Router overloaded
Router table address error
Security functions enabled
Server bus bandwidth overwhelmed
Server I/O (input/output) bound
Signal injector creating traffic
Slow NIC
SNMP messages saturating network
Static electricity strike
Store-and-forward message lost
Stray voltage corrupted memory
Too many distributed processes
Too many network nodes
Too many wireless stations
Too much network traffic
Translation gateway too slow
Translation protocol error
Twisted-pair bundle overutilized
Twisted-pair crosstalk
Twisted-pair substandard
Twisted-pair wire metal fatigue
Usage audit functions enabled
UTP instead of STP
Wireless RF frequency overlap
Wireless signal conflict
Wireless signal distorted by dust
Wireless signal too weak
Wireless stations too far apart
Workstation undergoing maintenance

Software problems

Application running across bridge
Application running across gateway
Application running across router
Application running on server
Bad interrupt request (DOS IRQ)
Bridge overloaded
CMIP messages saturating network
Device creating broadcast storm
Disk space fragmented
Driver configuration error
Encapsulation protocol error
File server disk too slow
File server jammed
File server memory error
Gateway overloaded
Improper shielding from noise
Inconsistent network software
Mismatched hardware
Network audit functions enabled
Network configuration error
Network out-of-spec error
Network tool stressing network
Network undergoing maintenance

No free disk space
Open break on network
Open short on network
Optical fiber break
Overloaded network
Protocol analyzer creating traffic
Protocol error
Remote query not optimized locally
Repeater overloaded
Router overloaded
Router table address error
Security functions enabled
Server bus bandwidth overwhelmed
Server I/O (input/output) bound
Signal injector creating traffic
SNMP messages saturating network
Static electricity strike
Stray voltage corrupted memory
Too many distributed processes
Too much network traffic
Translation gateway too slow
Translation protocol error
Usage audit functions enabled
User files corrupted

Workstation jammed

Bad interrupt request (DOS IRQ)
Bridge overloaded
Brouter routing error
CMIP messages saturating network
Coaxial cable metal fatigue
Corrupted database
Corrupted distributed database
Defective lobe/drop cable
Defective system software
Device creating broadcast storm
Disk space fragmented
Driver configuration error
Drop cable not properly connected
Drop cable polarity error
Encapsulation protocol error
Fan-out jammed
Faulty transceiver
File server disk too slow
File server jammed
File server memory error
Gateway overloaded
Inconsistent network software
Mismatched hardware
Network configuration error
Network out-of-spec error
Network tool stressing network
Network undergoing maintenance
No free disk space
No transceiver heartbeat
Optical fiber clarity degradation
Optical fiber ends not polished

Overloaded network
Protocol analyzer creating traffic
Protocol error
Repeater overloaded
Router overloaded
Router table address error
Server bus bandwidth overwhelmed
Server I/O (input/output) bound
Signal injector creating traffic
SNMP messages saturating network
Static electricity strike
Store-and-forward message lost
Stray voltage corrupted memory
Too many distributed processes
Too many wireless stations
Too much network traffic
Translation gateway too slow
Translation protocol error
Twisted-pair bundle overutilized
Twisted-pair crosstalk
Twisted-pair intermixed with RS-232
Twisted-pair not properly connected
Twisted-pair on live phone lines
Twisted-pair pairs reversed
Twisted-pair polarity error
Twisted-pair substandard
Twisted-pair wire metal fatigue
Wireless RF frequency overlap
Wireless signal conflict
Wireless signal distorted by dust
Wireless signal too weak
Wireless stations too far apart

Performance bottlenecks
Possible solutions

Generic solutions
Add disk space
Add local disk for temporary files and swap space
Add more disk space
Add more system memory
Allocate more memory to RAM disk
Allocate more memory to buffers
Allocate more memory to cache space
Apply tool during off-peak times
Archive and purge historial data
Archive files required infrequently
Ask for manufacturer for technical support
Backup data, reformat, and restore data
Backup disk, reformat, restore from backup media
Boost signal
Broadcast CMIP statistics during off-peak periods
Broadcast SNMP statistics during off-peak periods
Build routing tables manually
Check address table validity
Check configuration and allocation of memory
Check consistency/accurary of LLC and MAC addresses
Check for compatibility between drivers and OS
Check for compatibility between NIC PROMs and drivers
Check for extra (non-specified) ground
Check for parity errors
Check for proper IRQ settings
Check for sufficient memory
Check network for crosstalk, EMI or RF interference
Check NIC PROM release levels, and software drivers
Check proper tap configuration
Check that all grounds have same electrical potential
Check that memory speed is adequate for CPU
Check that NIC set for network tranmission speed
Check that tranceiver set for protocol version
Check that transceiver receiving A/C power
Clean up disk space
Cleanup hard disk; make more file space
Compress (ZIP, LZH, ARC) files required infrequently
Concentrate high volume users on same LAN segments
Configure NIC correctly
Connect properly/replace cable
Correct destination addresses
Correct LLC, MAC, or other address tables
Correct routing table entries
Create or enlarge disk cache space
Create subnets; reconfigure
Deactivate network downloading requests for node statistics
Deactivate stress tests
Decrease collision retries
Decrease deferral retries
Decrease the number of NICs in station

Generic solutions (continued)

Decrease timeout retries
Defragment disk
Defragment disk files
Defragment files
Defragment with software utility
Delete old files and records (increase free disk space)
Delete temporary files; restart operating system
Diagnose hardware and software
Diagnose infrastructure wiring problem
Diagnose memory
Diagnose short, break, MAU error, media or filter error
Disable all active CMIP functions
Disable all active SNMP functions
Disable audit functions
Disable auto routing tables
Disable automatic routing table
Disable functions
Disable IRQ interrupts; accept less performance
Disable network management alarms
Disable network management and alarms
Disable network management functions
Disable read after write disk operation
Disable security functions
Disable some CMIP functions
Disable some SNMP functions
Disable yellow page routing tables
Disable yellow pages or automatic routing tables
Disallow routing of packets with broadcast addresses
Disallow routing of packets with multicast addresses
Divide network into subnetworks
Divide workload between other servers
Ensure compliance of hardware and software to specification
Establish consistent LAN-wide ground potential
Establish hub in single-use PC
Fix it, replace it, restore it to service
Fix patch panel
Flatten directory structure
Format disk, reload system files
Format drive (low-level) to realign tracks to heads
Ground network cable and wires
Ground properly
Ground serevrs and workstations
Halt all processes; reinitialize NOS
Increase amount of memory allocated to disk cache
Increase amount of memory allocated to file buffers
Increase buffer space
Increase buffer space for packets (primarily incoming packets)
Increase capacity of server
Increase collision retries

Generic solutions (continued)

Increase CPU performance (faster CPU, more buffers or memory
Increase CPU speed (replace motherboard or system)
Increase deferral retries
Increase disk space
Increase number of message retries
Increase server CPU speed
Increase server memory
Increase size of disk, network buffer sp
Increase size of server cache
Increase the number of MAUs
Increase the packet address size
Increase timeout retries
Initiate audit of network hardware and software
Install (increase) local RAM
Install (increase) local RAM disk space
Install a memory management utility (for MS-DOS only)
Install application as standalone proces
Install bus master controller
Install caching controller
Install compatible software for all stations
Install cross-point switch matrix
Install crosspoint hubs
Install disk data compression driver
Install high-performance NIC
Install latest release of NIC software drivers
Install media filters
Install more file buffers
Install multitaps
Install network devices tolerant of high signal error rates
Install new wire
Install on-the-fly disk file compression utility
Install one controller per disk (do not daisy chain)
Install polarity sensing MAUs or NICs
Install signal repeater
Install spike, antistatic mats and AC power filters
Install UPS and AC power filters
Install UPS battery pack
Level the software on the network
Load application into local memory and C
Load system files over network from functioning node
Lower percentage of twisted pairs utilized in a bundle
Lower workload on gateway device
Minimize multicast and broadcast packets
Minimize network and routing protocols
Minimize the number of CMIP statistics broadcast from nodes
Minimize the number of protocols coexisting on network
Minimize the number of SNMP statistics broadcast from nodes
Move files to server, or, to local disk
Move security and login functions to secondary server
Move users files to local disks

Performance bottlenecks
Possible solutions

Generic solutions (continued)
Offload server functions to secondary servers
Optimize file directory structures
Optimize physical file placement
Optimize server configuration
Optimize software
Pack, purge, and defragment disk
Perform complete network audit
Phase out multiple protocols; standardize with single protoc
Purge old files and database records
Purge or pack files, and defragment chained files
Purge, pack, and reindex database
Readjust transmitter frequencies
Realign tranmitters and receivers
Reboot
Reboot servers; halt first with proper shutdown sequence
Reboot servers and workstations; restart OS or NOS
Rebuild address table, yellow pages, or routing table
Rebuild routing table (manually, if needed)
Rebuild, reindex, or reload database
Recable or rewire
Recode application to process at local C
Reconfigure
Reconfigure controller buffer
Reconfigure device drivers
Reconfigure network
Reconfigure network configuration
Reconfigure network to bypass construction area
Reconfigure or redesign network
Reconfigure system buffer space
Reconfigure transceiver
Redesign databases with more efficient structure
Reduce load on server
Reduce load on workstation
Reduce number of concurrent protocols
Reduce number of stacks
Reduce server workload
Reindex critical distributed database files
Reindex records
Reindex, purge, and pack bloated databases
Reinstall software
Reinstall system
Reinstall tap unit
Reinstall transceiver in new tap or with new unit
Reinstall transceiver in new tap or with new wires
Remove device from network
Remove or deactive signal generation
Remove stations from network; run locally
Reorganize FAT (DOS file allocation table)
Repair cable

Generic solutions (continued)

Repair yellow pages, TCP address table, reset NIC switches
Repair, remove stations from network, reboot OS or NOS
Repair, remove stations from network, reboot stations
Replace cable
Replace component hardware with compatible unit
Replace controller with 16-bit or 32-bit unit
Replace controller with another model
Replace CPU chip, motherboard, or station with another unit
Replace daisy-chained disks with multiple disk controllers
Replace defective device from network
Replace defective media filter
Replace defective NIC
Replace device
Replace device drivers
Replace disk controller with a caching controller
Replace disk controller with a faster unit
Replace disk controller with a wider data transfer bus
Replace disk controller with bus mastering controller
Replace disk with larger unit
Replace disk with unit with faster head access times
Replace inefficient software
Replace media filter
Replace multiple server disks with large single unit
Replace NIC
Replace NIC with 16-bit or 32-bit bus support
Replace NIC with more suitable unit
Replace or add wiring bundle
Replace server disk controllers with faster units
Replace server disk with faster units
Replace server with higher performance motherboard or unit
Replace software
Replace source system software media
Replace storage devices with a faster unit
Replace tap unit
Replace with bus mastering NIC
Replace with cross-point swicth match
Replace with cross-point switch matrix
Replace with functional unit
Replace with router
Replace, repair, or remove
Replace, tighten connectors, or repair cable break
Replace, upgrade, or remove
Reroute network
Reset IRQ settings
Restore damaged files from backup
Restore database from backup
Rewire to reverse polarity/replace cable
Run application in local workstation
Run database restoration utility
Run file restoration utility

Performance bottlenecks
Possible solutions

Generic solutions (continued)
Search for broadcast packet with defective addresses
Search for protocol, software, or gateway device error
Search for software bug
See also No free disk space
See Protocol errors and Address errors
Shorten lobe lengths
Shorten search path lengths
Subdivide network
Subnet
Substitute unit with faster seek times
Support daisy-chained disks with multiple disk controllers
Test IRQ settings with software (i.e. MACE)
Turn off signal injector
Unload database, reload data
Upgrade device
Use another media (substitute RF or IF)
Use SST-based transmission signal
Verify proper twisted-pair polarity
Verify tap (or microtap) polarity

Application running across bridge
Concentrate high volume users on same LAN segments

Application running across gateway
Concentrate high volume users on same LAN segments

Application running across router
Concentrate high volume users on same LAN segments

Application running on server
Add local disk for temporary files and swap space
Increase server CPU speed
Increase size of disk, network buffer space, file buffers
Increase size of server cache
Install (increase) local RAM
Install (increase) local RAM disk space
Install application as standalone process
Load application into local memory and CPU
Recode application to process at local CPU

Application running over repeater
Concentrate high volume users on same LAN segments

ARCnet hub in overloaded PC
Establish hub in single-use PC

ARL too long
Install signal repeater
Shorten lobe lengths
Subdivide network

Bad address
Repair yellow pages, TCP address table, reset NIC switches

Performance bottlenecks
Possible solutions

Bad interrupt request (DOS IRQ)
Disable IRQ interrupts; accept less performance
Replace component hardware with compatible unit
Reset IRQ settings
Test IRQ settings with software

Bad tap
Check proper tap configuration
Reinstall tap unit
Replace tap unit
Verify proper twisted-pair polarity
Verify tap (or microMAU) polarity

Bridge overloaded
Concentrate high volume users on same LAN segments
Reconfigure or redesign network
Replace with cross-point switch matrix
Replace with router

Broadcast storm
Disable automatic routing table
Disable network management functions
Minimize multicast and broadcast packets

Brouter overloaded
Concentrate high volume users on same LAN segments
Minimize network and routing protocols
Replace with cross-point switch matrix

Brouter routing error
Correct destination addresses
Minimize network and routing protocols
Rebuild routing table (manually, if needed)

CMIP messages saturating network
Broadcast CMIP statistics during off-peak periods
Disable all active CMIP functions
Disable some CMIP functions
Minimize the number of CMIP statistics broadcast from nodes

Coaxial cable metal fatigue
Recable

Corrupted database
Rebuild, reindex, or reload database

Corrupted distributed database
Purge, pack, and reindex database
Reindex records
Restore database from backup
Run database restoration utility
Unload database, reload data

Corrupted system files
Format disk, reload system files
Load system files over network from functioning node
Reinstall system
Restore damaged files from backup
Run file restoration utility

Performance bottlenecks
Possible solutions

CPU too slow
Replace CPU chip, motherboard, or station with another unit

Defective drop cable
Repair cable
Replace cable

Defective system software
Install latest release of NIC software drivers
Load system files over network from functioning node
Reinstall system
Replace source system software media
Restore damaged files from backup
Run file restoration utility

Device creating broadcast storm
Build routing tables manually
Correct routing table entries
Disable network management and alarms
Disallow routing of packets with broadcast addresses
Disallow routing of packets with multicast addresses
Remove device from network
Replace defective device from network

Disk space fragmented
Backup disk, reformat, restore from backup media
Defragment with software utility
Increase disk space

Disk too slow
Defragment disk files
Delete old files and records (increase free disk space)
Format drive (low-level) to realign tracks to heads
Increase amount of memory allocated to disk cache
Increase amount of memory allocated to file buffers
Install bus master controller
Install caching controller
Install disk data compression driver
Replace controller with 16-bit or 32-bit unit
Substitute unit with faster seek times

Disk too small
Archive files required infrequently
Compress (ZIP, LZH, ARC) files required infrequently
Delete old files and records (increase free disk space)
Install disk data compression driver
Move files to server, or, to local disk
Replace disk with larger unit

Driver configuration error
Reconfigure device drivers
Replace device drivers

Drop cable not properly connected
Connect properly/replace cable

Drop cable polarity error
Rewire to reverse polarity/replace cable

Performance bottlenecks
Possible solutions

Encapsulation error
Search for software bug

Encapsulation protocol error
Ask for manufacturer for technical support
Correct LLC, MAC, or other address tables

Excessive collisions (Ethernet)
Install cross-point switch matrix

Fan-out jammed (Ethernet)
Replace with cross-point switch match

Faulty transceiver
Check that tranceiver set for protocol version
Check that transceiver receiving A/C power
Reinstall transceiver in new tap or with a new unit
Replace with functional unit

File server disk too slow
Archive and purge historical data
Backup data, reformat, and restore data
Clean up disk space
Create or enlarge disk cache space
Defragment files
Install more file buffers
Install one controller per disk (do not daisy chain)
Optimize file directory structures
Optimize physical file placement
Redesign databases with more efficient structure
Reindex, purge, and pack bloated databases
Replace disk controller with a caching controller
Replace disk controller with a faster unit
Replace disk controller with a wider data transfer bus
Replace disk controller with bus mastering controller
Replace disk with unit with faster head access times
Replace inefficient software
Replace storage devices with a faster technology

File server down
Reboot

File server jammed

Cleanup hard disk; make more file space
Decrease collision retries
Decrease deferral retries
Decrease the number of NICs in station
Decrease timeout retries
Delete temporary files; restart operating system
Disable auto routing tables
Disable yellow page routing tables
Increase collision retries
Increase deferral retries
Increase timeout retries
Install crosspoint hubs
Reboot
Reduce load on server
Reduce load on workstation
Reduce number of concurrent protocols
Reduce number of stacks

File server memory error

Check configuration and allocation of memory
Check for parity errors
Check for sufficient memory
Check that memory speed is adequate for CPU

Performance bottlenecks
Possible solutions

File server overloaded
Decrease collision retries
Decrease deferral retries
Decrease the number of NICs in station
Decrease timeout retries
Disable auto routing tables
Disable yellow page routing tables
Divide workload between other servers
Increase collision retries
Increase deferral retries
Increase server memory
Increase timeout retries
Install crosspoint hubs
Install high-performance NIC
Install latest release of NIC software drivers
Move users files to local disks
Offload server functions to secondary servers
Optimize software
Purge old files and database records
Reconfigure network configuration
Reduce load on server
Reduce load on workstation
Reduce number of concurrent protocols
Reduce number of stacks
Reindex critical distributed database files
Replace daisy-chained disks with multiple disk controllers
Replace multiple server disks with large single unit
Replace NIC with 16-bit or 32-bit bus support
Replace server disk controllers with faster units
Replace server disk with faster units
Replace server with higher performance motherboard or unit
Replace software

Files marked deleted not purged
Purge or pack files, and defragment chained files

Gateway overloaded
Concentrate high volume users on same LAN segments

Improper coaxial grounding
Ground properly

Improper shielding from noise
Lower percentage of twisted pairs utilized in a bundle
Recable
Reroute network

In excess of 100 Ethernet taps
Subnet

Inconsistent network software
Install compatible software for all stations

Performance bottlenecks
Possible solutions

Insufficient buffer size
Add more system memory
Allocate more memory to buffers
Install a memory management utility (for MS-DOS only)

Insufficient cache space
Add more system memory
Allocate more memory to buffers
Install a memory management utility (for MS-DOS only)

Insufficient free disk space
Add more system memory
Allocate more memory to cache space

Insufficient free disk space
Install a memory management utility (for MS-DOS only)

Lack of SNMP agent
Replace device
Replace software
Upgrade device

Malfunctioning bridge
Establish consistent LAN-wide ground potential
Replace, repair, or remove

Malfunctioning gateway
Establish consistent LAN-wide ground potential
Replace, repair, or remove

Malfunctioning repeater
Establish consistent LAN-wide ground potential
Replace, repair, or remove

Mismatched device drivers
Level the software on the network

Mismatched hardware
Replace, upgrade, or remove

Multicast storm
Disable yellow pages or automatic routing tables

Network audit functions enabled
Disable functions

Network configuration error
Reconfigure

Performance bottlenecks
Possible solutions

Network jammed
Allocate more memory to buffers
Check consistency/accuracy of LLC and MAC addresses
Cleanup hard disk; make more file space
Create subnets; reconfigure
Decrease collision retries
Decrease deferral retries
Decrease the number of NICs in station
Decrease timeout retries
Delete temporary files; restart operating system
Disable auto routing tables
Disable yellow page routing tables
Establish consistent LAN-wide ground potential
Halt all processes; reinitialize NOS
Increase collision retries
Increase deferral retries
Increase timeout retries
Install crosspoint hubs
Install latest release of NIC software drivers
Reboot servers
Reduce load on server
Reduce load on workstation
Reduce number of concurrent protocols
Reduce number of stacks
Replace NIC with 16-bit or 32-bit bus support
Search for broadcast packet with defective addresses

Network out-of-spec error
Perform complete network audit

Network terminator missing
Replace, tighten connectors, or repair cable break

Network tool stressing network
Remove or deactivate signal generation

Network undergoing maintenance
Reconfigure network to bypass construction area
Remove stations from network; run locally
Repair, remove stations from network, reboot stations

NIC active on disabled node
Install latest release of NIC software drivers
Replace defective media filter
Replace defective NIC

NIC configuration error
Configure NIC correctly
Replace NIC with more suitable unit

NIC driver problems
Check for compatibility between drivers and OS
Check for compatibility between NIC PROMs and drivers
Reboot
Reinstall software

NIC errors
    Diagnose hardware and software
    Increase buffer space
    Install latest release of NIC software drivers
    Replace defective NIC
    Replace NIC with 16-bit or 32-bit bus support

NIC not inserting into ring
    Check NIC PROM release levels, and software drivers
    Install latest release of NIC software drivers
    Replace defective NIC
    Replace media filter
    Replace NIC with 16-bit or 32-bit bus support

No disk space
    Add disk space
    See also No free disk space

No free disk space
    Add more disk space
    Archive and purge historical data
    Clean up disk space
    Defragment disk
    Install on-the-fly disk file compression utility
    Redesign databases with more efficient structure
    Reindex, purge, and pack bloated databases

No transceiver heartbeat
    Reconfigure transceiver

Nodes missing from address table
    Rebuild address table, yellow pages, or routing table

Open break on network
    Reconfigure network to bypass construction area

Open short on network
    Reconfigure network to bypass construction area

Optical fiber break
    Reconfigure network to bypass construction area

Optical fiber clarity degradation
    Reconfigure network to bypass construction area

Optical fiber ends not polished
    Reconfigure network to bypass construction area

Performance bottlenecks
Possible solutions

Overloaded network
Decrease collision retries
Decrease deferral retries
Decrease the number of NICs in station
Decrease timeout retries
Disable auto routing tables
Disable yellow page routing tables
Divide workload between other servers
Increase collision retries
Increase deferral retries
Increase server memory
Increase timeout retries
Install cross-point switch matrix
Install crosspoint hubs
Install high-performance NIC
Install latest release of NIC software drivers
Move users files to local disks
Offload server functions to secondary servers
Optimize server configuration
Optimize software
Purge old files and database records
Reconfigure network configuration
Reduce load on server
Reduce load on workstation
Reduce number of concurrent protocols
Reduce number of stacks
Reindex critical distributed database files
Replace multiple server disks with large single unit
Replace NIC with 16-bit or 32-bit bus support
Replace server disk controllers with faster units
Replace server disk with faster units
Replace server with higher performance motherboard or unit
Replace software
Support daisy-chained disks with multiple disk controllers

Parity errors
Diagnose memory

Protocol address error
See Protocol errors and Address errors

Protocol analyzer creating traffic
Deactivate network downloading requests for node statistics
Deactivate stress tests
Disable network management alarms

Protocol error
Initiate audit of network hardware and software

Protocol incompatibilities
Minimize the number of protocols coexisting on network

Performance bottlenecks
Possible solutions

RAM disk too small
Add more system memory
Allocate more memory to RAM disk
Allocate more memory to buffers
Install a memory management utility (for MS-DOS only)

Records marked deleted not purged
Pack, purge, and defragment disk

Remote query not optimized locally
Optimize software
Replace software
Run application in local workstation

Repeater overloaded
Install cross-point switch matrix

Ring in panic resets
Diagnose short, break, MAU error, media or filter error
Establish consistent LAN-wide ground potential

Router overloaded
Install cross-point switch matrix

Router table address error
Rebuild routing table (manually, if needed)

Security functions enabled
Disable security functions
Move security and login functions to secondary server

Server also router or gateway
Increase capacity of server

Server bus bandwidth overwhelmed
Install cross-point switch matrix

Server I/O (input/output) bound
Decrease collision retries
Decrease deferral retries
Decrease timeout retries
Disable auto routing tables
Disable yellow page routing tables
Increase collision retries
Increase deferral retries
Increase timeout retries
Install crosspoint hubs
Install latest release of NIC software drivers
Reduce load on server
Reduce load on workstation
Replace NIC with 16-bit or 32-bit bus support

Server undergoing maintenance
Reconfigure network to bypass construction area
Remove stations from network; run locally
Repair, remove stations from network, reboot OS or NOS

Signal injector creating traffic
Apply tool during off-peak times
Turn off signal injector

Performance bottlenecks
Possible solutions

Signal strength error
Check network for crosstalk, EMI or RF interference
Diagnose infrastructure wiring problem

Signal timing error
Check network for crosstalk, EMI or RF interference
Check that NIC set for network tranmission speed
Diagnose infrastructure wiring problem
Establish consistent LAN-wide ground potential
Replace NIC

Slow NIC
Check for proper IRQ settings
Increase buffer space for packets (primarily incoming packets)
Increase CPU performance (faster CPU, more buffers or memory)
Install latest release of NIC software drivers
Replace NIC with 16-bit or 32-bit bus support
Replace with bus mastering NIC

SNMP messages saturating network
Broadcast SNMP statistics during off-peak periods
Disable all active SNMP functions
Disable some SNMP functions
Minimize the number of SNMP statistics broadcast from nodes

Static electricity strike
Check integrity and polarity of ground and power outlets
Check that all grounds have same electrical potential
Establish consistent LAN-wide ground potential
Ground network cable and wires
Ground servers and workstations
Install spike, antistatic mats and AC power filters
Install UPS battery pack
Reboot servers and workstations; restart OS or NOS

Store-and-forward message lost
Check address table validity
Increase number of message retries
Reconfigure network

Stray voltage corrupted memory
Check for extra (non-specified) ground
Check that all grounds have same electrical potential
Establish consistent LAN-wide ground potential
Ground network cable and wires
Ground servers and workstations
Install UPS and AC power filters
Reboot servers and workstations; restart OS or NOS

Tap probe not in contact with coax
Check that transceiver receiving A/C power
Check that transceiver set for protocol version
Reinstall transceiver in new tap or with new unit
Replace with functional unit

TCP/IP protocol error
Minimize network and routing protocols

Performance bottlenecks
Possible solutions

Too few buffers on controller
Reconfigure controller buffer
Reconfigure system buffer space
Replace controller with another model

Too many distributed processes
Reduce server workload

Too many network nodes
Divide network into subnetworks
Increase the number of MAUs
Increase the packet address size
Install multitaps

Too many statistics captured
Disable network management functions

Too many wireless stations
Realign transmitters and receivers
Use another media (substitute RF or IF)
Use SST-based transmission signal

Too much network traffic
Install cross-point switch matrix

Transceiver edge connector broken
Replace with functional unit

Transceiver tap probes broken
Replace with functional unit

Transceiver with improper frequency
Reinstall transceiver in new tap or with new wires
Replace with functional unit

Transceiver with improper voltage
Replace with functional unit

Translation error
Search for protocol, software, or gateway device error

Translation gateway too slow
Increase CPU speed (replace motherboard or system)
Lower workload on gateway device
Phase out multiple protocols; standardize with single protocol

Translation protocol error
Ask for manufacturer for technical support
Correct LLC, MAC, or other address tables

Twisted-pair bundle overutilized
Replace or add wiring bundle

Twisted-pair crosstalk
Establish consistent LAN-wide ground potential
Replace or add wiring bundle

Twisted-pair intermixed with RS-232
Replace or add wiring bundle

Twisted-pair not properly connected
Replace or add wiring bundle

Performance bottlenecks
Possible solutions

Twisted-pair on live phone lines
> Fix patch panel

Twisted-pair pairs reversed
> Install polarity sensing MAUs or NICs
> Recable

Twisted-pair polarity error
> Install polarity sensing MAUs or NICs
> Recable

Twisted-pair substandard
> Recable

Twisted-pair wire metal fatigue
> Recable

Usage audit functions enabled
> Disable audit functions

User files corrupted
> Load system files over network from functioning node
> Reinstall system
> Replace source system software media
> Restore damaged files from backup
> Run file restoration utility

UTP instead of STP
> Install media filters
> Install network devices tolerant of high signal error rates
> Install new wire

Wireless RF frequency overlap
> Readjust transmitter frequencies

Wireless signal conflict
> Realign tranmitters and receivers
> Use another media (substitute RF or IF)
> Use SST-based transmission signal

Wireless signal distorted by dust
> Use another media (substitute RF or IF)

Wireless signal too weak
> Boost signal
> Realign transmitters and receivers
> Use another media (substitute RF or IF)
> Use SST-based transmission signal

Wireless stations too far apart
> Boost signal
> Realign tranmitters and receivers
> Use another media (substitute RF or IF)
> Use SST-based transmission signal

Workstation undergoing maintenance
> Fix it, replace it, restore it to service

Performance bottlenecks
Possible solutions

Glossary

AC Abbreviation for *alternating current*. Electricity.

ARCnet A proprietary local area network protocol predominant in PC environments. ARCnet uses the a logical token passing protocol on either a bus or star topology. Transmission rate is 2.5 Mbits/s, although ARCnet *plus* supports 20 Mbits/s, and TCNS (Thomas-Conrad Network System) provides 100 Mbits/s with similar hardware and station drivers.

ARL *See* adjusted ring length.

AUI cable Attachment Unit Interface cable that connects a workstation to a transceiver or fan-out box. Often called a drop cable.

ANSI See American National Standards Institute.

abnormal preamble A packet error that occurs when the preamble doesn't match the legal 8-byte Ethernet synchronization pattern.

adapter board A PC board that plugs into any computer, including mainframe, minicomputer, personal computer, or workstation. Within the networking context it often refers to the network access unit or a controller and transceiver combination.

address A reference to a source station or destination station on a network.

address error A packet that is improperly labeled with either source or destination information.

adjusted ring length The driving transmission path length for a ring architecture when a node or segment fails, and the ring wraps to provide network service without interruption.

alignment error A packet that has not been synchronized correctly. It is usually uncovered as a packet that is not a multiple of 8 bits.

American National Standards Institute   A governmental agency that maintains standards for science and commerce that includes a list of acceptable standards for computer languages, character sets, connection compatibility, and many other aspects of the computer and data communications industries. Also known by the ANSI acronym.

analog   Something that bears a similarity to something else.

analog signal   A transmission in which information is represented as physical magnitudes of electrical signals.

application level   The seventh layer of the OSI reference model which supports identification of communicating partners, establishes the authority to communicate, transfers information, and applies privacy mechanisms and cost allocations. It may be a complex layer. The application layer supports file services, print services, and electronic mail.

average   The statistical value representing the middle point in a sample distribution. Also, the sum all sample values divided by the number of samples.

.BAT   Abbreviation for a *batch file;* usually refers to an MS-DOS or OS/2 script containing commands to execute. The file extent for an MS-DOS or OS/2 script file.

BMP   *See* burst mode protocol.

bandwidth   The range (band) of frequencies that are transmitted on a channel. The difference between the highest and lowest frequencies is expressed in hertz.

barrel connectors   A double-sided male coupling that interconnects coaxial sections.

baseband   A transmission channel which carries a single communications channel, on which only one signal can transmit at a given time.

beaconing   A term used to describe a malfunctioning node on a Token-Ring network that has not isolated itself from the ring. A constant signal, similar to an Ethernet jabber, collapses the ring segment.

benchmark   A measuring standard. LAN performance benchmarks include Mbits/s, throughput, error rates, and other less formal definitions.

bits per second (bps)   Rate at which data is transmitted over a communications channel.

bits/s   Rate at which data is transmitted over a communications channel. *See* bits per second.

bit time   The time for a network to transport 1 bit of data. It is equivalent to the reciprocal of the network transmission rate, and is a convenient measurement in network performance calculations.

break   A physical break (electrical or optical) in the network media that prohibits passage of the transmission signal. *See also* open.

bridge   A device that interconnects networks using *similar* protocols. The bridges provides service at level 2 of the OSI reference model. *See also* gateway and router.

broadband   A transmission coaxial cable with a wider frequency range (than baseband) that carries individual multiplexed communications channels.

broadcast   The transmission from one node on a LAN to two or more nodes on a LAN, or a packet with a destination broadcast address.

brouter   Combination or hybrid derived from *bridge* and *router.* A device that performs the function of a bridge while filtering protocols and packets specifically destined for a node on another interconnected network.

buffers   A temporary memory structure allocated for containing data. Usually refers to a memory structure for containing a block read or written to a hard disk.

burst mode protocol   A NOS enhancement implemented in Novell NetWare that optimizes the performance of intensive file transfer operations.

bus   A network topology in which nodes are connected to a linear configuration of cable. The data transfer path with a computer.

bus master   A specialized CPU and interface unit that controls the data transfer path and bypasses the computer CPU.

bus width   Refers to the size of the data units that the computer system to move through I/O. Usually represented by 8, 16, 32, or 64 byte units.

CCITT   *See* Consultative Committee for International Telephone and Telegraph.

CDMA   *See* Code-Division Multiple Access.

CI   *See* confidence interval.

CMIP   *See* Common Management Information Protocol.

CSMA   *See* Carrier Sense Multiple Access.

CSMA/CD   *See* Carrier Sense Multiple Access with Collision Detection.

CRC   *See* cyclic redundancy check.

CRC Error   *See* cyclic redundancy check error.

cable tester   A testing tool that verifies the integrity and performance of network wiring and cable . It tests for electrical breaks, shorts, impedance, capacitance, as well as for signal crosstalk and signal attenuation.

cache   A temporary memory structure that bffers data movement in a computer system to provide faster access to information and improve overall performance.

caching controller   A storage interface device that improves disk performance. *See* cache.

capacitance   The electrical properties of the coaxial cable and network hardware.

carrier sense   A signal provided by the physical layer to the data link layer indicating that one or more nodes are transmitting on the channel.

carrier-sense multiple-access A communication protocol in which (Ethernet) nodes contend for a shared communication channel and all nodes have equal access to the network. It is a channel access control protocol for multiple-access transmissions. Each node monitors the channel and transmits only if the channel is idle.

carrier-sense multiple-access with collision detection (CSMA/CD) A communications protocol in which nodes contend for a shared communications channel and all nodes have equal access to the network. Simultaneous transmissions from two or more nodes result in random restart of those transmissions. It is a refinement of CSMA because transmitting nodes cease transmission when a collision is detected.

chained files Files on disk stored in discontiguous blocks.

Channel An individual path that carries signals.

channel logic The logical functions between the transceiver cable and the data link layer that support the defined interface between the system and the hardware.

chatter The condition resulting when transceiver electronics fail to shut down after a transmission, and the transceiver floods the network with random signals.

claim token The signal propagated by a station which determines that a token is overdue, lost, or corrupted.

client A network "user," often a device or workstation.

client layer The collective term that is used to refer to the data link and physical layers of the OSI reference model.

client-server processing The establishment of a host computer (server) to provide end-user (client) services.

coax *See* coaxial cable.

coaxial cable An insulated, tinned copper conducting wire surrounded by foamed PVC or Teflon, and shielded by tinned copper braid or an aluminum sleeve. It can carry data transmissions at very high data rates with little loss of information and with a high immunity to outside interference.

code-division multiple access Wireless transmission technology that employs a range of radio-frequency wavelengths to transport multiple channels of communication signals. *See also* spread-spectrum technology.

collision The event occurring when two or more nodes contend for the network at the same time. This is usually caused by the time delay that the signal requires to travel the length of the network.

collision backoff The psuedo-random delay on Ethernet following a collision.

collision backoff algorithm The protocol on Ethernet for generating a psuedo-random delay following a collision. It should be an exponential backup based upon multiples of 96 μs, the maximum Ethernet slot time.

collision (error)   This network event is not an error in and of itself. It is an indication that two or more nodes attempted to transmit within the same slot. Unless the number of collisions is excessive, this is a "normal" condition.

collision detect   A signal provided by the physical layer to the data link layer to indicate that one or more other nodes are contending with a node's transmission.

collision detection (CD)   A node's ability to detect when two or more nodes are transmitting simultaneously on a shared network.

collision enforcement   The transmission of extra "jam" bits after a collision is detected, to ensure that all other transmitting nodes detect the collision.

.COM   The file extent for an MS-DOS executable application.

common carrier   Companies which provide communication networks (like AT&T).

common management information protocol   A network management protocol compatible with the OSI reference model. Also called *CMIP*.

common network interface protocol   A contender for standard network management protocols specified by ISO. This protocol provides a standard for managing large networks across bridges, routers, and gateways. *See also* simple network management protocol.

computer virus   Man-made software designed to disable, damage, or destroy computer hardware or read/write storage systems. Sometimes called incorrectly *worms*, *trojan horses*, and *trap doors*.

concentrator   A wiring hub.

Confidence Interval   A statistical range surrounding the average value.

congestion   A slowdown in a network due to a bottleneck.

Consultative Committee for International Telephone and Telegraph   An international organization that makes recommendations for networking standards like X.25, X.400, and CCITT facsimile data compression standards.

contention   The condition occurring when two or more more nodes access the channel at the same time, resulting in an Ethernet collision.

contention interval   The interval during which an Ethernet collision can occur.

contiguous file blocks   Storage units in a hard drive that are logically positioned next to each other.

core   The central conductor element in a coaxial cable, a large-diameter wire usually constructed of copper. *See* coaxial cable.

corrupt data error   Condition resulting when hardware components fail.

crosstalk   A technical term indicating that stray signals from other wavelengths, channels, communication pathways, or twisted-pair wiring have polluted the signal. It is particularly prevalent in unshielded twisted-pair networks or when telephone and network communications share wiring bundles.

cyclic redundancy check   A check sum—an error checking algorithm—that the transmitting station includes within a packet. The receiving station generates its own CRC to check against the transmitted CRC. If the results are different, the receiver usually requests a retransmission of the packet. This encoded value is appended to each frame by the data link layer to allow receiving NIC to detect transmission errors in the physical channel. *See also* frame check sequence (q.v.).

cyclic redundancy check error   An error caused by alignment errors and under- or oversized packets.

cylinder   Refers to a collection of tracks within a hard disk that are co-located on multiple platters.

DAS   *See* dual access station.

DC   Direct current. Electricity.

DECnet   Digital Equipment Corporation's vendor implementation of Ethernet.

DCE   Abbreviation for *distributed computing*.

DDE   Abbreviation for *dynamic data exchange*.

DDL   Abbreviation for *dynamic link library*. The file extent for an MS-Windows or OS/2 application overlay and executable code library.

DP   Acronym for *data processing*.

DTE   Acronym for *data terminal equipment*. A computer terminal.

data compression   A method of reducing the space required to represent data, either as bits, characters, or graphic images.

Data Link Layer   The second layer of the OSI reference model. It manages transmissions and error acknowledgment and recovery. Technically, the mechanical devices map data units to data link units, and provide physical error detection and notification, and link activation and deactivation.

decouple   A gateway (OSI application layer) process to notify an application that transmission will not be completed within the roundtrip delay limitations a LAN protocol. Instead, a completion message (for transmission success or failure) is given at some later time. This feature is critical for WANs, heterogeneous networks, and enterprise-wide facilities.

deference   The process by which an Ethernet controller delays its transmission when the channel is busy to avoid contention with an ongoing network transmission.

defragment   The process to rewrite files on disk stored in discontiguous blocks into a contiguous format to improve disk performance.

delni unit   A type of fan-out box, or wiring concentrator, for DECnet.

destination address   The receiving station's address. *See* address.

device   Any item on the network. This includes logical addresses that refer to software or hardware processes. It is refers to any physical node, including a PC, workstation, mainframe, minicomputer, bridge, router, gateway, remote probe, repeater, protocol analyzer.

digital   A representation of information by a unit of length or size.

digital transmission   A transmission of information represented by electrical units.

disk (head) seek time   The average time required for the read/write heads on a hard drive to reach a random block and sector.

disk transfer time   Average time required to read or write a block to a hard disk.

distributed computing   The technique of maintaining application software and data files on a centralized server for access by individual users on network nodes. *See also* file server.

distributed computing environment   *See* distributed computing.

downsizing   The replacement of computer equipment (and the operating environment) with a less expensive version.

driver   A software program to control a physical computer device (NIC, printer, disk drive, or RAM disk).

drop cable   *See* transceiver cable and AUI cable.

dropped packets   Packets lost in transmission.

dual access station   An FDDI station which connects into a dual ring.

duplex   The method in which communication occurs, either two-way as in full-duplex, or unidirectional as in half-duplex.

dynamic data exchange   Also called *DDE.* A method introduced by Microsoft with MS Windows to link cell information into a master document, spreadsheet, or other compound process running within the same CPU processor and memory stack. The cell content is not altered or duplicated, merely temporarily inserted for the master.

EEPROM   Abbreviation for *electrically erasable programmable read-only memory.*

EPROM   Abbreviation for *electrically programmable read-only memory.* A computer chip than holds structure in static memory.

EMI   *See* electromagnetic interference.

EMS   Abbreviation for either *enhanced memory services* or *expanded memory services.* Refers to a remapping and utilization of memory beyond the 640 K normally accessible to MS- DOS.

ESDI   Abbreviation for *enhanced small device interface.* A disk storage specification.

ETR   Abbreviation for *early token release.*

electromagnetic interference   Signal noise pollution from radio, radar, or electronic instruments.

end connector   A female coupling that attaches to the ends of a coaxial cable section to interconnect sections or to accept segment terminators.

Enet   *See* Ethernet.

enterprise networks   A wide area network that services all (or most) organizational sites. *See* enterprise-wide networks.

enterprise-wide networks   A wide area network that interconnects LANs at multiple sites.

error   A functional violation of a LAN protocol.

error rate   The number of errors during a duration of time divided by the number of *packets* tranmitted during that same interval. Errors might be reflected as a single bit error, but the rate should reflect errors as a basis not of bit throughput, but rather of packet throughput. *See also* throughput.

Ethernet   A popular example of a local area network from which the IEEE 802.3 standard was derived. Ethernet applied the IEE 802.2 MAC protocols and uses the persistent CSMA/CD protocol on a bus topology. Transmission rate is a maximum of 10 Mbits/s. Ethernet is a persistent transmission protocol.

.EXE   The file extent for an MS-DOS or OS/2 executable application.

FAT   Abbreviation for *file allocation table*. Refers to the MS-DOS table structures that maintain file directory information (size, name, placement, and block chaining.).

FOIRL   *See* fiber distributed optical interface.

FCS   *See* frame check sequence.

FCS error   *See* frame check sequence error.

FDDI   *See* fiber data distributed interchange.

ft   Abbreviation for an *SAE foot*.

facility   A WAN connection provided by a common carrier (such as Sprint, MCI, or AT&T).

fan-out box   A device that provides the capability to connect multiple workstations to a single transceiver. It also allows the construction of local area networks without coaxial cable, or the construction of concentrated clusters on a coaxial cable. It is often referred to as a delni, a multiport, or a multitap.

fiber data distributed interchange   Optical fiber network based upon the ANSI X3.139, ANSI X3.148, X3.166, ANSI X3.184, X3.186, ANSI X3T9.5 specifications. FDDI provides 125 Mbits/s signal rate with 4 bits encoded into 5 bits formats for a 100 Mbit/s transmission rate. It functions on single or dual ring and star local area network with a maximum circumference of 4 km, although copper-based (CDDI) hardware is an option.

fiber distributed optical interface   The interconnection protocol required to access FDDI optical fiber networks.

fiber optics   Thin glass or plastic cables that transmit data by modulating light pulses.

file (buffers)   A temporary memory structure allocated to contain names, locations, sizes, and other information about a file residing on a hard disk.

file server   A device that provides file services for other nodes. It is a shared resource often with higher speed, larger capacity, or better economies-of-scale than remote data storage.

firewall   A mechanism to protect network stations, subnetworks, and channels from complete failure caused by a single point.

firmware   Software that is encoded into a ROM BIOS or PROM chips.

force reduction   A method whereby the performance of slow application code is improved by simplifying algorithms or using hardware-based solutions. A typical example is applying an index to a file otherwise sorted, or by replacing multiplication operations by bit shifts.

forced collision   A collision that occurs when an Ethernet packet is transmitted even if traffic (carrier sense) is detected on the network, that is, if the packet will collide with other packets already on the network. When a packet is transmitted and collides, it is received at the destination node with either a CRC error or an alignment error, if it is received at all.

frame   *See* packet.

frame check sequence   A checksum value to verify correct receipt of the data packet. The checksum is based upon a cyclic redundancy formula. The encoded value appended to each frame by the data link layer to allow receiving controllers to detect transmission errors in the physical channel. Also called a cyclic redundancy check.

frame check sequence error   The condition occurring when the encoded value appended to each frame specifies the received frame as corrupt. *See also* cyclic redundancy check error.

frame relay   A switching interface to get frames or packets over parts of the network as quickly as possible. A packet switching device. *See* packet switching network.

framing   The process of assigning data bits into the network time slot.

Full-Duplex   A two-way transmission method that echoes characters to ensure proper reception.

GIS   Abbreviation for *graphical information system*. Generally refers to a database of graphical data, although it also can refer to an image storage and retrieval system.

Gateway   A device that routes information from one network to another. It often interfaces between dissimilar networks and provides protocol translation between the networks. A gateway is also a software connection between different networks; this meaning is not implied in this book. The gateway provides service at level 7 of the OSI reference model. *See also* bridge and gateway.

Gauss Meter   A device that measures the strength of a magnetic field.

Global Resource   Any hardware, software, server, or other resource generally available to all processes and users on a network.

HMA   *See* high memory area.

HPnet   Hewlett-Packard Corporation's vendor version of Ethernet.

half-duplex   A one-way transmission method that does not support characters echo.

handshaking   The exchange of signals between transmitting and receiving devices or their associated modems to establish that each is working and ready to communicate, and to synchronize timing. *See also* protocol.

heartbeat   *See* signal quality error heartbeat.

Hertz (Hz)   A unit of frequency that is one cycle per second. Ethernet is 20 million hertz, or 20 million cycles per second. Two cycles are required to represent a bit transition. Token-Ring is 8 or 31 million hertz depending upon its speed. FDDI is 125 million hertz since five bits are encoded as 4 bit cycles.

high-level language application programming interface   Also called HLLAPI. A standard for interconnecting processes running on host computers for data tranfer and user display.

high memory area   An MS-DOS memory region generally corresponding to any memory above 640Kb and below 1024Kb. Device controllers and VGA drivers can be loaded into this area for PC performance enhancement.

hub adapter   A network interface board that provides access for additional network nodes. This network interface unit essentially doubles as a concentrator unit.

hunt group   A series of telephone numbers in sequence that permits the calling party to connect with the first available line.

IDE   Abbreviation for *integrated drive electronics.* A composite unit consisting of a disk drive and controller components.

IEEE   The Institute for Electrical and Electronic Engineers.

IEEE 802   An IEEE standard for interconnection of local area networking computer equipment. The IEEE 802 standard describes the physical and link layers of the OSI reference model.

IEEE 802.2   A specification for media-layer communication typified by Ethernet and Token-Ring. *See also* logical link control.

IEEE 802.3   An Ethernet specification derived from the original Xerox Ethernet specifications. It describes the CSMA/CD protocol on a bus topology using baseband transmissions.

IEEE 802.5   A token ring specification derived from the original IBM Token-Ring LAN specifications. It describes the token protocol on a star/ring topology using baseband transmissions.

IES   An uncommon acronym for interenterprise network systems. *See* enterprise-wide networks.

I/O   Abbreviation for input and output from a computer. Refers to all memory movement with the bus, data moved to and from disks, user and screen presentations, and data packets placed to and from the network channel.

IPX   *See* Internet and Internet packet exchange.

ISO   Abbreviation for *International Standards Organization,* which created the OSI reference model.

impedance The mathematical combination of resistance and capacitance that is used as a measurement to describe the electrical properties of network cable and hardware.

In Abbreviation for an *SAE inch.*

IPX Abbreviation for *Internet packet exchange.* A Novell specification for OSI level-3 data exchange.

inductance The property of electrical fields to induce a voltage to flow on the coaxial cable and network hardware. It is usually a disruptive signal that interferes with normal network transmissions.

interface A device that connects equipment of different types for mutual access. Generally, this refers to computer software and hardware that enable disks and other storage devices to communicate with a computer. In networking, an interface translates different protocols so that different types of computers can communicate together. In the OSI model, the interface is the method of passing data between layers on one device.

interface error A condition indicative of hardware or software incompatibilities.

interframe spacing The 96-μs waiting time between transmissions to allow receiving Ethernet controllers to recover.

Internet A government-sponsored mail communication network that gave rise to TCP/IP protocols.

Internet address An address applied at the TCP/IP protocol layer to differentiate network nodes from each other. This is in addition to the station hardware or protocol address.

Internet packet exchange A common network-level protocol proposed and applied by vendors, including Novell. IPX is based upon the original XNS frame specifications.

Internet protocol *See* Transaction Control Protocol/Internet Protocol.

internetworking Communication between two or more different networks through a bridge, a gateway, a modem, or other routing equipment.

interoperability The process of different network protocols, network hardware, and host mainframe systems to communicate.

jabber To talk without making sense. The condition when a transceiver's carrier senses electronics malfunction, and the transceiver broadcasts in excess of the specified 150-μs range time limit and creates an oversized frame.

jabber frame A frame that exceeds 1518 bytes in the data field and violates the Ethernet IEEE 802.3 specifications.

jam A short encoded sequence emitted by a transmitting node overriding other colliding packet signals. It is the method by which Ethernet indicates to all network nodes that a collision has occured.

jitter A network failure that occurs when a 10BASE-T network segment preamble and the packet signal are out of phase. The transmission signal distortion, decay, frequency, and timing errors on a token-based LAN.

jitter budget   The allowed range for signal distortion on a token-based LAN.

k   Abbreviation for a metric kilometer, or a unit representing 100 meters. It can also be represented by km.

KB   Abbreviation for *kilobytes* (1024) of memory.

LAN   Acronym for local area network (q.v.).

LAN operating system   *See* network operating system.

LLC   *See* logical link control.

late collision   A collision, indicated by an oversized runt frame, usually indicative of a network exceeding length or size specifications.

latency   The waiting time for a station desiring to transmit on the network.

learning bridge   A smart device that interconnects two local area networks using similar protocols. It learns what nodes are on each connecting segment and routes only that information that is destined for the other segment, therefore improving network performance. The learning is a simple router that provides service at level 3 of the OSI reference model.

lease line   A dedicated common carrier circuit providing a point-to-point or multipoint network connection. Also called a *private line.*

link control field   A data field contained within an an Ethernet packet as part of the Internet Protocol.

linkage product   Any unit that provides an interface between network segments. This includes gateways, bridges, and other specialty components.

load balancing   A technique to equalize the workload over peer and client network components. This includes workstations, storage disks, servers, network connectivity devices, and network transmission channels.

lobe   A section of cable or wire extending from a MAU, hub, or concentrator to a network station or network node.

local area network   Also referred to by the acronym LAN. A network limited in size to a floor, building, or city block.

logical device   A description that lists how the network references physical devices (q.v.).

local echo   A host implementation for capturing and displaying individual keystrokes on terminal or serial network connections.

logical link control   A data link control field occupying the first few bytes of the data frame data field that initiates, maintains, and terminates any communication.

long packet   A packet that exceeds the specified protocol length maximum.

loop-back test   A test for faults over a transmission medium where received data is returned to the sending point (thus traveling a loop) and compared with the data sent.

low-level format   A process that creates (or overwrites) the pattern of tracks and sectors on a a hard or floppy disk while the disk head is moving across the spinning media.

m   Abbreviation for a *metric meter* (39.25 SAE in).

Mb   Abbreviation for a *megabit* (1024) of memory.

MB   Abbreviation for a *megabyte* (1024) of memory.

MAN   metropolitan area network. A network that spans buildings, city blocks, a college or corporate campus. Optical fiber repeaters, bridges, routers, packet switches, PDN and PBX services usually supply the network links.

MAU   *See* multiple access unit.

MFM   Abbreviation for *modified frequency modulation* encoding method used for storing data a hard disk. A disk storage specification.

MPS   Megabits (1,000,000 decimal units) per second (Mbits/s). This is a channel bandwidth. *See also* bandwidth and Mbits/s.

ms   Abbreviation for a *millisecond.*

μs   Abbreviation for a ***millisecond.***

Manchester encoding   A digital encoding technique in which there is a transition in the middle of each bit time period. A 1 is represented by a high level during the first half of the bit time period whereas a 0 is represented by a low level during the first half of the bit time period.

mean   *See* average.

media access control   A hardware-level protocol for networking corresponding to ISO level 1. Also called the *MAC-layer protocol.*

memory paging   The process of moving memory within the CPU or temporary computer memory to other parts of memory, to screen, or to a disk.

meter   Unit of measurement equivalent to 39.25 SAE in, or 3.27 ft. Meter is abbreviated as *m*.

metrics   A formal measuring standard or benchmark. LAN performance metrics include Mbits/s, throughput, error rates, and other less formal definitions.

microMAU   A transceiver device that converts standard coaxial Ethernet to 10BASE-T twisted pair. *See also* network access unit.

millisecond 1×10^{-6} seconds.

misaligned frame   A frame that trails a fragmentary byte (1 to 7 residual bits), and has an FCS error, or an Ethernet packet that was framed improperly by the receiving station and therefore a synchronization error (q.v.).

mode   The most likely single value in a data sample. The single value in a random set most likely to occur, or the value sample distribution with the most occurences.

modem   A device that converts digital to analog signals and restores analog signals back into digital signals for transmission over a network.

Monte Carlo experiments   Repetitive experiments using sophisticated variance reduction techniques to approximate the behavior of a random process.

monitor   *See* protocol analyzer.

multicast   The ability to broadcast to a select subset of nodes.

multimeter   A test tool that measures electrical voltages (units in V) and resistances (units in Ω). It is also called multitester. It is sometimes called an ohmmeter.

multiple access unit   This network concentrator connects directly to a coaxial cable and broadcasts and receives information over that cable. It is often called a *hub.*

multiport   *See* multitap.

multitap   Fan-out box. A multiple-socket box that provides for a multiple number of workstations to connect to a single node.

multitester   A test tool that measures electrical voltages (units in V) and resistances (units in Ω).

multithreading   A concurrent processing of messages commonly implemented in OS/2, UNIX, and VMS operating systems.

NAU   Abbreviation for *network access enit.* This term represents the combination of a controller and transceiver into a single module as found in most 10BASE-T or Token-Ring adapter boards. *See also* controller.

NDIS   *See* network device independent specification.

ns   Abbreviation for **nanosecond.**

NetBEUI   Abbreviation for network NetBIOS extended user interface. A version of NetBIOS from Microsoft (LANManager).

NetBIOS   Abbreviation for network basic input output system. The first level of network software which controls network hardware. A specification for OSI level-1 data exchange.

NETBLK   network block transfer protocol.

NIC   *See* network interface controller.

NIDL   *See* network interface definition language.

NIU   Abbreviation for *network interface unit. See* Ethernet controller.

NOS   *See* network operating system.

nanosecond 1×10^{-10} seconds.

network   Hardware and software that allow computers to transmit data over both local and long distances.

network computing   The ability of underutilized workstations to broadcast their status and provide automatic parallel compute power.

Network DDE   *See also* dynamic data exchange. A method for linking cell information (such as spreadsheet cells, text blocks, audio or graphic elements) into master documents, spreadsheets, or other compound processs accessible by LAN, WAN, or enterprise-wide networks. These TSR or shell processes define the location of the cell, type of information, method of access, complete address, or frequently the means to establish remote links and initiate remote processes to fetch the cell contents.

network device independent specification. Some vendors define it as network driver interface specification. An effort to create a standard for bridging different type of network adapter cards and multiple protocol stacks. This network-level protocol is supported by IBM LAN Manager and new Microsoft networking products.

network interface controller The network access unit that contains the necessary hardware, software, and specialized PROM information for a node to communicate across the network.

network interface definition language IEEE proposed model for parallel processing and logical process partitioning across a distributed network. *See also* network computing.

network layer The third layer of the OSI reference model, which activates the routing with network address resolution, flow control in terms of segmentation and blocking, and in the case of Ethernet, collision handling. Also, this layer provides service selection, connection resets, and expedited data transfers. The Internet protocol (IP), a common LAN software, runs at this level.

network monitor *See* protocol analyzer.

network operating system A platform for networking services that combines operating system software with network access. This is typically not application software, but rather an integrated operating system. Abbreviated as *NOS*.

no-backoff error A transmission state that results if a transceiver transmits when there is no carrier, but does not wait for the necessary 9.6-µs delay.

node A logical, nonphysical interconnection to the network that supports computer workstations or other types of physical devices on a network. Alternatively, a node might connect to a fan-out unit providing network access for many devices. A device might be a terminal server, or a shared peripheral such as a file server, printer, or plotter.

noise Electrical signal interference on a communications channel that can distort or disrupt data signals. Generally, this refers to electromagnetic interference (EMI) or radio-frequency interference (RFI).

non-isolating error A catch-all term to describe a Token-Ring error that does not initial a beacon, claim token, or other protocol-based error recovery sequences.

ODI *See* open data-link interface.

OLE *See* object linking and embedding.

OSI reference model Open systems interconnection reference model defined by the International Standards Organization (ISO), which has determined a data communication architectural model for networking.

OTDR *See* optical time domain reflectom.

object linking and embedding   Also called *OLE.* A method introduced by Microsoft with MS Windows not merely to link specific data cells but also to include the latest versions of entire documents, graphic images, full-motion video, and sounds into a master document, spreadsheet, or other compound process or object. Changes made to objects linked thusly within this master framework are simultaneously reflected and updated within the individual and original cells, processes, or objects. Additionally, other masters, including objects with multiple OLE links, would see such changes simultaneously. *See also* dynamic data exchange and network DDE.

ohmmeter   *See* multimeter.

open   A partial physical break (electrical or optical) through one or more signal conductors in the network media that prohibits passage of the transmission signal. Open circuits usually do not refer to a complete cut of the media. *See also* break.

open data-link interface. Also called *ODI.* An interoperability standard. Novell has proposed this network-level protocol and built IPX/SPX with this protocol specification. This is the LLC control standardized by Novell.

operating system   The software required to control basic computer operations (disk access, screen display, and computation).

optical fault finder   *See* optical time domain reflectometer.

optical fiber   A glass or plastic material drawn into a cable that carries data communications via light modulation.

optical time domain reflectom   Test equipment that verifies proper functioning of the physical components of the network with a sequence of time delayed light pulses. Primarily, this tool checks for contiguity and isolation of optical fiber.

overhead   CPU, disk processing, and/or network channel bandwidth allocated to the processing and/or packaging of LAN data.

oversized packet   A packet that exceeds the maximum packet size defined by a protocol.

PBX   *See* private branch exchange.

PDN   *See* public data network.

PROM   Abbreviation for programmable read-only memory. A computer chip with software designed into its structure.

PVC   polyvinyl chloride. An extensively used insulator in cable coatings and coaxial cable foam compositions.

packet   A self-contained group of bits representing data and control information. The control information usually includes source and destination addressing, sequencing, flow control, and error control information at different protocol levels. Packet length can be fixed or variable depending upon the protocol.

packet buffers   A structure created in computer memory to build, disassemble, or temporarily store network data packets.

packet burst   An (overwhelming) broadcast of packets requesting LAN and station status information, source or destination addresses, or indicating panic error messages. Not to be confused with packet burst protocol.

packet burst protocol   A Novell enhancement protocol that overcomes some limitations of routing information between different addressed networks. This may provide an performance increase.

packet switching network   A network transmission methodology that uses data to define a start and length of a transmission for digital communications. A process of sending data in discrete blocks.

paging   *See* memory paging.

peer-to-peer exchange   The ability of computer workstations from the same or different vendors to interconnect and communicate.

performance profiler   A software tool that measures where resources are used within another software application or hardware device.

persistence   A statistical term refering to a protocol's method of accessing the network. Ethernet is *persistent* in transmitting, while other protocols are *non-persistent* and wait for a permission token.

phantom voltage   The voltage differential (5 V DC) maintained between the transmit and receive wire pairs in a 10BASE-T, twisted-pair network.

physical address   The unique address associated with each workstation on a network. A physical address is devised to be distinct from all other physical addresses on interconnected networks. A worldwide designation unique to each unit. *See* Ethernet address.

physical channel   The actual wiring and transmission hardware required to implement networking.

physical device   Any item of hardware on the network.

physical layer   Level 1 of the OSI reference model, which insulates the data link layer from the medium-dependent physical characteristics.

ping   A protocol request to poll a subset of network stations for an active status.

polling   An access method involving a central node asking each node in a predetermined order if it has data to send. This is often used in mainframe environments, and the order is often determined as a function of priority.

position-dependent unfairness   A situation common to LANs where some stations receive better service due to proximity to other stations or a central location in a bus-structured LAN.

preamble   The 64-bit encoded sequence that the physical layer of Ethernet transmits before each frame to synchronize clocks and other physical-layer circuitry at other nodes on the network transmission channel.

premises network   *See* enterprise-wide network.

presentation layer   This is the sixth layer of the OSI reference model, which transfers information from the application software to the network session layer of the operating system. At this level, software performs data transformations, data formatting, syntax selection (including ASCII, EBCDIC, or other numeric or graphic formats), device selection and control, and last, data compression or encryption.

print server   A device that provides print services for other nodes. It is a shared resource often with higher speed, larger capacity, or better economies-of-scale than local printers.

private branch exchange   Also called a *PBX*. A telephone system used to connect calls between offices in the same complex and to switch calls between the site and a larger phone network.

profiler   A tool to visibly explore where an application is requiring an extraordinarily large share or CPU, system, or network resources.

protocol   A formal set of rules by which computers can communicate. This includes session initiation, transmission maintenance, and termination.

protocol analyzer   Test equipment that transmits, receives, and captures data packets to verify proper network operation.

public data network   Also called a *PDN*. An analog or digital wide area communication link. This term usually refers to a common carrier such as AT&T, Sprint, or MCI.

queueing model   A statistical model describing a system of event arrivals (q.v. packets or transmission requests) and service times (q.v. tranmission delivery times, network channel loading, and performance levels). Sometimes refered to as a *queuing model*.

RAM disk   A temporary random access memory disk created in memory that functions as a fast disk drive.

RF   Acronym for *radio-frequency* (q.v.).

RFI   Acronym for *radio-frequency interference* (q.v.).

RLL   Abbreviation for the run length limited data encoding method used for storing data on a hard drive. A disk storage specification.

ROM   Abbreviation for read only memory. Refers to the basic information required by most computers to check memory, initialize the bootstrap, and load operating systems and networks.

RS-232   A standard for interfacing data communications between peripheral devices and the computer.

radio-frequency interference   Electronically propogated noise from radar, radio, or electronic sources. *See also* electromagnetic interference.

radio-frequency switch   A remote radio-frequency trigger relay that electrically switches sections of network wiring or coaxial cable and alters network topology. Sometimes called an isolation switch or a *firewall*.

random A statistical term referring to a process with outcomes in a defined sample space. Random does not mean chaotic, indiscriminate, or arbitrary.

random variable A numerically valued function defined over a sample space.

redirector A software driver that diverts commands to access local devices and routes them to network devices for data storage and retrieval and printing.

reliable A description of the day-to-day performance of a network, infrastructure, or software application subject to error conditions and traffic loading levels.

repeater A device that boosts a signal from one network segment and continuing transmission to another similar network segment. Protocols must match on both segments. The repeater provides service at level 1 of the OSI reference model.

resistance The measurement of the electrical properties of the wiring or coax and network hardware that describes their ability to hinder the passage of electrons.

ring A network topology that has nodes in a circular conflguration.

ring purge A Token-Ring protocol operation where a node initiates a a request to create a new token.

roundtrip propagation time The worst-case bit time required for the transmitting node's collision detect jam signal to propagate throughout the network. It is the two-way travel time because the transmitting node needs to receive acknowledgment from all the contending nodes. This delay is the primary component of slot time.

router A device that interconnects networks that are either local area or wide area. Routers often provide intercommunication with multiple protocols. Routers provide service at level 3 of the OSI reference model. *See also* bridge and gateway.

runt frame An Ethernet frame that is too short. A runt frame has fewer than the 60 bytes in the data fields required by the IEEE 802.3. If the frame length is less than 53 bytes, a runt frame indicates a normal collision. A frame less than 60 bytes, but at least 53 bytes, indicates a late collision.

s Abbreviation for a *second.*

SAS *See* single access station.

SCSI Abbreviation for *small computer system interface.* A hardware device controller specification.

SEF *See* source-explicit forwarding.

SNA Abbreviation for *system network architecture.* IBM host mainframe connection protocol.

SNMP *See* simple network management protocol.

SPX Abbreviation for *system packet exchange.* A Novell specification for OSI level-4 data exchange.

SQE *See* signal quality error heartbeat.

SST *See* spread-spectrum technology.

STA *See* spanning-tree algorithm.

STP   *See* shielded twisted-pair.

sector   A pie-shaped structure on a hard disk.

server   A dedicated processor performing a function such as printing, file storage, or tape storage. *See also* file server and print server.

session layer   The fifth layer of the OSI reference model. It recognizes the nodes on the LAN and sets up the tables of source and destination addresses. It also establishes, quite literally, a hand-shaking for each session between different nodes. Technically, these services are called *session connection, exception reporting, coordination of send-receive modes,* and of course, the actual *data exchange*.

service address point   A data link status value contained within the logical link control field of each frame data field that initiates, maintains, and terminates any communication.

shield   A barrier, usually metallic, within a wiring bundle or coaxial cable that is intended to contain the high-powered broadcast signal within the cable. The shield reduces **electromagnetic interference (EMI)** and radio-frequency interference (RFI), and signal loss.

shielded twisted-pair   Pairs of 22- to 26-gauge wire clad with a metallic signal shield.

short   A physical discontinuity (usually electrical, rarely optical) such that one or more signal conductors in the network media leaks signal into other conductors. Usually, a short refers to an electric short circuit between signal conductor and the shield or grounds. It can also refer to a short between receive or transmit pairs.

short packet   An Ethernet packet smaller than the minimum packet size defined by a protocol.

signal   A transmission broadcast. The electrical pulse that conveys information.

signal injector   A tool applied in conjunction with a time domain reflectomer, optical time domain reflectomer, transceiver tester, ring scanner, or cable tester for analyzing the integrity and performance of a local area network. The signal injector creates a signal which mimics the electrical or optical characteristics of the transmission medium.

signal interphasing   A technique of overlapping multiple transmission signals simultaneously to achieve higher transmission rates.

signal quality error heartbeat   A signal from the transceiver to the node peripheral indicating that the transceiver is functioning correctly.

simple network management protocol   A contender for standard network management protocols becoming widely implemented by NIC hardware and software vendors to provide management of heterogeneous networks. *See also* common network interface protocol.

simplex   A transmission standard that does not echo characters.

simulation   A technique to model or represent a real-world situation using computerized tools (*LANModel*).

single access station   An FDDI station that connects into a concentrator, but not into the dual optical fiber ring.

slot time   A multipurpose parameter to describe the contention behavior of the data link layer of OSI reference model. It is defined in Ethernet as the propagation delay of the network for a minimum size packet (64 bytes). Slot time in token-based protocols is either the waiting time for a token or the maximum token hold timer (i.e., the longest packet). Slot time provides an upper limit on the collision vulnerability of a given transmission, an upper limit on the size of the frame fragment produced by the collision runt frame, and the scheduling time for collision retransmission.

soft error   A catch-all term to describe a Token-Ring error that does not initial a beacon, claim token, or other protocol-based error recovery sequences.

SONET   Synchronous Optical Network. A common carrier fiber optic transmission link providing basic bandwidth in blocking units of 50 Mbits/s. Multiple streams can support bandwidths up to 18 billion bits per second.

source address   The transmitting station's Ethernet address.

source-explicit forwarding   A security feature provided by a bridge, router, or gateway that permits only packets from a specified list to be forwarded to another network.

spanning-tree algorithm   IEEE 802.1 standard that detects and manages logical loops in a network. When multiple paths exist, the bridge or router selects the most efficient one. When a path fails, STA automatically reconfigures the network with a new active path.

spectrum analysis   A technique that tests the radio, electrical, or optical signal frequencies to ascertain that the transmission signal conforms to requirements.

spread-spectrum technology   Wireless radio-frequency signal transmission that utilizes multiple frequencies to transmit an identical signal to defeat jamming, background noise, and lower the required power requirements.

stable   A description of the consistency for a network protocol, infrastructure, or application subject to error conditions and traffic loading levels.

standard deviation   The square root of the variance. This statistical value provides a range of values about the average sample value for analysis. The term is abbreviated as *STD*. *See* variance.

star   A network topology that has all nodes joined at a central location.

StarLan   A TCP/IP and Ethernet version that uses twisted pair or telco wiring in place of coaxial cable. It operates at transmission speeds of 1 Mbits/s although 3 Mbits/s or 10 Mbits/s are possible.

station　A single addressable node on Ethernet, generally implemented as a standalone computer or a peripheral device such as a printer or plotter, connected to Ethernet with a transceiver and Ethernet controller. This sometimes referes to a workstation.

stochastic　A process that is random, or probabilistic.

subnet　A terminated Ethernet segment that is a portion of a larger network.

subnetwork　A terminated Ethernet segment that is a portion of a larger network.

swap file　A temporary file established on a local workstation to buffer network data access, provide rapid storage for image displays and work files, and to provide a linearly mapped memory for construction of database views and complex data processing.

synchronization　The event occurring when transmitting and receiving stations operate in unison for very efficient (or inefficient) utilization of the communications channel.

synchronization Error　An Ethernet packet that was framed improperly by the receiving station.

synchronized Ethernet transmission　IEEE 802.3F proposal to transmit overlapping and multiple Ethernet packets (on fiber) without modulating the data signal with a baseline quiet period for a substantially greater effective channel bandwidth.

TCP/IP　Acronym for transaction control protocol/internet protocol. Although commonly referred to as TCP/IP, a complete implementation of this networking protocol includes Transmission Control Protocol (TCP), Internet Protocol (IP), Internetwork Control Message Protocol (ICMP), User Datagram Protocol (UDP), and Address Resolution Protocol (ARP). Standard applications are File Transfer Protocol (FTP), Simple Mail Transfer Protocol (SMTP), and TELNET which provide virtual terminal on any remote network system.

TCNS　Abbreviation for Thomas Conrad Network System; 100 Mbits/s ARCnet variant.

TDR　*See* time domain reflectometer.

TSR　*See* terminate-and-stay resident.

TRT　Abbreviation for *token rotation time*.

Teflon　Trade name for fluorinated ethylene propylene. A nonflammable material used for cable foam and jacketing.

telco　A reference to modular telephone wiring.

10BASE2　An uncommon reference to the Ethernet standard, specifically Cheapernet and Thinnet variations. The number scheme designates that these networks are baseband networks with transmission rates of 10 Mbits/s, with maximum contiguous coaxial segment lengths of 2×10^{10} m (200 m).

10BASE5　An uncommon reference to the Ethernet standard. The number scheme designates that these networks are baseband networks with transmission rates of 10 Mbits/s, with maximum contiguous coaxial segment lengths of 5×10^{10} m (500 m).

10BASE-T   A reference to the Ethernet standard supplemental definition, specifically to twisted-pair wiring and connectors and twisted-pair variations. The number scheme designates that these networks are baseband networks with transmission rates of 10 Mbits/s. The maximum contiguous cable segment lengths is usually limited to 100 m because of the extreme signal interference on the unshielded cabling, although 200 m is nominally supported for distances between a concentrator (hub) and a workstation. There are two versions. One supports bidirectional signaling with dual-pair (4-wire) telephone wiring thus allowing hardware to see collisions. The other version uses single-pair to support daisy-chaining of multiple workstations. Note that signal repeaters are required for the dual-pair twisted-pair wire to boost signal between the concentrator (hub) and the workstations.

terminal server   A computer device that provides low-speed DTE network access. A device for connecting terminals to a network.

terminate-and-stay resident   Also called *TSR*. A PC- and MS-DOS program that is permanently loaded into memory for access by a unique keystroke sequence or event sequence. It can be likened to an extension to the operating system functionality.

throughput   A measurement of LAN work accomplished. Measurements are presented in percentages, bits/s, packets/s, or other user-defined gauges.

time delay reflectometer   An incorrect reference to a device called a time domain reflectometer.

time-division multiplexer   A method using specific time slots to access a communication link. This is accomplished by combining data from several devices into one transmission.

time domain reflectometer   Test equipment that verifies proper functioning of the physical components of the network with a sequence of time-delayed electrical pulses. Primarily, this tool checks for contiguity and isolation of coaxial cable.

time domain reflectometry   The process of testing transmission lines for proper electrical functioning.

token   The protocol-based permission that is granted to a station in a predetermined sequence. The permission allows that station to transmit on network.

Token Ring   Reference to *Token-Ring*.

Token-Ring   A popular example of a local area network from which the IEEE 802.5 standard was derived from original IBM working papers. Token-Ring applies the IEE 802.2 MAC protocols and uses the non-peristent token protocol on a logical ring although physical star topology. Transmission rate is a 4 Mbits/s, with upgrades to 16 Mbits/s and an early token release option.

token acquisition time   The waiting time for a station awaiting permission to transmit to acquire the token. This is sometimes refered to the *latency*.

token hold timer The time measurement and measuring device that sets the time a station might hold a token (while transmitting data), and thus implicitly refers to the size of the longest possible legal packet.

Token-Ring An IBM network protocol and trademark.

token ring An physical networking configuration.

Token-Ring address The hardware address of contained within a NIC PROM. The logical ring position relative to position 1 on a MAU.

token rotational time The time for a token to circulate once around the network. *See* token.

topology Layout of a network. This describes how the nodes are physically joined to each other.

track A circular (ring-shaped) structure on a hard disk.

traffic A measure of network load that refers to the packet transmission rate (frames per second or frames per hour).

Transaction Control Protocol/Internet Protocol Common communication protocol servicing the network and transport layers that provides transmission routing control and data transfer. This represents logical connectivity at levels 2 and 3 of the OSI reference model, although the protocol does not conform in point-of-fact to this model. Also known by its acronym, *TCP/IP.*

transceiver The Ethernet physical layer electronics that connect directly to the coaxial cable. *See* network interface unit.

transceiver cable A four-pair, shielded cable that interconnects an Ethernet workstation to a transceiver or fan-out box. Often called a drop cable or AUI cable.

transceiver chatter *See* chatter.

transceiver exerciser *See* transceiver tester.

transceiver jabber *See* jabber frame.

transceiver tester A testing tool that verifies the integrity and performance of Ethernet transceivers, transceiver attachment cables (AUI), and activates the built-in functions of the transceiver, including the loop-back test. It is also called a *transceiver exerciser*

transmission deferred The act of not transmitting when such transmission would create an Ethernet collision. This is sometimes called an *avoidance of contention.. See also* deference.

transmission error Catch-all term for a CRC Error. Such errors are caused by alignment errors, undersized packets, or oversized packets (q.v.), plus a variety of application, system software, or hardware failures.

transport layer The fourth layer of the OSI reference model, which controls data transfer and transmission control. This software level is called Transaction Control Protocol (TCP), the common LAN software.

twisted-pair Telephone-type wire twisted over its length to preserve signal strength and minimize electromagnetic interference.

type error   A packet that is improperly labeled with protocol information.

UDP   Abbreviation for *user datagram protocol.* A simplified version of the Transmission Control Protocol (TCP) for application-level data.

UMB   *See* upper memory blocks.

UPS   Uninterrupted Power Supply. A backup power supply in case the main electrical source fails.

UTP   *See* unshielded twisted-pair.

undersized packet   A packet that contains less than 64 bytes, including address, length, data, and CRC fields.

unshielded twisted-pair   Pairs of 22- to 26-gauge wire usually in bundles of 25 pairs installed for telephone service.

upper memory blocks   An MS-DOS memory area that is accessible above 1024Kb. MS Windows and some application software can be loaded into this memory when special memory access software is installed. Both *enhanced* and *expanded* memory services reside within UMB. Expanded memory tends to provide the better MS-DOS performance, although it provides the more restricted utility.

VSAT   Abbreviation for *very-small-aperture terminal.* Synonomous with satellite data communication.

variance   A statistical term reflecting the sum of the squared differences between sample values and the sample average. *See* average.

WAN   Abbreviation for *wide area network.* A network that spans cities, states, countries, or oceans. PBX services usually supply the network links.

virus   *See* computer virus.

wiring concentrator   *See* wiring hub.

wiring hub   Central wiring concentrator for series of 10BASE-T nodes.

workstation   A single addressable site on Ethernet, generally implemented as a stand-alone computer or a peripheral device, connected to Ethernet with a transceiver and Ethernet controller. Also termed a **station.**

XNS   Abbreviation for *Xerox Network System.* An original-vendor implementation of Ethernet.

Yellow Pages   A Sun Microsystem network management TCP/IP routing table.

Bibliography

Bickel, Peter J. and Kjell A. Doksum, *Mathematical Statistics: Basic Ideas and Selected Topics,* Holden-Day, San Francisco, CA., 1977.

DEC-INTEL-XEROX, *The Ethernet, A Local Computer Network, Data Link Layer and Physical Layer,* Version 1.0, September 30, 1980.

Haller, Ted, *Cookbook approach to troubleshooting in the Token-Ring environment,* 1992 Communication Test Symposium, Hewlett-Packard.

Hiller, Frederich S., and Gerald J. Lieberman, *Operations Research,* Holden-Day, San Francisco, CA., 1974.

IEEE Standards for Local Area Networks: Logical Link Control Procedures, IEEE, New York, 1985.

Internet Protocol Transition Workbook, March 1981, SRI International, Menlo Park, CA, 94025.

LAN and Enterprise Network Performance Queueing Model, SST Associates, PO Box 771, Brookline, MA, 02146-0771.

Larsen, Andy, ARCnet trade Association, Arlington Heights, IL 60004.

Lee, Ronald, Senior Consultant, Novell, Inc. 122 East 1700 South, Provo, UT 84606-6194.

Network Performance Institute, Inc. Post Office Box 41-4371, Miami Beach, FL 33141-9998.

The Seybold Report on Publishing Systems, Vol. 20, No. 10/11, Autumn 1990.

Shannon, C. E., *The Mathematical Theory of Communications,* University of Illinois Press, Urbana, IL, 1964.

Shoch, John F. and Jon A. Hupp, *Performance of an Ethernet Local Network—A Preliminary Report,* Local Area Communications Symposium, Mitre and NBS, Boston, MA, May 1979.

Shotwell, Robyn, *The Ethernet Source Book,* Elsevier, Amsterdam, 1985.

Wang, P. T. and Michael McGinn, Mitre Corporation, *Performance of a Stochastically Optimized CMSA Network,* /0742/1303/85/000/0061 IEEE, 1979.

Index

Other Bestsellers of Related Interest

**BUSINESS APPLICATIONS
SHAREWARE**—*PC-SIG, Inc.*

Shareware allows you to evaluate hundreds of dollars worth of software before buying it. Once you decide, you simply register the shareware you want at a fraction of the cost of buying commercially marketed packages. This resource shows you a wide variety of these programs including: PC Payroll, Bill Power Plus, Painless Accounting, Graphtime, PC Inventory Plus, Formgen, and more. 312 pages, 81 illustrations. **Book No. 3920, $29.95 paperback only**

**MAINTAIN AND REPAIR YOUR
COMPUTER PRINTER AND SAVE A
BUNDLE**—*Stephen J. Bigelow*

A few basic tools are all you need to fix many of the most common printer problems quickly and easily. You may even be able to avoid printer hangups altogether by following a regular routine of cleaning, lubrication, and adjustment. Why pay a repairman a bundle when you don't need to? With this time- and money-saving book on your printer stand, repair bills will be a thing of the past! 240 pages, 160 illustrations. **Book No. 3922, $16.95 paperback, $26.95 hardcover**

ONLINE INFORMATION HUNTING
—*Nahum Goldmann*

Cut down dramatically on your time and money spent online, and increase your online productivity with this helpful book. It will give you systematic instruction on developing cost-effective research techniques for large-scale information networks. You'll also get detailed coverage of the latest online service, new hardware and software, and recent advances that have affected online research. 256 pages, 125 illustrations. **Book No. 3943, $19.95 paperback. $29.95 hardcover**

FOXPRO® PROGRAMMING
—**2nd Edition**—*Les Pinter,*
Foreword by Walter Kennamer,
COO, Fox Software

If you've been looking for a book that concentrates entirely on the FoxPro language and not on the product itself, then look no further! This book is a gold mine of fully-tested techniques, ready-to-run source code, and application templates to use as is or build upon in your own programs. You'll get complete programming models for creating FoxPro report generators, screens, menus, spreadsheets, multiuser interfaces, network support, and much more. 384 pages, 150 illustrations. **Book No. 4057, $22.95 paperback only**

CONVERTING C TO TURBO C++
—*Len Dorfman*

Discover how to move existing C applications into the OOP/GUI environment—often without changing a single line of code! This book explains the principles of OOP and outlines the procedures you should follow to develop commercial-quality graphical interfaces with C++. You'll develop C++ class libraries for all functions—display, window, keyboard, sound, and mouse—of software development and a complete object-oriented user interface. 352 pages, 100 illustrations. Includes 5.25″ disk. **Book No. 4084, $29.95 paperback, $39.95 hardcover**

VISUAL BASIC: Easy Windows™
Programming—*Namir C. Shammas*

Enter the exciting new world of visual object-oriented programming for the Windows environment. *Visual Basic* is chock-full of screen dumps, program listings, and illustrations to give you a clear picture of how your code should come together. You'll find yourself referring to its tables, listings, and quick-reference section long after you master Visual Basic. As a bonus, the book is packaged with a 3.5-inch disk filled with all the working Visual Basic application programs discussed in the text. 480 pages, 249 illustrations. **Book No. 4086, $29.95 paperback**

MACINTOSH HARD DISK MANAGEMENT—*Bob Brant*

Keep your hard drive healthy. This comprehensive guide takes a close look at the disk itself—how it works, how to keep it running properly, and how to fix it if it breaks down. In addition, you'll explore how to make the most of your Mac hard disk's storage capacity and capabilities. Several utilities, such as ADB Probe, Connectix Mode 32, RAM Check, System Picker, DisKeeper, Speedometer, and Layout, are included on an accompanying 3.5" disk! 344 pages, 150 illustrations. **Book No. 4087, $29.95 paperback only**

BUILD YOUR OWN 386/386SX COMPATIBLE AND SAVE A BUNDLE —2nd Edition—*Aubrey Pilgrim*

Assemble an 80386 microcomputer at home using mail-order parts that cost a lot less today than they did several years ago. Absolutely no special technical know-how is required—only a pair of pliers, a couple of screwdrivers, and this detailed, easy-to-follow guide. 248 pages, 79 illustrations. **Book No. 4089, $18.95 paperback, $29.95 hardcover**

HIGH-PERFORMANCE C GRAPHICS PROGRAMMING FOR WINDOWS® —*Lee Adams*

Take advantage of the explosive popularity of Windows with the help of computer graphics ace Lee Adams. He offers you an introduction to a wide range of C graphics programming topics that have interactive commercial applications. From software prototypes to finish applications, this toolkit not only explores graphics programming, but also gives you many examples of working source code. 528 pages, 224 illustrations. **Book No. 4103, $24.95 paperback. $34.95 hardcover**

BATCH FILES TO GO: A Programmer's Library—*Ronny Richardson*

Ronny Richardson, respected research analyst and programmer, has assembled this collection of ready-to-use batch files featuring over 80 exclusive keystroke-saving programs. These fully developed programs—all available on disk for instant access—can be used as they are, or altered to handle virtually any file management task. 352 pages, 100 illustrations. 5.25" disk. **Book No. 4165, $34.95 paperback only**

THE INFORMATION BROKER'S HANDBOOK—*Sue Rugge and Alfred Glossbrenner*

Start and run a profitable information brokerage. You'll examine all of the search and retrieval options today's successful information brokers use, everything from conventional library research to online databases, special interest groups, CD-ROMs, and bulletin board systems. No successful information broker should be without this valuable reference tool for his or her office. 408 pages, 100 illustrations. **Book No. 4104, $29.95 paperback, $39.95 hardcover**

EASY PC MAINTENANCE AND REPAIR—*Phil Laplante*

Keep your PC running flawlessly—and save hundreds of dollars in professional service fees! This money-saving guide will show you how. It provides all the step-by-step instructions and troubleshooting guidance you need to maintain your IBM PC-XT, 286, 386, or 486 compatible computer. If you have a screwdriver, a pair of pliers, and a basic understanding of how PCs function, you're ready to go to work. 152 pages, 68 illustrations. **Book No. 4143, $14.95 paperback, $22.95 hardcover**

BUILD YOUR OWN MACINTOSH AND SAVE A BUNDLE—2nd Edition—*Bob Brant*

Assemble an affordable Mac with inexpensive, easy-to-obtain mail-order parts. This helpful book includes all-new illustrated instructions for building the Mac Classic, Mac portable, and new 68040-based machines (LC, IIci, and Quadra 700). It also provides valuable tips for using System 7, outlines ways you can breathe new life into older Macs with a variety of upgrade options, and updates prices on all peripherals, expansion boards, and memory upgrades. 368 pages, illustrated. **Book No. 4156, $19.95 paperback, $29.95 hardcover**

MICROSOFT® MONEY MANAGEMENT —*Jean E. Gutmann*

Written especially for first-time Windows users, this is a complete guide to effective financial record-keeping with Microsoft Money—the new money management software for Windows that's perfect for individuals and small businesses that don't need a full-fledged, double-entry accounting package. With this user-friendly guide, you'll become a pro in no time as you take advantage of the expert hints and proven techniques not found in software manuals. 272 pages, 132 illustrations. **Book No. 4172, $17.95 paperback only**

Look for These and Other TAB Books at Your Local Bookstore

To Order Call Toll Free 1-800-822-8158
(24-hour telephone service available.)

or write to TAB Books, Blue Ridge Summit, PA 17294-0840.

Title	Product No.	Quantity	Price

☐ Check or money order made payable to TAB Books

Charge my ☐ VISA ☐ MasterCard ☐ American Express

Acct. No. _____ Exp. _____

Signature: _____

Name: _____

Address: _____

City: _____

State: _____ Zip: _____

Subtotal $ _____

Postage and Handling
($3.00 in U.S., $5.00 outside U.S.) $ _____

Add applicable state and local
sales tax $ _____

TOTAL $ _____

TAB Books catalog free with purchase; otherwise send $1.00 in check or money order and receive $1.00 credit on your next purchase.

Orders outside U.S. must pay with international money order in U.S. dollars drawn on a U.S. bank.

TAB Guarantee: If for any reason you are not satisfied with the book(s) you order, simply return it (them) within 15 days and receive a full refund.   **BC**